Charles Ashton, James Ott Crosby

A hand book of Iowa,

Or The discovery, settlement, geographical location, topography, natural resources, geology, climatology, commercial facilities, agricultural productiveness, manufacturing advantages, educational interests, healthfulness, governm - Vol. 1

Charles Ashton, James Ott Crosby

A hand book of Iowa,

Or The discovery, settlement, geographical location, topography, natural resources, geology, climatology, commercial facilities, agricultural productiveness, manufacturing advantages, educational interests, healthfulness, governm - Vol. 1

ISBN/EAN: 9783337775223

Printed in Europe, USA, Canada, Australia, Japan

Cover: Foto ©ninafisch / pixelio.de

More available books at **www.hansebooks.com**

IOWA STATE CAPITOL.

A HAND BOOK OF IOWA,

....OR.....

THE DISCOVERY, SETTLEMENT, GEOGRAPHICAL LOCATION, TOPOGRAPHY, NATURAL RESOURCES, GEOLOGY, CLIMATOLOGY, COMMERCIAL FACILITIES, AGRICULTURAL PRODUCTIVENESS, MANUFACTURING ADVANTAGES, EDUCATIONAL INTERESTS, HEALTHFULNESS, GOVERNMENT, AND THE EXCELLENCE OF THE SOCIAL AND MORAL LIFE

........OF........

THE STATE OF IOWA.

The Brightest Star in the American Constellation.

CHARLES ASHTON, JAMES O. CROSBY AND J. W. JARNAGIN

Committee on Archæological, Historical and Statistical Information, Iowa Columbian Commission.

PUBLISHED BY THE COMMISSION A. D., 1893.

TABLE OF CONTENTS.

	PAGE.
I. Introductory Remarks	1
II. The Name Iowa. Origin. Meaning	1
III. Discovery. By whom. Time. Place	1
IV. Settlement. Providential Circumstances. Rapid Development	3
V. Boundaries and Area	5
VI. Geographical Location	6
VII. Topography. Elevations. Landscapes. Rivers. Lakes. Spirit Lake Massacre	7
VIII. Iowa a Prairie State. Advantages for Settlement. Changed Conditions.	12
IX. Geological Surveys	14
X. The Geology of Iowa. Relation of Geology to Agriculture. Formations. Rocks. Soils. Coal, Etc.	14
XI. Climatology. Importance of climatic conditions. General climatic features. Precipitation. Temperature, Etc.	28
XII. Natural Resources. Water. Medicinal Waters. Soil. Clays. Sands. Stone. Gypsum. Coal. Iron. Lead. Zinc	42
XIII. Commercial Facilities. River Navigation. Railroads. First Projected. Construction. Land Grants in aid of. Present Mileage. General Distribution. Present Taxable Valuation. Tonnage Carried. Earnings. Number of employees. Salaries, etc.	51
XIV. Postal Facilities. Telegraphs. Telephones	57

XV.   PAGE.

Banking. State and Savings Banks. Capital. Deposits, Etc. Private Banks. Loan and Trust Companies. National Banks. Capital. Deposits... 57

XVI.

Insurance. Fire and Life. Home and Foreign Companies. Volume of Business, Etc... 58

XVII.

Development of Wealth. Demonstration of Figures. Comparative Growth of Population and Wealth.............................. 59

XVIII.

Finance and Taxation.. 62

XIX.

Agricultural Excellence and Productiveness. Rank of State, in Area and Population. Grain Productiveness. Demonstrative Figures. Value of Agricultural Production................................. 64

XX.

The Oldest Legends of the Origin of Maize........................... 68

XXI.

The Live Stock Industry. Its Growth. Comparative Values. Grain Products and Live Stock. Six Leading States—Iowa Leading. Cattle. Sheep. Swine. The Grasses. Flax..................... 75

XXII.

The Dairy Industry. Number of Milch Cows in the Country. Value, Etc. Number and Value of Milch Cows in Iowa Compared with Other Leading States. Iowa Dairy Display at the Centennial and the New Orleans Expositions. Value of Iowa's Dairy Products. Their Importance in our Agricultural Industry.......... 79

XXIII.

Horticulture. Nurseries. Their Number. Value. Employees. Value of Products. Fruit Production. Shipments. Vegetable Production. Hands Employed. Productions. Growth of the Industry. Floriculture. Florist Establishments. Male. Female Employees. Seed Farms. Value of Products. State Encouragement. State Societies. State and other Fairs. Poultry....................... 81

XXIV.

The Native Flora of Iowa... 86

XXV.

Forests and Artificial Groves. Growth of Woods, Etc................ 89

XXVI.

Manufacturing Interests. Inviting Outlook for Manufacturing Industries.. 90

XXVII.

The Iowa Fish Commission and its Work........................... 95

XXVIII.

Education in Iowa. First Schools. Law of 1858. The System

	PAGE.
Described. School Houses. School Finances. Educational Associations. State Schools. Closing Summary..................	96

XXIX.

Public Libraries 105

XXX.

Churches and Church Work in Iowa. Growth. Denominational Organizations. Statistical Table. Denominational and Non-Sectarian Colleges and Universities. Parochial Schools.......... 105

XXXI.

Iowa Palaces. Corn Palace, Flax Palace, Blue Grass Palace, Coal Palace... 115

XXXII.

Iowa Books and Authors.. 119

XXXIII.

Iowa and Patriotism.... 127

XXXIV.

Iowa and Art 130

XXXV.

Iowa in World's Expositions. At Paris. At New Orleans. In the World's Columbian Exposition.............................. 130

XXXVI.

Population tabulated. 1840, 1850, 1860, 1870, 1880, 1890............. 141

XXXVII.

State Government and Institutions.................................. 143

XXXVIII.

Pauperism... 153

XXXIX.

The Newspaper Press...... 153

INTRODUCTORY...

Of Iowa we write. Our task is to set forth its discovery, settlement, geographical location, topographical features, geology, climate, soils, minerals, rivers, agricultural advantages and productiveness, its commercial opportunities, educational facilities, development, progress and the excellence of its intellectual, social and moral life. The subject is broad yet inviting, the duty is a pleasant one, yet in many respects one difficult of accomplishment. The artist who would attempt to present with the brush the grandeur of hue and majestic form of the bow of promise would find the task to lie beyond the reach of his culture or the grasp of his endowments. So the pen is inadequate to present in its bright and winsome reality this realm of topographical beauty, rich resources, gracious climate and excellent development which earth's millions now know as the State of Iowa.

THE NAME, IOWA.

Prior to the settlement of the region a tribe of the aboriginal inhabitants were designated by a term from which we have the name of Iowa. An intelligent and early pioneer of the territory now forming the state, well acquainted with its native tribes and their languages, Mr. Antoine Le Claire, stated that this word, used by its original inhabitants to designate the portion of the country which they occupied, signified "This is the land." Pre-eminently among its sister states Iowa is "the land."

DISCOVERY.

Iowa was first seen by white men in the summer of 1673, two hundred and twenty years ago. The French settlers then occupying Lower Canada, in exploring the great lakes and their connections, had reached Mackinaw, and the Catholic church had formed at that place a missionary settlement. In their association with the Indians its missionaries heard of a great river in the west that came out of the north and flowed into the far-away south, and a wonderful land along its shores. So enrapturing were the descriptions given of the "Father of Waters" and the beauties of the treeless land bordering it, that an educated missionary, then laboring at Mackinaw for the conversion of the Indians, became possessed of an intense desire to explore it.

Louis Joliet, a young man of Canadian birth, but of French descent, well educated, active and ambitious, traveling under the authority of the government of Quebec, reached Mackinaw in one of his adventurous voyages of exploration. There he met Jacques Marquette, an educated missionary priest. These two energetic men with five French-Canadian attendants, left Mackinaw on the thirteenth day of May, 1673, in two bark canoes to reach, if possible, the great river of which they had heard, and explore "the beautiful land." Father Marquette and his companion, Joliet, were both intent on enlarging the dominion of the French government, but the former was more directly concerned in propagating the Catholic faith among the native tribes in the then unknown interior region of this then unknown west. Leaving Mackinaw in their two canoes, frail vessels for such a voyage, with "some Indian corn and some dried meats as their stock of provisions," these intrepid Christian leaders coasted along the western shores of Lake Michigan into Green Bay. On reaching the mouth of the Fox River they entered it and ascended to the portage, where, being directed by Indian guides, they transferred their canoes and provisions to the Wisconsin river and descended the stream. On the seventeenth day of June when near its mouth they looked across a greater stream, the "Missi," great, and "Sepe", river, on the western shore of which rose the high bluff on which, in 1805, Lieut. Pike planted the United States flag. Then had they the first view ever enjoyed by white men of the strange land on the sunset side of the great river which their venturous voyage was made to discover.

Of the thoughts and emotions of those men, forming that day the vanguard of our present Christian civilization in this central west, we have no record. Something of the strange musings they indulged as they rode in their fragile vessels amidst their strange, weird surroundings, we are left to imagine. Gliding slowly down the great stream on that June day, the valley and the not far away hills that bound it were clothed in summer luxuriance. As they entered the Mississippi to their right, but little above them on the Wisconsin shore lay a beautiful prairie, reaching miles up the great stream and some three miles back from the river, but this they did not see. In front of them on the Iowa side of the larger river were the high bluffs, but turning down the stream they were soon in a delightful river archipelago. The first Iowa prairie they beheld was that on which the town of Guttenburg was built. In all this varying scenery they saw no sign of human form or habitation. It is said they rode on the river four days before the first sign of human inhabitant was seen. Then they beheld human footprints in the sand.

How profound the solitude in which they rode!

How wonderfully different that great valley now from its condition, then! Those men must have been conscious that they were in a vast inhabitable region, but had but slight conception of its present wonderful development and civilization, more beneficent than any which in their day shed blessings upon humanity; which in this celebrative year graces with its wealth of happiness the dwellers in the great central region which they then discovered, but now having world-wide fame alike for its beauty and its productiveness.

In this commemorative year which calls the millions of the nation to the shores of the great lake, from which those men began their voyage, should any of these millions traverse this interior region they will find on the shores of the great river then discovered, ten Christian commonwealths, all free, powerful states, yet parts of this one powerful Nationality. Those ten states have a population of nineteen millions of Christian

THE FIRST SPOT IN IOWA SEEN BY ITS DISCOVERERS.

people, and possess a wealth surpassing the riches of the wealthiest nation of as recent date as Iowa's discovery; while on that tree-clad, western shore, on which those men first looked with inquiring anxiety, there is now this beautiful state, the home of two millions of the most prosperous, intelligent, orderly and happy people of earth, In the intervening years, this region, then nameless to those adventurous voyagers, largely covering the fertile peninsula formed by the two largest rivers of the country, then an unexplored, herbage-covered land, inhabited only sparsely by an uncultured, savage race, has made a progress in civilized attainment that must ever be the marvel of the country's history. Here are now commercial facilities, manufacturing forces, educational advantages, and a Christian freedom and liberality unknown to the world when this beautiful portion of the country was discovered.

THE SETTLEMENT OF IOWA.

The territory bordering the Mississippi river extending eastward of that stream to the Alleghanies and westward to the Rocky Mountains, and from the Gulf by which thrives the stately palm and fragrant orange, to the great lakes, was by right of discovery subject to the crown of France. In the course of human events that portion of this interior territory west of the Mississippi and reaching from Lake Superior to the Gulf of Mexico passed under the dominion of the Spanish crown. In 1800 Spain receded this great territory to the French government. That part of the original French possessions in this region lying north of the Ohio and east of the Mississippi had, by the conquest of Canada, become subject to the British crown, and by the fortunes of war in the American Revolution had subsequently become United States territory. In 1803, by the treaty arrangement known as the Louisiana Purchase, France ceded its possessions along the Mississippi river to the United States government. The wise action of the Jefferson administration in extending the western frontier of the country to the Rocky Mountains, secured to this fertile prairie-interior the advantages, forever, of free government and liberal laws.

When the Revolutionary war closed settlements soon began to extend west of the Alleghanies from New York, Pennsylvania, Virginia and the New England states. In 1802 Ohio was admitted into the Union. In 1730 the French had formed a settlement at Vincennes and in 1809 Indiana was given state government. Yet in 1810 its population numbered only 23,890 white persons. In 1720 the French had formed a settlement at Kaskaskia. In 1818, lacking but two years of a century thereafter, Illinois was given a place as a state in the Union. Yet in the centennial anniversary year of the founding of that settlement at Kaskaskia that state contained a population of only 53,788 white persons. A French settlement was formed at Detroit, Michigan, in 1701 but the census of 1830, taken 129 years thereafter, reported the population of the Michigan territory at only 31,346. Several more years passed before the American Congress gave it statehood.

At the close of the first third of the present century the population of the four states formed out of the old Northwestern Territory covering the region between the Ohio river, the Mississippi and the Great Lakes had a population only a little in excess of one and a half millions of white persons. In 1870, forty-three years after the permanent settlement of Iowa began, it had a larger population than Michigan, the settlement of which was commenced a century and a half before the first settlement was founded in Iowa.

For 113 years after the discovery of Iowa by Joliet and Marquette it remained virtually an unknown land. In that cycle of slow transportation, limited reading, but numerous discoveries of new lands, the discovery of this interior portion of the North American continent had failed to attract public attention. No effort was made to effect any settlement within the borders of what is now the state of Iowa, until the fall of 1788. Julien Dubuque, an adventurous French trader, having secured from the Indians a grant of land extending southwardly from the Little Maquoketa river seven leagues along the Mississippi by three leagues inland, embracing about 121,000 acres, formed a settlement thereon. On it, it is said Dubuque "improved an extensive farm, built houses to dwell in, erected a horse mill, cultivated the farm and mined lead." He died in 1810 and his possessions were soon controlled by others. The Indians became dissatisfied with the lead mining and other conduct of their French and half breed neighbors, drove them from their mines and homes, and broke up the settlement.

In March 1799 Louis Honori obtained a grant of land from the government of Upper Louisiana in Lee county, where the town of Montrose now stands, near the head of the rapids in the Mississippi river. The tract was sold from him in 1803 and a settlement, founded by him, was abandoned.

Various venturesome parties of hunters, trappers and Indian traders made temporary settlement along the Mississippi, within the limits of Iowa, from 1820 to 1830, but did not permanently remain. In 1809 a military post had been established on the present site of Ft. Madison. The troops however did not long occupy the post, its establishment having been in violation of treaty stipulation made with the Indian occupants of the region it was abandoned by the government.

The city of St. Louis was founded in 1764. It soon had trade with the Indians. In 1801 that city, the river approaches of which were then navigated by only flat boats and Indian canoes, passed, by the Louisiana Purchase, under the dominion of the United States government. Three years later Robert Fulton made his successful trial trip on the Hudson with the "Clermont", and steam, as a motive power on American rivers, was demonstrated to be a practical force, and soon had large application. In 1817 the first steamboat reached St. Louis. That city then passed from its primal stage, as a mere trading post for Indians and hunters, to a growing and important commercial center. Steam navigation being applied on the Ohio and Mississippi brought settlers into southwestern Illinois and northeastern Missouri and prepared the way for the settlement of Iowa.

The western border of Iowa was first traced in 1805 by the Lewis and Clark expedition on its famous journey across the continent by way of the Missouri and Columbia rivers. Maj. Pike traced its eastern border as he ascended the Mississippi river to its source about the same time. The reports of these expeditions published by the government, with the reports of the journeys of hunters and Indian traders through the territory, spread knowledge of the remarkable beauty and natural excellence of this then far western region. When the Indians were finally subdued by the defeat of Black Hawk at the "Bad Axe" in 1832, and permanent safety was thereby assured to venturesome pioneers, settlements rapidly formed on the Iowa side of the Mississippi. No region, ever opened for settlement, offered more inviting advantages to home seekers, and they were rapidly embraced.

In 1833 the area now comprising the state of Iowa was a part of the territory of Michigan. Its legislature organized two counties within what is now Iowa, naming them Des Moines and Dubuque. Three years later, namely in 1836, Congress organized the territory of Wisconsin--Iowa constituting a part of that territory. In 1838 the territory of Iowa was constituted by act of Congress, and Robert Lucas of Ohio was appointed to the office of Governor. The first legislature of the Iowa territory assembled November 12th, 1838, at Burlington. Iowa, as a territory, embraced a considerable portion of what is now the state of Minnesota, and had almost unlimited expansion toward the setting sun.

On the opening of Iowa for settlement in 1833 settlers rushed into the lead mining regions surrounding Dubuque, and that city was founded. In 1836, three years after Iowa was opened for settlement, the population of the territory numbered 10,315. Two years later the population had increased to 22,850. In the census of 1840, taken but seven years after the territory was opened for settlement, the population numbered 43,112. Six years later a state enumeration found the population to be upward of 100,000. The star of empire was taking its way westward, the people of the timber-clad east had heard of the beauty and richness of this prairie land where a farm could be made in a season with a yoke of oxen and a plow, and were coming in by thousands to enjoy the beauty of its broad landscapes, the glory of its sunshine, the purity of its waters and the fertility of its acres. In 1850, but seventeen years after the building of the first cabin in its permanent settlement, the second national enumeration therein reported a population of 192,214 free men and women. December 8, 1846, but thirteen years after its first permanent settlers entered upon its soil, Iowa was admitted into the Union. The fame of its wonderful natural meadows and the beauty and fertility of its prairies had spread, not only over this country, but had crossed the seas and the people of other countries, as well as the states in the east were crowding in to find homes in this richly inviting region of the prairie west.

BOUNDARIES AND AREA.

The constitution under which Iowa was admitted into the Union fixed the boundaries of the state as follows "Beginning in the middle of the main channel of the Mississippi river at a point due east of the middle of the mouth of the main channel of the Des Moines river, thence up the middle of the main channel of the said Des Moines river, to a point on said river where the northern boundary line of the state of Missouri, as established by the constitution of that state, adopted June 12th, 1820 crosses the said middle of the main channel of the said Des Moines river, thence westwardly along the said northern boundary line of the state of Missouri as established at the time aforesaid, until the extension of said line intersects the middle of the main channel of the Missouri river; thence up the middle of the main channel of the said Missouri river to a point opposite the middle of the main channel of the Big Sioux river, intersected by the parallel of forty-three degrees thirty minutes north latitude, (a range of latitude possessing a temperate climate most highly favorable for agricultural production.) The area of the state covers on the forty-second parallel six ranges of townships east of the fifth P. M., the fourteenth meridan west of Washington and the ninetieth west from Greenwich, and on the same parallel forty-five townships west of that meridan. Estimating each township at six miles the state has an extreme length east and west of 300 miles by a breadth of about 204 miles, including in its breadth thirty-four surveyed townships. According to a report made by the Secretary of the Treasury to the United States Senate in March, 1863, it embraces 55,044 square miles, or 35,220,200 acres—an area larger than Scotland, almost as large as England, four times the size of the kingdom of Denmark, five times as large as Belgium; three times as large as the kingdom of Greece, that made the world's pre-Christian history interesting by it glorious deeds and the splendor of its philosophy and architecture; and it is five times the area of the land of Judea, that gave to the world its noblest ethical code, and to the race its Redeemer.

Such is the state of Iowa in its location and area; greater than many powerful, wealthy kingdoms in extent, and the equal of great empires in natural resources. The free bestowment of the beneficent Creator, its productive capabilities are yet unmeasured, its every acre being fertile. Barren, rocky, sterile, sandy or great swamp areas being unknown in its extent, its ultimate wealth producing power cannot be estimated.

GEOGRAPHICAL LOCATION.

An artist once represented Columbus as standing and surveying the North American continent. When his eyes rested upon the brightest spot, central in the vast expanse, that spot was named Iowa. Geographically it is centrally located in this union of states. On the forty-second parallel its eastern boundary is upwards of one thousand miles from the Atlantic's tide by Plymouth Rock, while on the same parallel from its western border to the Pacific's surf-beaten shore, fifteen hundred miles intervene. From the northern line of the state to the British possessions by the Lake of the Woods, the distance is four hundred miles, while between the southern border of the state and the Gulf coast lie the states of Missouri, Arkansas and Louisiana, covering an expanse of 760 miles. A position so central in the richest, freest and most powerful nation of modern times, and central in the vast system of river navigation connected with the great streams that form its eastern and western boundaries, and so situated that the principal lines of railway binding ocean to ocean must cross its territory, must ever possess incalculable advantages in the security its location affords, the markets it assures, and the commercial advantages that must ever accrue to its citizens.

TOPOGRAPHY.

Iowa is not only princely in its area and highly fortunate in its geographical location, but it is winsome in its topography. In the days of a geographical ignorance, which an intelligent world remembers now with smiles, Iowa may have been placed in school-book maps in "The Great American Desert." But if this beautiful and fertile state was ever a desert, then surely it was that one of which the Lord's prophet spoke when he declared "The wilderness and the solitary place shall be glad for them and the desert shall rejoice and blossom as the rose. * * * * * * The glory of Lebanon shall be given unto it and the excellency of Sharon." No grander cedars ever grew on Lebanon than now adorn Iowa homes, and no more beautiful or fragrant roses ever bloomed along the sunny slopes of Sharon than now grow in this realm of Edenic loveliness.

One of the more noticeable features of the topography of Iowa is the entire freedom of the state from barren, rocky elevations, or other waste lands. It has no Saharas, dismal swamps, nor fever-breeding everglades.

From railroad surveys and other sources of information we have definite knowledge of the elevation of the chief portions of the state. Low water in the Mississippi at the southeastern corner of the state, its lowest point, being 444 feet above sea level.

The point recognized as its highest elevation is on the summit divide near Spirit Lake, Dickinson county, it being estimated at 1250 feet above low water at Keokuk, giving the highest point in Iowa an elevation of only 1,694 feet; between these extremes in elevation lies all of Iowa. To show more clearly by comparison the moderate elevations of this area, we notice that its highest point is 165 feet lower than the Union Pacific railroad grade in the Platte valley at Grand Island, Nebraska, the grade at that station being 1,860 feet above tide.

The water in the Big Sioux river at the northwestern corner of the state is 1344 feet above the tide level. This is the descent from that point to the Gulf of Mexico via the Missouri and Mississippi rivers.

The crest of the state or the summit forming the water shed between the waters of the Mississippi and the Missouri lies diagonally across the state; its general trend being from the northwest to the southeast. Entering Iowa from Minnesota where it separates the waters of the Des Moines and Little Sioux rivers, it leaves the state entering Missouri near the southeast corner of Appanoose county, there separating the waters of the Chariton river from the Fabius creek, having crossed in its course through the state Dickinson, Clay, Buena Vista, Sac, Carroll, Audubon, Guthrie, Adair, Madison, Union, Clark, Lucas, Monroe and Appanoose counties.

The altitude of this important ridge is shown by the elevations at which it is crossed by the five chief railroad lines crossing the state from east to west. The most southern of these lines is the Chicago, Burlington and Quincy. It touches this great water-shed twice. First at Chariton, Lucas county, at an elevation of 1,080 feet, and the second time at Murray, Clark county, thirty-seven miles west of Chariton at an altitude of 1,268 feet. This line of road reaches its highest altitude in the state at Creston, Union county, 1,355 feet, on the divide separating the Platte and Grand rivers, affluents of the Missouri. The Chicago, Rock Island and Pacific railroad, the next line north of the one first named, crosses this watershed in the northwestern part of Adair county, at the town of Adair, at an elevation of 1,389 feet. The summit of the divide at this point is fifty feet above the railroad grade. The Chicago and Northwestern railroad crosses this watershed at or near Arcadia, in Carroll county, at an elevation of 1,437 feet. The Dubuque and Sioux City (Illinois Central) crosses it at Alta. Buena Vista county, at an altitude of 1,521 feet. Thus the three roads named reach their highest elevations in the state at the crossing of this divide.

The Chicago, Milwaukee and St. Paul railway crosses it at or near Ruthven, Palo Alto county, at an elevation of 1,424 feet, but this road reaches its summit elevation at Sanborn, O'Brien county, 1,537 feet above tide, on the divide separating the east and west branches of the Floyd river.

The facts here stated show the evenness of the altitude of the summit of the state and that there is a very moderate and easy descent across the state from the northwest to the southeast. From Sanborn to Chariton the descent is 475 feet. The distance is two hundred miles in a direct line, the descent averaging 2.37 feet to the mile.

Any map of Iowa will show that the rivers in that part of the state which lies east of the great watershed, trend toward the southeast and flow into Mississippi, and that in the portion lying west of that summit all the rivers flow into the Missouri with a southwesterly trend. The traveler crossing Iowa soon discovers that, although a prairie state, and lying under the moderate elevations given, it is not a breadth of swampy levels, but a realm of beautiful undulations,—in some places rising from the streams somewhat abruptly but seldom precipitously. The divides separating the numerous streams generally rising to an altitude of 175 to 250 feet, afford a constant succession of changing scenery. No country affords more graceful landscapes, when clothed in summer's green or when its groves are dyed in their autumn robes of silver, scarlet, gold and purple. Iowa landscapes are grandly beautiful, and the traveler sees a breadth of farm homes beautiful in situation and surroundings. The great fields of growing grain, in their season, add beauty to the delighting panoramas by every shade of green, covering the broad and billowy areas over which the eye extends. In the summer season great herds and flocks feed amid blooming flowers and rich herbage, and add enchanting variety to the inviting picture. In that season the enriching, life-giving sunshine paints the floral gemmed-meadows with a brilliancy of hue that makes the broad landscapes over which the vision reaches, constantly discovering new charms, superbly winsome. Paraphrasing the language of inspiration we may truly say, "beautiful for situaion, and the joy of her people" is beautiful, fertile Iowa.

RIVERS.

Iowa is a realm of beautiful, perennial streams flowing in deep channels and with rapid current. Prof. White in the first volume of his report on the geology of the state, tabulates the descent of the principal rivers of the state according to railroad surveys and other sources of information which we here copy.

A FARM HOME ON THE CREST OF IOWA.

RIVERS.

NAME OF RIVER.	PART OF COURSE.	SLOPE PER MILE.		AUTHORITY.
		FT.	IN.	
Mississippi	From Lansing to the Confluence of the Missouri		6	J.E. Ainsworth.
Missouri	From Sioux City to Council Bluffs	1		R. R. Surveys.
Des Moines	From Fort Dodge to Ottumwa	2	4	R. R. Surveys.
Des Moines ..	From Ottumwa to its mouth	1	11	R. R. Surveys.
Raccoon	From Forks near Van Meter to mouth	2	11	R. R. Surveys.
North Raccoon	From Jefferson to Forks near Van Meter	4		R. R. Surveys.
Skunk	From Oakland to its mouth	1	6	R. R. Surveys
Skunk	From Colfax Station to Oakland	2	2	R. R. Surveys.
Iowa	From Iowa Falls to Iowa City	3	1	R. R. Surveys.
Iowa	From Iowa City to its mouth	2	4	R. R. Surveys.
Cedar	From State boundary to Cedar Falls	3	7	R. R. Surveys.
Cedar	From Cedar Falls to Moscow	2	5	R. R. Surveys.
Wapsipinicon .	From Independence to mouth	2	10	J.E. Ainsworth.
Maquoketa	From Manchester to the mouth	3	4	J.E. Ainsworth.
Turkey	From Crane Creek to the mouth	5		R. R. Levels.
Upper Iowa...	From Decorah to the mouth	8	6	R. R. Levels.
E. Nishnabotna	From C. R. I. & P. R. R. to mouth	2	5	R. R. Levels.
W Nishnabotna	From C. R. I. & P. R. R. to mouth	2	8	R. R. Levels.
Boyer	From Denison to its mouth	3	3	R. R. Levels.
Big Sioux	From Indian Creek to mouth	1	4	Estimated.
Big Sioux	From N. W. corner of State to Indian Creek..	3	2	Estimated.
Little Sioux ..	From Cherokee to Sm'aland	2	6	R. R. Levels.
Little Sioux ..	From Smithland to its mouth		4	R. R. Levels.
Floyd	From fork of Willow Creek to mouth	3		J.E. Ainsworth.

From this table it will be seen that the rivers of Iowa are not sluggish, stagnant streams. The Little Sioux has rapid fall from its source in the lakes in Dickinson county, on the summit divide, to Smithland. The stream furnishes many water powers in its course through Clay and other counties. Below Smithland it strikes the broad flood-plain of the Missouri, and so its small descent below that town is explained.

The Skunk is perhaps the flattest stream in the state, yet it flows with a strong current in its labyrinth of bends through the broad flood-plain in which its channel is cut. The traveler who had to cross this river in early days will never forget the "Skunk bottoms." But now with graded and bridged roads, its wide bottom lands are grand pastures and wealth producing properties.

Lying in the peninsula bounded by the rivers forming its eastern and western boundaries, Iowa is not situated to afford interior navigable streams. Its largest interior river, the Des Moines, has its source in Minnesota, and flows with a southeasterly trend east of the great watershed and empties its volume into the Mississippi at the southeast corner of the state. From Fort Dodge to Ottumwa, a distance in a direct line of 150 miles, its descent of two and a half feet per mile gives it a rapid current precluding any great value as a navigable stream but rendering it of great value for manufacturing purposes. At Bonaparte, Ottumwa, Des Moines and other places it is made to furnish important water power. Before the advent of railroads, steamboats plied on this river in the spring and early summer, an occasional small boat running up as far as Fort Dodge. Steam boats occasionally, in those days, plowed their way up the Iowa and

Cedar rivers, but the advent of railroad facilities rendered those streams unnecessary for navigation and they have been given up to manufacturing purposes. Many of the rivers of Iowa and their affluents furnish numerous and valuable water powers. Some are improved for grist and other mill purposes, but many of the most valuable yet invite improvement. The Cedar furnishes water power of great value at Cedar Falls where the river descends about twenty-two feet in three-quarters of a mile. At Waterloo and also Cedar Rapids it furnishes important hydraulic power. The Iowa and many other streams also furnish valuable water powers at numerous places.

The rivers of Iowa are classed in two systems. The one embracing the streams east of the watershed, the other the streams west of that ridge. The principal streams in the eastern system are the Upper Iowa, Turkey, Maquoketa, Wapsipinicon, Cedar, Iowa, Skunk and the Des Moines and its affluents, the principal of which are South, Middle and North rivers, the Raccoon with its branches and the Boone. In the western system we name the Floyd, Rock River, Little Sioux, Maple, Boyer, Nishnabotna, Nodaway, Platte, Grand and the Chariton. These are mostly perennial, many of them serviceable in the milling and manufacturing power afforded. Along their course were many fine native groves that attracted early settlers. All flow in fertile valleys bordered by sloping uplands and are sources of pleasure as well as utility and add beauty by giving variety to the luxuriant landscapes through their course.

LAKES.

The people of Iowa do not boast of the magnitude of their lakes nor the surrounding grandeur of their "unsalted seas." Yet there are numbers of lakes with charming surroundings, several of which are becoming famous as places of resort for rest and pleasure. Iowa's lakes all lie in the central third of the northern half of the state, and its most elevated portion, where the watersheds are developed into broad table lands. None of her lakes are of value in aiding commerce by furnishing important water transportation. In the sporting season they are inviting to sportsmen, as they are visited by immense numbers of migrating waterfowls, as geese, ducks, brants, swans, pelicans, cranes, etc., and furnish large quantities of fine fish, it being true of them in this particular that "The waters brought forth abundantly." The lakes are mostly bodies of clear, pure water. On the shores of many of them are beautiful groves of native timber, located in breadths of charming scenery and are specially inviting to rest seekers and those desiring health-giving recreation. Clear Lake, in Cerro Gordo county, is about five miles in length by two in breadth. Rice Lake, Silver Lake and Bright's Lake in Worth county are small bodies of water from one to two miles long, Rice Lake lying partly in Winnebago county. Crystal Lake, Eagle Lake, Wood Lake, Lake Edwards and Twin Lakes are in Hancock county, Eagle Lake being the largest of the three. Lake Gertrude, Elm Lake, and Wall Lake, beautiful bodies of water, lie in Wright county, the largest of the three Wall Lake, being about three miles long by two broad. Twin Lakes in Calhoun county are becoming a noted resort for fishing and pleasure parties; the Des Moines and Northwestern R. R. making them easily accessible. The two cover a length of about four miles. They are separated by a narrow belt of land through which is cut a narrow stream. Some twenty-five miles from these Twin Lakes lies Wall Lake in Sac county, which is becoming a famous health and pleasure resort.

The maps of Iowa show three separate lakes within the state denominated Wall Lake, one lying in Sac county, one (the largest of the three) in Wright county, and one (the smallest of the three) in Hamilton county The idea has been entertained that at some time in the ante-historic period some strange people built veritable stone walls along portions of the shores of these lakes; but that idea is a myth. Over that region in which those lakes lie, when vast icebergs or ponderous glaciers were exerting their mighty forces in forming the wonderful drift coverings of the region, great numbers of boulders were borne by these forces from the north country and deposited about these fresh water bodies. The forces of winter frosts and ice have lifted these boulders in the shallow portions of these lakes and have piled them by their shores. Fancy has conjured them into walls and so they have their name, and thus the stories of the "Walled lakes of Iowa" had their origin.

In addition to the above named lakes we notice Swan Lake in Emmet county, which is one of the largest of Iowa lakes. It lies in the central portion of that county and is readily accessible from Estherville, the county seat. It is a beautiful pleasure resort. Storm Lake, one of the most beautiful lakes of Iowa, lies in Buena Vista county, on the line of the Illinois Central railroad and by it is the beautiful town of Storm Lake. The largest lakes in Iowa are Spirit Lake and the Okoboji, in Dickinson county. These lie on the great watershed and near the Minnesota line and being accessible by the B., C. R. & N. and the C., M. & St. P. railways have become very popular summer resorts.

In the winter of 1857 a band of Sioux Indians passed southwardly through northwestern Iowa, and on their return passed through Sac, Cherokee and Dickinson counties. The winter was a severe one and in the first week of March the ground was covered with deep snow. The Indians had trouble with the few white settlers then dwelling in Sac and Cherokee counties, stealing and destroying the settlers' property. Reaching the Okoboji Lakes they perpetrated a fearful massacre of white settlers who were then dwelling in the surrounding groves.

The few families settled in those groves, on account of the inclement weather and the deep snow covering the wide unsettled prairies of northern Iowa, were unable to seek protection from the distant settlements, there being no possibility of relief nearer than Fort Dodge, a hundred miles distant. Upwards of forty persons were killed outright by those savages. The settlers' cabins were burned and their property destroyed, and some three or four females were carried off as prisoners. When the news of the massacre reached Fort Dodge a force was immediately raised to go to the relief of these settlements. The sufferings of that brave band of civilian soldiers were terribly severe. Two of them were frozen to death. The Indians immediately after the massacre fled into Minnesota and could not be overtaken by the pioneer force.

Perhaps the only battle ever fought on Iowa soil between United States troops and Indian warriors took place some thirty miles east of Spirit Lake.

A company of United States dragoons under command of Captain N. Boone, about 1842, while crossing the state had a skirmish with an Indian band. Iowa has but a brief history of the heroic in Indian wars, or the sorrowful in the massacre of its early settlers by Indian foes.

PRAIRIE.

Iowa was early known as a prairie state. Its broad, treeless areas were its glory. Its prairies were not in their natural condition vast marshes, or great breadths of sterile sand, barren of productive power, nor were they regions of cold barren clay. They soon became known as of the finest land, awaiting the plow to turn them into productive farms. On the fourth day after Monsieurs Marquette and Joliet entered the Mississippi they had their first view of an Iowa prairie in its summer dress of green and bloom. This great central region of the country was largely treeless then. How long it had existed thus is only known to Him who created it. Why, how, or when these breadths of fertile acres and beautiful landscapes became treeless, would be useless for us to inquire.

Iowa's being so largely prairie favored its rapid settlement. Its first settlers had known something of the toilsome, slow process of making farms with a mattock and an axe in a heavily wooded country. In 1845 a man went into northwestern Ohio, bought an axe and commenced on a piece of timbered land to make a farm. He found it slow work. He afterwards came to Iowa, bought a half section of "raw prairie," went upon it with a breaking plow and team and broke the first furrow made on the tract a mile in length without a rock, grub, tree or stump to hinder the plow. That was a speedier, saying nothing about its being an easier, way to make a farm. Then there was the continuous advantage of a stumpless field. When he settled in the Ohio woods he could not have cut a ton of hay on a hundred acres of his land; when he came to Iowa he could go out on the prairie with a mowing machine, cut the finest of blue-joint and make all the hay he wanted; as fine as was ever fed a horse. He visited a neighbor, an old settler, and going into his hay-yard he asked: "How much hay have you there Mr. S———?" "I guess about 800 tons," was the reply. Every stem of it made from wild grass. The settler in Iowa soon saw there was a distinction with a difference between making a farm on eastern wooded lands and the prairies of Iowa. Infinite wisdom contrived seven-eighths of Iowa's surface to be prairie that Iowa might the more speedily and easily be turned into a paradise. The prairies of Iowa did not invite settlers merely by the ease by which they were turned into fine farm homes, but the beauty of the views they afforded, the breadth and grandeur of the great natural meadows and pastures they offered, and the ease of communication they provided between neighbors and neighborhoods were potent influences in inducing settlers from the heavily wooded east.

The facility of intercourse offered by the Iowa prairie was no mean factor in inviting their rapid settlement. In driving across them there was no climbing over stumps and logs. A few trips indicated a road which was soon worn, if not into a straight, at least into a fine smooth, traveled way. The Iowa farmer had use for a carriage from his first settlement on the prairie. The writer knows something from experience of opening and traveling new roads in the east. Talk about the settler there having use for a carriage from its first settlement, he scarcely had use for such a vehicle in the first generation of its settlement.

It has been objected that there are terrible blizzards and awful cyclones on these Iowa prairies. We admit that there are storms in Iowa, but are there no tornadoes, no terrible storms and blizzards in timber covered countries? We know there are tumults in nature's domain in all regions. Men are helpless before nature's forces in all places, but destructive tornadoes in Iowa, like destructive earthquakes in California, are of but rare occurrence.

There have been severe winters in Iowa but they have been few in its history. There may have been danger for pioneer settlers in journeying across Iowa prairies from winter blizzards in the past, but those dangers are now matters of history. Iowa winters on Iowa prairies are desirable now for the benefits and pleasures which they afford.

The prairies, yet beautiful, are not now as they were when the pioneer chased over them the agile deer and the fleeing elk. Their great breadths were then open commons with sloughs and streams unbridged. Fire, in the fall, swept off their summer vegetation and left naught to hold in place the falling snow. The settlers' cabins, built in grove or sheltered nook, were far apart. The great breadths of open prairie were houseless and many of the pioneer settlers were poor and thinly clad. Then there was nothing to mark the traveled road in the winter's snow storm, and the traveler seeking to cross the broad prairie may have been in danger when such a storm overtook him, distant from his home or a shelter. But terrible, life-destroying blizzards have been of rare occurrence in our history, while mild, beautiful, healthful winters, giving months of delightful sunshine and the smoothest, possible roads for winter travel, have been common.

Our broad prairies, originally beautiful, have been made more grandly so by human handi-work, directed by cultured mind. Terrible prairie fires may be read about in our history, but they will never more be seen. Our great prairies now are broad realms of finely improved, or improving, productive and enclosed farms. Good roads are common and the farms distinctly mark them. Streams and sloughs are bridged. Thrifty villages and thriving towns and cities are multiplied while the whole breadth of the country is flecked by beautiful artificial groves. Now, every where over Iowa prairies there are human habitations and the danger to a traveler in a winter blizzard is passed forever.

But with all of this improvement and change made by human intelligence and industry there are some things pertaining to the prairies of Iowa which are unchanged. The depth, the richness, the porousness of the soil, qualities which give it superior excellence for agricultural productiveness, are yet unchanged. Proper culture never diminishes but increases its productive power. The perennial streams coursing through these broad prairies, yet flow in the same channels cut deep into the earth, with the same, ever continuing, rapid current, yielding untold advantages in their surroundings. The prairies of Iowa, no longer grand in their wild luxuriance, have been made more truly beautiful by the art and industry inspired by our Christian civilization, and will ever be renowned for their agricultural superiority. Beautiful, fertile and exuberantly productive, their possessors are truly a fortunate people.

GEOLOGICAL SURVEYS.

The first geological explorations in Iowa were made by Dr. D. D. Owen, under United States authority. His field of work embraced parts of Wisconsin, Minnesota and Iowa. His report was published, a large quarto volume one.

The first geological survey in the state was made under the direction of Professor James Hall, State Geologist, in parts of the years 1855, 1856 and 1857, with J. D. Whitney as chemist and mineralogist. Their reports were published in two illustrated volumes by authority of the General Assembly of 1858.

In the years 1866, 1867, 1868 and 1869 a second and more extensive geological survey of the state was made by Dr. Charles A. White, State Geologist, Orestes H. St. John, assistant; and Rush Emery, chemist. Their work is reported in two volumes printed by F. M. Mills, state printer, in 1870.

The twenty-fourth General Assembly, deeming a new geological survey of Iowa desirable, made an appropriation for the work and appointed a commission to select a suitable geologist to make the survey. This commission selected Professor Samuel Calvin of the State University to take charge of the work, Dr. Charles R. Keyes, Assistant State Geologist and Professor G. E. Patrick, chemist. It is believed that this survey will lead to an enlarged development of the mineral interests of Iowa, and a fuller knowledge of the extent and value of its coal fields.

A SKETCH OF THE GEOLOGY OF IOWA.

By Charles R. Keyes, A. M., Ph. D., Assistant State Geologist.

Iowa is so pre-eminently an agricultural state that usually her mineral resources are almost entirely overlooked. Yet her geological features are none the less interesting scientifically, none the less important from an economic standpoint.

The mineral wealth of a community can only be developed through a liberal appreciation of its proper functions. Geology ranking first among the useful sciences, has for one of its leading objects the investigation of the natural resources of a region. It considers the characters of the different soils and their capabilities for agricultural purposes; the extent and value of the different deposits of coal and lead, iron and other ores; the distribution, properties and uses of the exhaustless beds of valuable clays; the accurate determination of the areas for artesian waters; the analysis of the mineral, well and river waters; the relative value and durability of the numerous kinds of building stones; and all kindred subjects which are of the utmost importance to the great body of citizens.

Agriculture and geology are daily becoming more intimate in their relations. Nowhere has their inter-dependence been more clearly understood and nowhere have the benefits been more apparent than in certain

European countries. Some of the older states of the Union, especially those along the Atlantic border, have followed the same line of work with the most happy results. To-day it is almost universally conceded that a good geological map of a region is practically a soil map also. The proper comprehension of the close relations of the two sciences cannot fail, therefore, to impress the truth of the statement.

In pointing out the various mineral deposits a knowledge of the distribution of the geological formations is of prime importance. Iowa possesses a measureably complete sequence of strata. The Paleozoic beds, from the Cambrian to the Upper Carboniferous, are very fully represented. The Mesozoic deposits, of Cretaceous age chiefly, are found in considerable thickness. Over all spreads a thick mantle of drift or glacial debris.

Below the soft, unconsolidated drift material the indurated sediments are everywhere exposed through erosion. The complete vertical section of the rocks in the state shows a thickness of about five thousand feet.

ALGONKIAN ROCKS.

Sioux Quartzite. The rocks exposed within the limits of the state which are usually regarded as the oldest geologically are those, called the Sioux quartzite or Sioux "granite," which form outcrops of considerable extent in the extreme northwestern corner of the state. While there is no doubt that all the stratified sediments of Iowa rest at no very great depth upon the fundamental complex of crystallines which probably support all the sedimentary rocks of the globe, the Sioux quartzite and its associated masses are the only truly metamorphosed or massive crystalline rocks having a surface exposure in the state. The common phase of the rock under consideration is a completely vitreous type not unlike red jasper in general appearance and properties. Other parts of the mass are less indurated; and still others are simply loose sand. In places the formation is distinctly conglomeratic. Although the quartzite has been rendered in places so thoroughly crystalline since its original deposition, no igneous rocks have been noted in the vicinity until very recently.

A few months ago Professor G. E. Culver found in the midst of the Sioux quartzite of southeastern Dakota, within a few miles of the Iowa boundary, a large exposure of black trap rock, which extends for more than a mile along one of the minor streams flowing into the Big Sioux river. Dr. W. H. Hobbs, who has made careful microscopical examinations of the rock, finds it to be a coarse-grained olivine diabase—a massive basic rock unquestionably igneous in origin. It seems not improbable that further search will reveal other masses of the same rock or even other types of eruptives very similar.

In quarrying, the quartzite presents numerous difficulties; but the labor in getting out the material is greatly reduced by the fact that it is everywhere jointed and cracked in such a manner as to enable it to be removed readily in convenient sizes for handling. It is one of the most compact and durable building stones in the northwest. For architectural purposes it forms a very beautiful stone and is used for all kinds of construction throughout the region. Some of the leading churches and office buildings in Sioux City, Omaha, Council Bluffs, Des Moines, Burlington, and other places have been erected from this rock, with very pleasing effects.

It has also been used with good results as a paving material both in blocks and macadam. The chief quarries in Iowa are near Rock Rapids, in Lyon county, where the development of the quarry industry, though not so great as a few miles northward and westward, is capable of great expansion, since the stone may be obtained in practicaly inexhaustible quantities.

Reference has been made to the occurrence of igneous rocks near the state boundary. It may be of considerable interest therefore to mention the fact that in sinking a number of deep wells in different parts of northwestern Iowa the drills have passed completely through sedimentary rocks into the crystalline basement below, penetrating the latter in some cases to the extent of several hundred feet. At one of the latest borings, at Hull, in Sioux county, several thick beds of flint-like rocks were passed through, the different layers being separated by sands and gravels. These flint-like layers were found to be typical quartz-porphyry, a truly igneous rock, or lava, very acid in nature and essentially identical with granite, but cooling under somewhat different physical conditions.

The presence of these massive crystalline rocks is very suggestive of agencies that may have been involved to some extent in metamorphosing the old Sioux sandstone.

CAMBRIAN.

Saint Croix Sandstone. In the extreme northeastern corner of Iowa, at the base of the high bluffs along the Mississippi river and its tributaries there is exposed a thick unconsolidated sand bed, which has been called by Minnesota geologists the Saint Croix sandstone. Its greatest thickness shown in Iowa is about two-hundred and fifty feet; but it is known to have a thickness of not less than one thousand feet, as has been disclosed by borings. While for the most part it is a soft sandstone wearing away rapidly under atmospheric influences there are in places clay seams and thin layers of lime-rock frequently developed. In the neighboring states the calcareous and argillaceous beds assume a much greater importance and form shales and shaley limestones which are charged with the remains of trilobites. This sandstone has been called by most writers on the geology of the Upper Mississippi Valley the "Potsdam," and has been regarded as the western extension of the formation known by that name in New York. There is but little doubt, however, that the Saint Croix is very distinct from the Potsdam sandstone of the Appalachian region, though the fauna is possibly equivalent to the similiar one of the New York horizon.

Although the formation has such a thickness in Iowa no subdivision of it into minor beds has been attempted. It does not have so great an importance in this state as in the neighboring regions of Wisconsin and Minnesota.

As a whole the Saint Croix sandstone of Iowa is of little economic value. At Lansing and some other localities there are thin beds of this formation which are sufficiently compact to furnish building stones of inferior quality. These layers are as yet only used for rough masonry. As most of the sandstone is very incoherent, it will furnish unlimited quantities of coarse and fine building sand; while certain light colored layers could be used for the manufacture of glass.

SILURIAN.

Oneota Limestone. The name of this formation is that proposed by

McGee for the rock usually known as the Lower Magnesian limestone. Though attaining a thickness of between two and three hundred feet it is exposed only over a small area in the northwestern portion of the state. Along the borders of the Mississippi it rises above the soft Saint Croix sandstone in bold escarpments and castellated walls. For the most part the rock is a rather impure dolomite with occasional thin sandstone layers in the upper part. In color it is buff to brown. It is often vesicular and cavernous. In Wisconsin and Minnesota the lower Magnesian limestone embraces other layers than those represented in Iowa. The principal beds thus referred to are called the Willow river limestone and New Richmond sandstone in Wisconsin and the Shakopee limestone and white sandstone in Minnesota.

The Oneota limestone is quarried at Lansing, Waukon, McGregor and other places in Clayton and Allamakee counties. For all ordinary masonry it supplies unlimited quantities of good material. Lime of a very good quality is also manufactured from this rock at a number of places. In certain localities considerable amounts of lead ore are found, but as yet this mineral has not been mined to any great extent in the lower Magnesian limestone.

Saint Peter Sandstone. Overlying the Oneota limestone is a heavy bed of pure silicious sandstone, very friable and with few lines of stratification. It is sometimes somewhat indurated, but as a rule incoherent. This is the formation that has long been known in the Upper Mississippi region under the name of the "pictured" rocks, best exposed perhaps in the vicinity of McGregor. Along the boundary of the state northward thin limestone layers are often intercalated. In places this sand formation graduates downward by a rapid increase of calcareous matter into the Oneota limestone. Economically it is of considerable importance in Iowa. Many of the layers are very pure and form excellent material for the manufacture of glass.

Trenton Limestone. Contrasting sharply with the other Silurian limerocks of Iowa the Trenton is an ordinary blue limestone instead of a dolomite. For the most part it is a very compact rock, and often fossiliferous. Owing to its difference in lithological characters as compared with the other Silurian limestones it is honeycombed in places by cavities and caverns of greater or less extent. "It constitutes a conspicuous feature of the Mississippi river bluffs from above McGregor to near Eagle Point, Dubuque, and occurs as the surface rock over all or part of the counties of Allamakee, Howard, Winneshiek, Fayette and Clayton. The Trenton limestone is interesting to the scientist on account of the number and beauty of the fossil remains inclosed in some of the strata. Here occur the oldest types of life that have been preserved in any degree of perfection within the limits of the state. The old Potsdam trilobites are few and fragmentary, and their structural characters are very obscure. In the Trenton are found countless multitudes of organic remains literally crowded together, and retaining in absolute perfection every structural feature even to the minutest detail. Owing to the slight southerly or southwesterly dip the strata pass successively below the level of the Mississippi river, and so just above Dubuque the Trenton limestone disappears from view." (Calvin.)

The Trenton limestone is quarried in numerous places throughout the counties mentioned. Lime of very good quality is made of this stone. Certain of the clay shales afford good material for the manufacture of light colored brick.

Galena Limestone. Overlying the Trenton limestone in northeastern Iowa is a heavily bedded brown dolomite which attains a miximum thickness of between two and three hundred feet in the vicinity of Dubuque. In many places it is very coarse, vesicular and unevenly textured. It frequently contains some cherty matter. The entire bluffs at Dubuque are formed of this limestone. Some sandy material is present in different portions of the formation. The partings are usually argillaceous and are more massive and important toward the top where the formation gradually passes into the overlying shales. As shown by Chamberlain, the conditions of the deposition, in southwestern Wisconsin and vicinity were changed somewhat from those which had existed during the Trenton.

One of the most characteristic features of the Galena limestone is the surface fissures which everywhere traverse this formation. Sometimes they are mere vertical cracks or horizontal partings of the strata, but often widen out into broad cavities. In these openings are found the lead and zinc ores of the region. The metallic ores taken from this limestone form perhaps one the most important economic characters. It was in the Dubuque region that the lead ore of the upper Mississippi valley was first mined in a systematic way.

The Galena limestone furnishes a considerable quantity of good material for heavy masonry. The chief quarries are located at Dubuque, though everywhere throughout its geological range the rocks are adapted and used for ordinary building purposes. A superior quality of lime is also manufactured from this rock.

Maquoketa Shales. Along the entire western slope of Turkey river and below the mouth of that stream on the Mississippi as far as Clinton county, there is exposed between the Galena limestone and the Niagara an extensive bed of bluish or greenish clay-shale. Disintegrating readily under the influence of weathering, these shales allow the massive overlying dolomities to form a bold, mural escarpment which extends the entire length of the river mentioned. The shales have not been reported north of the Iowa boundary. Beginning at a point in Winneshiek county about twenty miles from the Minnesota line the Maquoketa shales have a thickness of over a dozen feet or more. This thickness rapidly increases till at its southernmost exposure it attains a vertical measurement of more than one hundred and twenty-five feet. At Dubuque a few feet of these shales are seen in isolated patches in the summits of the bluffs. For the most part these shales form alternating bands of dark and light colored clays with occasional thin seams of impure limestone. On the upper Maquoketa where the typical locality is situated, the shales are highly charged with many species of fossils. This formation is of small economic importance, unless the clays can be utilized in the manufacture of brick and pottery.

Upper Silurian. The "Niagara" escarpment which rises in great prominence on the western slope of Turkey river and continues southward along the Mississippi nearly to Davenport is one of the most important topographical features in northeastern Iowa. The upper Silurian limestones which form this elevation in Iowa are massive dolomities yellowish or brown in color, having a very considerable thickness. Although presenting great uniformity in texture there are locally large amounts of cherty material in bands or irregular nodules. Silicious material is also often disseminated in fine particles throughout the rocks, but as a rule it is concentrated into the masses already referred to.

Chemical analysis of the limestone itself shows that most of the formation is a very pure magnesian limerock or dolomite with scarcely any foreign material. In different layers the percentage of lime and magnesia vary somewhat. In a few cases the latter is almost entirely wanting and the beds assume the condition of a normal limestone.

From its southern exposure where it is thought to attain a thickness of more than five hundred feet it rapidly thins out northward until just beyond the Iowa-Minnesota line its vertical measurement is very insignificant. At the southern end it is heavily bedded. In many places the inclination of the beds is very considerable, sometimes as high as sixty degrees. Lying directly upon the inclined strata are often seen perfectly horizontal beds. At first sight it appears as if there was a marked unconformity. But from a careful examination of some of the exposures it seems probable that the apparent dip is in some cases due to false-bedding on a large scale. In other instances it may be that very decided disturbances have occurred in the strata.

The exact subdivisions of the upper Silurian rocks in Iowa is yet somewhat undetermined. Hall in 1858 regarded the limestone as made up of an upper member which he termed the Le Claire limestone and a lower portion which was regarded as the same formation to which in New York the name Niagara had been applied. With the exception of White, all geologists who have examined the upper Silurian strata in Iowa regard these rocks as made up of at least two distinct formations. These subdivisions greatly differ not only faunally but in a less marked degree in stratigraphical and lithological characters. For the reason set forth above, Hall's Le Claire appears to be a desirable name for the upper member as now understood; while Niagara, for the present, will be retained for the lower member. For the latter term some other name will probably have to be substituted after a further investigation of these rocks has been made.

Perhaps no other geological formation in the state furnishes a better quality of building stone for general purposes than the upper Silurian strata. The great extension of these rocks both in thickness and surface area make the supply inexhaustible. They form also the best lime in the world. This industry has already begun to assume very considerable proportions in this state.

DEVONIAN.

The broad belt of Devonian rocks in Iowa is traversed medially its entire length by the Cedar river, the beds of this age extending from fifteen to twenty-five miles on each side of the stream. The formation is made up chiefly of massive limestones with magnesian layers. These rocks form one of the most important geological horizons in the state. Although widely known in a general way their details are as yet little understood, as the various minor subdivisions recognized by different writers readily show. Until much additional information has been obtained it seems desirable to recognize now only four sections of the Devonian in Iowa. Some of these formations will probably require further breaking up as the rocks become better understood. Regarding the equivalents of the Iowa Devonian beds with the more eastern formations much has been written, but as yet no satisfactory results have been obtained.

Independence Shales. For a long time the Devonian beds of Iowa were regarded as made up almost entirely of limestones. Hall and others found clay beds in the northern part of the state; while still more recently Calvin has discovered important shales layers at the base of the Devonian, in Buchanan county. The latter beds are made up of dark carbonaceous clays with thin bands of impure concretionary limerock. In places the shales are so highly charged with bituminous matter that considerable excitement has been caused at different times, on account of their supposed nearness to coal deposits. Remains of plants have been found scattered through these clays; and they have also accumulated so abundantly locally as to form thin veins of true coal. The shales also yield a very considerable number of animal remains.

Cedar Valley Limestones. As already remarked the greater portion of the Devonian in Iowa is made up of limestones, for which it seems desirable to revive Owen's old name of Cedar Valley. These limerocks present very considerable differences in lithological characters. Although for the most part they are ordinary limestones they pass rapidly into argillaceous, dolomitic or even bituminous phases. Many of the beds are very massive though others are somewhat shaley. Everywhere the rocks of this age are highly charged with fossils of many kinds.

Some of the most valuable building and ornamental stones occurring in Iowa are of Devonian age. Perhaps the best limestones for heavy masonry found anywhere in the state are those quarried on the Iowa river north of Iowa City. The old state house at the place just mentioned, and the basement of the new Capitol building at Des Moines were both constructed of this rock. Unlimited quantities of good building stone are accessible in the Devonian throughout the exposed area. Abundant supplies for the manufacture of quick-lime are present everywhere but the quality of lime is not as good as that furnished by the upper Silurian strata.

Montpelier Sandstone. This name is applied to certain arenaceous beds that are well exposed in Muscatine county, and which have been recently differentiated by Calvin from the lower Carboniferous sand-rocks found farther to the southward. They are Devonian in age, but were formerly regarded as being identical with the Kinderhook sandstone exposed in the vicinity of Burlington. The Montpelier sandstone lies immediately above the Devonian limestone. The chief exposures of this rock are near the mouth of Pine Creek in the county mentioned. It is composed of yellowish or brownish material, somewhat friable, but in places indurated sufficiently to afford blocks for common masonry. Large quantities of this rock have been quarried and used for the rip-rap which extends for many miles along the Mississippi above Muscatine as a protection for the railroads from the waters of the river.

Lime Creek Shales. These beds have long been supposed to form the uppermost member of the Devonian in Iowa. The are well exposed in many places in Floyd county especially. Some of the most important outcrops being at Rockford and along Lime Creek. At the latter place there is exposed a vertical thickness of about one hundred feet of dark argillaceous shales which are highly fossiliferous. They disintegrate rapidly under the influences of the weather, forming a plastic clay which will probably prove quite valuable for the manufacture of brick. The geographic extent of these shales is not known at present; nor is their stratigraphic position fully understood.

CARBONIFEROUS.

Lower Carboniferous or Mississippian Series.

At the base of the Carboniferous rocks as represented in Iowa and forming one of the most important geological formations exposed within the limits of the state is the great series of limestones which have commonly been termed the "Subcarboniferous." These rocks in Iowa form a sinuous belt twenty-five to forty miles in width midway between the Cedar and Des Moines rivers. The zone mentioned thus extends from the southeastern corner of the state northwestward as far as the Minnesota line.

In southeastern Iowa the lower Carboniferous rocks form percipitous bluffs along the Mississippi and Des Moines rivers and their tributaries. The Mississippian series as represented in the continental interior is made up of four distinct formations. Only three of these however are exposed in Iowa. They are the Kinderhook, Augusta and St. Louis formations.

Kinderhook Beds. In the southeastern part of the state the Kinderhook beds are largely hard clay-shales with occasional bands of limestone. At Burlington these shales attain a thickness of over two hundred feet, not all of which, however, are exposed above the water level of the Mississippi river.

Lithologically this formation as exposed at Burlington is a massive clay-shale, often highly calcareous and in the upper part contain silicious matter in the form of fine yellow sand which occasionally assumes the character of a soft sandstone. Below the sandy portion these shales have long been supposed to be destitute of fossils, but recent exposures have disclosed faunas of a most interesting and instructive character. A short distance below Burlington near the mouth of the Skunk river these shales disappear below the water-level. At Keokuk, as has been shown by recent borings, they are in the neighborhood of one hundred and fifty feet below the water-level in the Mississippi. At Burlington immediately beneath the Burlington limestone are several beds a few feet in thickness of limestone and oolite. These are separated by clay shales. The exact relation of these beds to the rocks farther southward in Missouri is not known at present. Beyond the immediate vicinity of the Mississippi river the shales in question are not exposed at the surface in Iowa; but they apparently have a considerable geographical extent and are thought to be recognizable in a number of deep well sections in different portions of the southeastern part of the state.

A hundred miles northwest of Burlington, in Tama and Marshall counties, rocks which have been referred to the Kinderhook are well exposed along the Iowa river and some of its tributaries. The exact correlation of these beds with those of southeastern Iowa has not as yet been fully made out. As shown in the LeGrand quarries the formation is chiefly a rather soft, somewhat irregularly bedded, buff limestone, probably containing a considerable percentage of magnesia. It seems from an examination of the fossils contained in the Le Grand beds that a part of them at least correspond to the limestone at Burlington.

In southeastern Iowa no good quarry rocks have been found in the Kinderhook formation. Occasionally the oolitic beds are used, but they withstand weathering only a short time. The clay-shales at Burlington have recently been brough into prominence in the manufacture of paving brick.

Toward the northern limit in Iowa the Kinderhook assumes a calcerous facies. It is extensively quarried at numerous places in Humboldt, Hardin, Grundy, Tama and Marshall counties. In the latter localities the rock is a fine-grained limestone and forms a very durable building stone. It has been used largely for bridge piers and architectural purposes. Portions of it contain ferric-oxide in narrow veinings. It takes a fairly good polish and is extensively used for interior work in place of ordinary marble. The lower part of the Le Grand section is made up of very compact oolitic rock which withstands very well all weathering influences, as is shown in the court house at Marshalltown which is constructed almost entirely of this stone.

Augusta Limestone. The two formations commonly known as the Burlington and Keokuk limestones have recently been found to form properly but a single sequence of rocks. The Burlington and the Keokuk groups are called after the cities of the same name in southeastern Iowa. At these localities the rocks have been regarded as typical developments. A careful examination of the fossils contained and of the relations of the different beds indicate that the limestones under consideration which were formerly considered as two distinct formations should be included under a single term. The lower portion of the formation commonly known as the Burlington limestone is a coarse-grained, encrinital rock, usually white and very pure in certain layers. It often contains considerable ferric-oxide and consequently a reddish hue is imparted to it upon exposure. The lithological characters of this rock are remarkably constant over broad areas. There are also in certain places silicious beds, the lowermost of which have thickness of twenty-five feet or more. They are made up largely of nodular masses and irregular bands of chert with some calcareous matter. There are other layers of flint of equal if not greater importance in the Augusta beds than those just mentioned. The so-called Keokuk limestones are essentially the same as the Burlington rocks. They are usually more compact, less fossiliferous and have a bluish cast instead of the pure white color. The upper portion of the formation also contains beds of clay-shales.

The Augusta Limestones are quarried rather extensively; the chief localities being at Columbus Junction, Burlington and vicinity, Ft. Madison, Keokuk, Bonaparte, and Bentonsport. The rocks at Burlington are used for ordinary masonry; some of the layers, the more massive ones, forming fairly good material for building. Large quantities of good lime could be manufactured, but at the present time only a few small kilns are in operation. Farther southward in Missouri, the Burlington limestone is quarried largely for the manufacture of lime as well as for ordinary masonry. The lower layers at Keokuk have been used for bridge work and all kinds of common masonry. A good quality of lime is burned at various points in the vicinities of the places just mentioned. The sandy magnesian layers at the top of the Keokuk limestone have been extensively used for building and a number of churches and other structures are composed of this material. Along the Des Moines river the rocks of this formation were formerly used in the construction of dams at the time when slack-water navigation was proposed for the Des Moines river.

St. Louis Limestone. The rocks of this stage have commonly passed under the name of Concretionary limestone. But they are the same as those developed at the mouth of the Missouri river which Shumard called after the city of St. Louis. The northern limit of these rocks is one hundred miles beyond any known exposure of Augusta rocks. From this northern border nearly to the mouth of the Missouri river the limestone is comparatively thin; but southward from the latter point it thickens rapidly until it attains a measurement of more than two hundred feet. Everywhere over the northern area of the St. Louis, characteristic brecciated rocks are seen. In Iowa this formation has probably a surface exposure much greater than any other member of the Lower Carboniferous. It is usually a fine-grained, compact, bluish rock breaking with concholdal fracture. The upper portion of the formation is often covered by a white, highly fossiliferous marl.

The St. Louis limestone is made up largely of pure calcium carbonate. Quick-lime is manufactured at numerous places everywhere throughout the range of the formation. At Tracey, and elsewhere in Marion, Wapello and Van Buren counties certain of the St. Louis rocks furnish excellent material for heavy constructional purposes, bridge piers and foundations

COAL MEASURES.

From an economic standpoint the most important geological formation in the state is that yielding coal. The strata of Iowa furnishing this valuable product form the northernmost extension of the great interior coal field of the American continent. The beds occupy the southern third of the state and are distributed more or less extensively through one-half of the entire number of counties. The area covered by the Carboniferous strata is therefore not far from twenty thousand square miles. It must not be inferred, however, that the coal is equally distributed over all this district, for such is not the case. The broad belt running southeast and northwest and traversed its entire length by the Des Moines river from Fort Dodge to Keokuk has heretofore been found to be much more productive of coal than other parts of the region. Lately in many places outside of the belt named, coal has been discovered in abundance, often where its presence was unsuspected before.

Taken as a whole there are two kinds of beds, sharply contrasted, which go to make up the Coal Measures of the state. The first is marked by a great predominance of clay shales and sandstones, often to the total exclusion of the limestone. The individual beds have usually a very limited extent and replace one another in rapid succession. On the other hand, the second class of sediments above mentioned is made up chiefly of calcareous shales with heavy beds of limestone. The layers are evenly bedded and extend over very considerable areas.

As the conditions of deposition were evidently those of a slowly sinking shore the marginal deposits as a whole practically underlie the open sea formations, the former being regarded as the "Lower" Coal Measures and the latter as the "Upper" Coal Measures. At the same time it must be remembered that this does not necessarily imply that the "Lower" measures are to be considered much older than the "Upper;" but rather that along the great and successive planes of sedimentation different beds of the upper and lower divisions were laid down contemporaneously. The limits of the two formations in Iowa thus assume somewhat different lines from those that have commonly been recognized.

It has been proposed, therefore, to divide the Coal Measures, or Upper Carboniferous, into:

(2) The "Upper" Coal Measures, or Missouri Stage.
(1) The "Lower" Coal Measures, or Des Moines Stage.

The Des Moines formation represents the Lower Coal Measures or marginal deposits of the upper Carboniferous. It takes its name from the Des Moines river which flows for more than two hundred miles directly through the beds of this terrane. It extends into Missouri forming the northern and western boundaries of the Ozark mountains and extends still farther southward into Kansas and Indian Territory.

The Missouri formation corresponds essentially to the upper Coal Measures, representing the more strictly marine deposits. It is the formation typically developed in the northwestern part of Missouri. The Missouri river also winds its way for more than four hundred miles through the beds of this stage, exposing numerous fine sections on both sides of the stream throughout the entire distance.

In the order of their abundance the rocks of the Coal Measures are clay-shales, sandstones, limestones and coals. The secondary part that the calcareous beds play in the Coal Measures of the state, especially in the lower division, contrasts this formation with the other paleozoic rocks. Below, the Coal Measures rest on a great basement of massive limestones with but few clayey or sandy beds of separation. Not less striking is the relative thinness, as a rule, of the individual layers which replace one another upwards and laterally in rapid succession. If the upper and lower divisions of the Coal Measures in Iowa were to be contrasted upon lithological characters alone it would be found that the former is prevailingly lime bearing; the latter largely clayey.

Little need be said here concerning the quality of the coals of the state. They are all of the bituminous variety and are fully described in another place. The carbonaceous seams vary from a few inches to seven or eight or even ten feet in thickness; the average of the veins at present worked is between four and five feet. These beds are deposited not in two or three continuous layers over the entire area, as has been commonly supposed, but in more or less lenticular masses varying from a few feet to several miles in extent.

The stratigraphical importance of the coal seams is not so great as has been generally supposed, since the bituminous beds are, with very few exceptions rather limited. Only a single case is at present known in which the geographic extent of a coal stratum is more than a few miles, and for a part of this distance the coal is but two or three feet in thickness. On the other hand, the amount of coal in the state, is probably very much greater than has been commonly supposed.

For reasons which need not be stated in detail here, considerable difficulty has been encountered in working out the structural features of the Coal Measures of Iowa. The general inclination of the beds is to the southwestward. Careful estimates indicate that the greatest thickness of the Lower Coal Measures in the state is probably in the neighborhood of four hundred feet; and that the maximum vertical measurement of the upper division is thrice that figure. Erosion has removed much of the coal bearing strata of this district and the original thickness of these rocks is not now represented at any one place.

The basal coal seams of the Lower Coal Measures of Iowa appear to be much more extensive than those toward the top, where they are only a few inches in vertical measurement and perhaps a hundred yards in extent. The coal may therefore be regarded as disposed in numerous basins of greater or less area, thickened centrally, but gradually becoming attenuated toward the margins. These are arranged in various horizons interlocking with one another, but separated by varying thicknesses of sandstone and shale. Thus at any one point a dozen or more seams may be passed through in sinking a shaft, several perhaps being workable.

The disposition of the coal in numerous limited lenticular basins instead of a few layers extending over broad areas is of the utmost importance from a purely economical standpoint. In all mining operations and in all prospecting it is very essential that this fact be kept constantly in mind. With methods of boring more modern than those commonly in vogue throughout the western states there is every reason to believe that in the Lower Coal Measures especially the large majority of good coal seams twelve inches in thickness and over encountered in prospecting may be traced readily and easily to localities where they are thick enough for profitable working.

In Iowa the restrictions upon the distribution of the individual seams are not numerous as compared with other regions. Yet there are disturbances of various kinds which break the continuity of the coal strata, locally interfering slightly with mining operations. They are referable to the three general agencies of deposition, erosion and dislocation.

From careful estimates made from reliable sources the production of coal for the past year amounted to more than 5,340,000 tons, valued at $7,750,000. By comparisons it will be seen that Iowa as a coal producer ranks first among the states west of the Mississippi river and fifth among the states of the Union.

Throughout all of the Coal Measures in Iowa occur unlimited quantities of clay of excellent quality for the manufacture of paving, pressed, fire and other kinds of brick. An excellent quality of potter's clay and material for tiling, terra-cotta, and in fact nearly all other kinds of clay products, are plentiful.

CRETACEOUS.

Although formerly known to be exposed only over a small area near Sioux City, the Cretaceous rocks of Iowa have recently been found to occupy a very considerable district in the northwestern portion of the state. On account of a thick mantle of drift over all this portion of the state there is considerable difficulty in locating the exact boundary along the eastern margin of the deposits. From numerous borings, however, the Cretaceous beds have been recognized over more than a dozen counties, showing that the approximate eastern boundary is a somewhat sinuous line running through a point midway between Sioux City and Council Bluffs nearly to Fort Dodge and thence bending northward. Beyond the limits of this line numerous outliers have been recognized, some appearing more than fifty miles beyond the boundary mentioned.

There are four formations in Iowa which are probably referable to the Cretaceous, though the exact stratigraphical equivalents of two of these, the Fort Dodge gypsum deposits and the Nishnabotna sandstone are at present somewhat doubtful.

Nishnabotna Sandstone. Although the beds under consideration have usually been referred to the Cretaceous they have never been directly traced to the outcrops of the Woodbury shales. The geographical distance between the nearest exposures of the two formations as at present known is very considerable. If the Nishnabotna is Cretaceous it may be the equivalent either of the Woodbury shales or of the Niobrara chalk; which one it is cannot now be stated. In regard to the gypsum beds their formation indicates a saline lake deposit such as might be left by a retreating ocean. This fact taken in connection with the probable great eastern extension of the Niobrara suggests that the Fort Dodge beds were formed during the retreat of the Niobrara waters through Iowa. At the present time it seems best not to attempt a specific correlation of the gypsum deposits, nor of the Nishnabotna sandstone, but merely to regard them as Cretaceous in age. The sandstones and loose sands that have been called Nishnabotna are to be regarded as shore deposits; along with numerous other beds of similar character which occasionally are found as outliers through central and northern Iowa.

The Nishnabotna as reported by White has a thickness of fifty to seventy-five feet, and is seen exposed in the southeastern part of Guthrie county, southern Montgomery county, and elsewhere in the western part of central Iowa.

Quarries have been opened in these rocks at Lewis, in Cass county. In its lithological characters the formation is a coarse-grained, ferruginous sandstone, dark brown in color and usually quite friable. Occasionally thin clay seams are intercalated.

Fort Dodge Beds. This name is applied to the gypsum deposits and certain associated beds which are well exposed in the neighborhood of Fort Dodge. The gypsum attains a vertical measurement of from two to thirty feet, its average thickness being perhaps about fifteen to sixteen feet. It occupies an area, in the central part of Webster county, of about twenty-five square miles. It is traversed north and south its entire length by the Des Moines river and is cut through by many of this stream's smaller tributaries

Probably more than one-half of the entire deposit has been removed through erosion by the chief water course. The most extensive exposures now open are about six miles below Fort Dodge.

To some extent the massive gypsum of Fort Dodge has been quarried for building purposes. A number of buildings and foundations have been constructed of this material. It has also been used quite extensively for heavy masonry. Its most important use, however, is its manufacture into stucco and land-plaster. During the past year more than fifty thousand tons of these materials were prepared in the vicinity of Fort Dodge.

Woodbury Shales. As already intimated, the typical outcrops of this formation are to be seen in Woodbury county along the Big Sioux river. The formation corresponds essentially with the Dakota and Fort Benton groups of Hayden. The beds represent shore deposits and it seems desirable to retain the name in preference to the two proposed by Hayden. "Woodbury" as defined by White expresses more accurately than any other name yet proposed the lithological features of the rocks as represented in Iowa.

The Woodbury shales are made up in certain places largely of the sandstone, which sometimes form hard concretionary masses not unlike quartzite. In some localities these masses are so near together that they may be quarried to advantage for building stone. The most important of these openings is in the vicinity of Sioux City and is now known as the Rees' Granite quarry. The rock has apparently all the qualities of the regular crystalline massive rocks. The greater portion of the Woodbury shales is argillaceous and afford inexhaustible quantities of good clay for the manufacture of pottery, fire and paving brick.

Niobrara Chalk. These beds in their chalky facies have been observed in Iowa in the vicinity of the Big Sioux river. They are probably represented farther eastward by more strictly shore deposits. They consist of fine soft calcareous layers appearing not unlike clay at first glance. These chalky layers in connection with the clays form excellent material for the manufacture of Portland cement. This industry has already begun under favorable circumstances on the Missouri above Sioux City.

PLEISTOCENE, OR SURFACE DEPOSITS.

Over all Iowa, covering the indurated rocks to a depth of from a few inches to two or three hundred feet, is a mantle of loose incoherent material. This material is chiefly of three kinds; known as the drift, loess, and alluvium. The latter may be regarded as the deposits of the modern rivers, the two former as glacial debris.

Alluvium. Little need be said here in regard to the alluvial deposits. They are the fine sediments laid down in the river valleys making up what is commonly known as the flood plain. Many of the river terraces are also alluvial. These materials will be treated at length in another place in connection with an account of the soils of the state.

Drift. To the heterogeneous mixture of clay, sand, gravel and boulders which is seen everywhere throughout the state there has been applied the name of drift. Everwhere the proportions of these drift constitutents vary. It changes rapidly from place to place passing from one kind into another. The clays form by far the largest portion of the mixture and is usually mingled with more or less fine sand. In color it has a characteristic brown or buff tint. When excavated the surface exposed quickly breaks up into small cubic or angular fragments commonly known as joint-clay. The sand and gravel often form considerable beds yet they are usually quite limited in extent. The boulders are chiefly of crystalline rocks of northern origin. They represent a great variety of eruptive and metamorphic types.

The drift is largely of glacial origin. It has been shown in Iowa to be made up of two sheets. The lowest or earliest drift forms a part of the great drift mantle extending over northern United States. In the Mississippi valley it has its southern boundary along the line of the Ohio and Missouri rivers. The upper till belongs to a later glacial epoch and is included within the area bounded by what is known as the moraine of the Des Moines lobe of the second great ice invasion. This forms a narrow triangle in Iowa with its apex reaching to the city of Des Moines.

Loess. This deposit is well displayed along the Missouri and Mississippi rivers and at numerous places throughout the interior of Iowa. It is a fine homogeneous clay-like material which seldom shows any tendency toward stratification. It is friable enough to be impressed with the finger but resists weathering in a remarkable way.

The surface deposits of the state belong chiefly to the Quaternary age of geology. Over a great part of Iowa the soils are formed directly through these deposits. The purer clays afford good material for the manufacture of brick; while certain portions afford sand which can be utilized in glass making.

CLIMATOLOGY OF IOWA.

By John R. Sage, Director Iowa Weather and Crop Service.

The prime factors of agricultural prosperity are a fertile soil and a favorable climate, the latter being the more important. There are in this country millions of acres of soil, which, though abundantly supplied with the elements of fertility are comparatively worthless, because of unfavorable climatic conditions. Nothing can fully compensate for the lack of rainfall in the growing season, for only a small portion of any arid region can be made productive by irrigation.

The claim may be made in behalf of Iowa that in respect to these two essentials, soil and climate, it stands foremost among the agricultural states of the Union. There is no question as to the exceeding richness and depth of its soil, for it has maintained a large measure of its original fertility under a system of continual cropping which would have reduced to barrenness the thinner soils of less favored sections. And its climate has served as a fit complement of its soil in the production of those vast crops which have figured so conspicuously in the agricultural statistics of the country.

The establishment of the National and State weather bureaus has incited public interest in questions relating to the climate of the different sections of our greatly diversified country. And the census reports have revealed the fact that the settlement of the country and increase of population bear a very definite ratio to the average yearly precipitation, mean temperature and the general climatic conditions affecting crop production and the public health. People who are about to emigrate, to better their condition in life, are largely influenced in their choice of a new home by such facts as they are able to obtain relative to climate. With the larger number this is very properly a consideration of chief importance.

WEATHER REPORTS.

Fortunately we have at hand ample meteorological records to illustrate the constants of temperature, humidity, wind movement and the general characteristics of the climate of Iowa. Weather observations were begun at the military posts in the territory as early as the year 1820, and records were made with some degree of regularity under military auspices until 1849, when the Smithsonian Institution, aided by the general government, took up the work of systematic observation, establishing stations wherever intelligent observers could be secured. Since 1871 this work has been done under the auspices of the National and State weather services. There is, therefore, no lack of material, in the form of official records, from which we may obtain a knowledge of the more important features of Iowa's climate. A careful study of the voluminous data will convince any one interested in the subject that for all-the-year-round residence, for the promotion of health, physical vigor and agricultural prosperity there is no more favorable climate in America than in this favored section of the great Mississippi valley.

GENERAL CLIMATIC FEATURES.

Situated near the geographical center of the United States, the climate is strictly continental. This term being used in contradistinction to marine climate implies that it has winters of considerable severity, and summers of unusual warmth, with large seasonal and daily temperature ranges, a generally dry and salubrious atmosphere, small percentage of cloudiness and large percentage of sunshine. The altitude of the State ranges from 444 feet above sea-level at the confluence the Des Moines and Mississippi rivers, to 1,650 feet at a point near Spirit Lake; and as there are no mountain ranges nor extensive forests the physical conditions give to the State a homogeneous climate, with only such variations of temperature, rainfall and other meteorological elements as result from latitude and elevation.

Despite its remoteness from the sea its climatic characteristics are remarkably constant; in fact, no section of the country enjoys a greater degree of uniformity of the conditions favorable to the production of the staple crops. In attestation of this it may be stated that, while there have been seasons of variable productiveness, there has never been a total failure of the principal crops in this State since the virgin soil was first broken by the plow-shares of the white settlers.

The climate of this section is affected by the general topography of the continent, the great mountain ranges, and the oceanic and atmospheric currents, all of which must be duly considered in a thorough study of the subject. A glance at the map of the continent will show a great central depression extending from the Gulf of Mexico to the Arctic sea, formed by the vast mountain ranges at the west and the lesser uplift skirting the Atlantic coast. This interior valley is much wider and somewhat lower at the north than at the south, and two-thirds of the drainage of the continent flows northward. The upper Mississippi valley, of which Iowa is a part, forms the water-shed about midway between the Gulf and Hudson Bay. It has been stated that in time of high water a canoe can be rowed from the Mississippi up the Minnesota to its source in Big Stone Lake, and thence across a slough to Traverse Lake, the source of the Red River of the North. The altitude at this point where the waters of the Gulf and the Arctic ocean are in touch is less than one thousand feet above sea level.

Through this vast channel in ancient geologic periods the glaciers pushed their way, forming the drift deposits, and laying the foundation of soil of the most productive empire on the surface of the globe. And now, in these latter years, this mid-continent depression gives free passage to the boreal breezes from the north and the humid winds from the south, which here meet and commingle to refresh the earth with copious showers in the season when they are most needed. It is easy to see what an important part is borne in the climate of the interior by the great physical feature herein described. If the mountain ranges crossed the continent east and west, instead of north and south, this central valley would be a veritable desert, instead of the garden and granary of the western hemisphere. The cool waves from the north and the vapor-laden winds from the south are equally important factors in making this a habitable, productive and prosperous region.

PRECIPITATION.

The moisture precipitated over Iowa and contiguous portions of the Mississippi and Missouri valleys comes almost entirely, either directly or indirectly, from the Gulf of Mexico. The warm southerly winds, heavily laden with humidity from that source, drawn hither by the passage of low area storms from the west, deposit a portion of their moisture in advance of the storm centers as they move toward the Atlantic. Following in the rear of these depressions the cold and dry air from the northward condenses the remaining moisture in the rear quadrants of departing storms. These alternating currents flowing northward and southward through the valley, with their sharp contrasts of temperature, brought thus into action by the passage of low areas across the continent, form the warp and woof of the fabric of the weather of this section. And as the Gulf, which is the great fountain of humidity whence our annual supply of moisture is drawn, is permanent, and the atmospheric waves of high or low pressure are constantly passing, there is no danger that this region will become arid and unproductive. The people may safely bank upon the permanence of their climate and an ample supply of moisture.

Various early historic publications placed the average yearly precipitation of Iowa at forty-four to forty-seven inches. These figures are too high, being obtained from insufficient data. The correct mean obtained from all available records, covering a considerable number of years in all sections of the state is about thirty-five inches.

Blodget's rain chart for the continent shows the average annual precipitation in the eastern and southeastern counties to be forty-two inches; through the central belt from southwest to northeast it is thirty, and in the extreme northwestern section twenty-five inches. In the United States

Army Meteorological Register, published in 1855, Mr. Blodget, referring to the precipitation in the Mississippi Valley, says:

"There is an exceptional district in eastern Iowa having a great rain fall, which requires some explanation, especially in its contrast with the small quantities at Lake Michigan. The exception is due apparently to the elevation of central Missouri in comparison with lower Iowa, causing an atmospheric eddy similar to that of the lower Mississippi."

A careful study of meteorological data covering the period since the above was published does not show so wide a difference between the average annual precipitation of the eastern, central and western districts of the State. For example, the average at Keokuk, from 1872 to 1892, is 35.87 inches; at Muscatine, 1845 to 1892, 39.21 inches; at Davenport, 1872 to 1892, 34.70 inches; at Dubuque, 1874 to 1892, 37.00 inches; at McGregor, 16 years record, 34.97 inches. These stations are all in the eastern part of the State, and it will be seen the average is below the figures of Blodget's rain chart. In the central and western sections of the State, the following averages are obtained: Des Moines, 35.06 inches; Sioux City, 25.58 inches; Council Bluffs, 33.36 inches; Logan, 35.50 inches; Sac City, 30.82 inches; Glenwood, 31.70 inches. These figures indicate that there is a more equable distribution of rainfall than the earlier charts and tables showed. And it may be stated further that in the western half of the State the precipitation in the winter months is considerably less than in the eastern half, while the rainfall in the summer months is greater in the western than in the eastern districts.

COMPARISON WITH EASTERN STATES.

The annual precipitation in Iowa is equal to the averages in the northern, central and western portions of New York, northern Vermont and New Hampshire, northwestern counties of Pennsylvania, northern Ohio and the larger part of Michigan. In fact it compares favorably with all the Atlantic and Middle States on the same latitude, except points along or near the sea coast, or in the mountainous districts. The following yearly averages are from the United States Weather Bureau tables of recent date:

STATIONS.	INCHES.	STATIONS.	INCHES.
Charlotte, Vt	33.79	Fort Niagara, N. Y	25.52
Hanover, N. H	30.94	Buffalo, N. Y	38.55
Portland, Me	41.55	Pittsburgh, Pa	38.29
Fitchburg, Mass	38.07	Cleveland, Ohio	37.90
Woodstock, Vt	37.90	Toledo, Ohio	32.94
Albany, N. Y	38.88	Detroit, Mich	33.83
Cooperstown, N. Y	35.60	Alpena, Mich	36.00
Madison Barracks, N. Y	27.07	Escanaba, Mich	33.93
Rochester, N. Y	35.52	Marquette, Mich	33.93
Ithaca, N. Y	31.73	Lansing, Mich	33.75

Comparison of these yearly averages with the accompanying tables of annual precipitation at a large number of Iowa stations will show that the eastern states on this parallel have no advantage over Iowa in respect to the yearly supply of moisture.

And it will be seen that these figures do not sustain the theory that the annual precipitation of a locality is affected by contiguity to the lakes or extensive forests. In fact, local evaporation, whether from marshes, lakes or forests does not materially affect the rainfall of the interior of the continent. The following from the United States Army Meteorological Register is to the point:

"The lake district presents a somewhat anomalous result, in comparison with the interior portions, as it has less rainfall than the valley of the Mississippi in their latitudes. The effect of these bodies of water is clearly to diminish the quantity of rain for the whole period of the warm season. This deficiency appears very clearly in the mean for the spring, and it is conclusive proof that local evaporation adds little or none to the quantity of rain of these interior districts. The valley of the Mississippi, and its extension in the Ohio valley, strikingly contrast with the rainfall in the lake districts.

DISTRIBUTION BY SEASONS.

A peculiar feature of the climate of the trans-Mississippi region is that it has its minimum of precipitation in the winter, and its maximum in the spring and summer, or in the crop growing season. This characteristic of the climate is of great economic importance, since it insures an abundance of food products even in years of the greatest variability in the distribution of moisture. In this respect Iowa has a most decided advantage over the eastern states which have a much heavier annual rainfall, for in this State two-thirds of the yearly moisture comes in the six crop growing months, when it is most needed. Professor Blodget, in his American Climatology, refers to this feature as follows:

"For the whole period of the warm months, in which May and September should be included, the quantity of rain distributed over the Mississippi valley is comparatively very great, and there is no great area so far in the interior which presents a similar result. The quantities are absolutely as well as relatively large, and they considerably exceed those of the plains of the Atlantic coast in the same latitude. The line of fifteen inches for the three (summer) months goes only to 38 of latitude on the Atlantic coast, yet it rises nearly to 44 in the Mississippi valley, and occupies a very wide area below the fortieth parallel. The measure of twelve inches is equally more extensive in the interior, though neither of these stretches upon the plains beyond 100 west longitude."

The fact here stated is undoubtedly due to the prevalence during the summer months of southerly winds laden with vapor from the Gulf, the great thermal fountain whence is drawn the bulk of the precipitation of the interior valleys. The following table gives, as a basis of comparison, the average rainfall for the four critical months of the year, viz: May, June, July and August, at a number of stations in the Atlantic states and in Iowa:

EASTERN STATIONS.	INCHES.	IOWA STATIONS.	INCHES.
Albany, N. Y.	15.21	Des Moines	17.20
Rochester, N. Y.	12.47	Council Bluffs	19.10
Buffalo, N. Y.	13.28	Logan	19.50
Oswego, N. Y.	11.66	Dubuque	17.35
Cleveland, Ohio	11.68	Muscatine	18.50
Atlantic City, N. Y.	13.88	Keokuk	16.30

It should be noted that these four months make the corn, as also the other staple crops of this region, excepting hay, and a glance at the figures of the above table will show the great advantage enjoyed by the Mississippi valley in the distribution of summer rainfall. The average rainfall of Iowa for the four months named is as follows: May 4.15 inches; June 4.95; July 4.30; August 3.60. Total for the four months 17.00 inches.

But let us take the six crop months, adding April and September to the four above named, and we have a total average rainfall of 23.25 inches, or an average of 3.87 inches per month. This amount of moisture in the soil, and a mean summer temperature of 71 degrees, give a hot-house development to the staple crops of this region.

Dr. Gustavus Hinrichs, who originated the Iowa Weather Service and served over twelve years as its director, said in his last annual report: "While Iowa has a continental climate in regard to temperature, it enjoys the fertilizing advantages of a high and well distributed rainfall usually restricted to the coasts only. In fact there is no region in the interior of any continent that has a climate like that of Iowa, in which the extremes of temperature are coupled with an abundance of fertilizing moisture. Right close to the south, the immense boiler of the Gulf is furnishing vapor; the heated continental expanse north causes the southerly current prevailing throughout the summer. These southerly winds carry the moisture of the Gulf all over the Mississippi valley, where it descends normally in great abundance, making it the best watered valley in the world."

In Hall's Geology of Iowa the following statement occurs in the opening chapter: "The most marked feature in the distribution of moisture precipitated in the form of rain and snow through the year is a relative increase in the quantity falling in the spring and summer, and a very considerable diminution in winter; which condition becomes more and more marked as we advance westward from the Mississippi. The diminution in the quantity of snow, as compared with the eastern States on the same parallel, is one of the features of the climate which is practically most felt by settlers in that region."

The climatic feature has a favorable effect upon the health and comfort of the inhabitants of this region, the relatively dry atmosphere enabling them to easily withstand the low temperature prevalent in the winter months. Those who have experienced the chilling atmosphere and "eternal drizzle" of the so-called milder climates of the sea coast region can appreciate the difference.

CROPS IN DROUGHTY SEASONS.

While a high average of summer rainfall has been recorded for the past fifty years, this State like all other sections of the country is subject to fluctuations or variability in the seasonal precipitation, and occasional droughty seasons have been experienced. But as a compensation there is a peculiar quality of the Iowa soil which enables it to withstand droughts and produce abundantly with an average summer rainfall that would be totally insufficient in eastern and southern states. This fact was noted by Prof. T. S. Parvin some years ago, who in a contribution to the American Journal of Science, Vol. XXIII, said:

"In 1854 occurred the great drought in this and the western States generally; but owing to the porous nature of our soil the crops with us turned out much better than in the States east of the Mississippi."

"1856. This season was very dry; the total quantity of rain in the summer months was only 6.78 inches, or 10.20 below the summer mean. The crops were, notwithstanding, more than an average yield, both of corn and small grain; and the three or four dry seasons we have had abundantly prove that the soil and climate of Iowa are unsurpassed on the continent for farming purposes."

These facts so well stated by Prof. Parvin have been remarked in the occasional dry seasons that have occurred since the above was written, justifying the assertion that there has never been any very near approach to absolute failure of crops in Iowa since its settlement by civilized man. And the years of severe drought in the summer months have been very few in comparison to the number suffered in some of the States which have a larger average annual rainfall.

The severest drought in recent years, affecting the lower part of the State, occurred in the mid-summer of 1890. The average amount of rainfall in July was only 1.98 inches, and in August, 3.41 inches. And the severity of the drought was greatly increased by very high winds during the periods of high temperature. And yet in that year of untoward conditions, Iowa produced 239,000,000 bushels of corn, 71,368,000 bushels of oats, 2,979,081 bushels of flax, 8,332,000 bushels of potatoes, 4,991,000 tons of hay, and over $50,000,000 worth of poultry products. There is no danger of a famine in a country, which, in the worst seasons, can produce such vast amounts of food stuffs.

The same porous nature of the soil which causes it to withstand severe droughts, also gives it the requisite quality to take up a considerable surplus of rainfall, making it fairly productive in abnormally wet seasons. These extremes, however, are exceptional, by far the greater number of years being normal and abundantly productive. The State is favorably situated in the heart of the valley, escaping frequent liability to the extremes of wet and dry to which other sections are subject.

Prof. W. I. Chamberlain, of Ohio, who served about five years as president of the Iowa Agricultural College, gave the following unbiased testimony concerning the soil and climate of this state:

"One thing has surprised me each spring and summer, viz: that the spring is considerably earlier here than it is a hundred miles further south in Ohio, and the summer is much hotter and surer to mature the corn crop before frost. The proportion of clear sky and hot days and nights is far greater, and the power of the sun's rays upon the black soil is immense. I believe Iowa to be on the whole the best and surest corn State in the Union, the surface is more rolling, the soil more porous and sandy and better drained by nature than most of the prairie soils in other States. Hence the corn is not so subject to damage from too much rain here as in Illinois and Missouri. It dries out for cultivation quicker."

TABULATED PRECIPITATION DATA.

The following table gives the average monthly and annual precipitation (rain and melted snow) in inches, at a number of Iowa Stations, covering the records of years named in the last column. The United States Weather Bureau furnished the data from various official sources:

STATIONS.	JAN'RY	FEB'RY	MARCH	APRIL	MAY	JUNE	JULY	AUGUST	SEPT'R	OCTOB'R	NOV'B'R	DEC'B'R	ANNUAL	NO. OF YEARS
Algona	.92	1.55	1.52	2.20	3.46	4.62	3.04	3.82	3.23	2.33	1.30	.89	27.77	16
Amana	1.51	1.36	2.08	2.45	3.19	4.95	3.84	2.91	3.53	3.13	2.00	1.64	34.07	11
Ames	1.01	1.01	1.54	2.43	3.81	1.08	4.51	3.74	3.76	2.33	1.42	1.36	30.96	9
Brookside	.85	1.65	1.43	3.00	4.82	5.74	5.95	5.21	1.60	3.62	2.11	1.02	40.96	11
Brookville	1.26	1.25	1.00	2.06	3.85	4.55	2.82	3.89	3.00	3.59	1.64	1.02	32.21	15
Cedar Rapids	1.22	1.73	1.45	2.51	3.47	5.11	4.20	3.21	2.64	3.04	1.63	1.42	33.83	20
Creco	1.34	1.00	1.07	2.33	1.89	5.95	5.23	3.34	3.45	3.04	1.10	.99	31.45	13
Council Bluffs	.80	1.18	1.57	2.12	4.47	1.63	5.12	2.68	3.15	2.96	1.00	1.02	31.45	15
Clinton	1.92	2.21	2.16	2.69	4.40	4.36	3.91	3.04	3.16	2.59	2.05	2.11	35.70	20
Davenport	1.74	1.63	2.31	3.12	3.96	5.82	4.12	3.63	4.33	2.24	1.85	1.66	37.19	23
Dubuque	1.89	1.56	1.46	2.69	4.22	4.96	4.55	4.32	3.15	2.36	1.45	1.35	35.06	18
Des Moines	1.40	1.31	1.73	2.56	3.28	4.22	3.19	3.71	4.40	3.03	1.64	.96	33.34	21
Denmark	1.02	1.21	1.46	2.33	4.28	4.96	3.28	3.22	4.03	2.73	1.70	1.02	31.31	13
Dysart	1.50	1.74	1.73	2.13	3.13	4.56	4.62	3.02	3.00	3.06	2.05	1.98	34.71	12
Elkader	1.50	1.66	1.78	2.36	3.55	4.47	4.14	1.66	4.17	3.07	1.64	.88	34.58	11
Fairfield	1.73	2.18	2.77	3.13	5.13	5.03	4.85	4.43	4.28	3.45	2.03	1.46	34.28	22
Ft. Madison	1.14	1.17	1.46	2.61	1.10	5.81	1.72	3.25	3.56	3.04	1.34	.80	39.65	7
Guttenburg	1.46	1.96	1.96	3.33	2.76	5.03	4.69	3.91	3.33	3.17	1.53	.74	31.78	21
Glenwood	1.57	1.05	2.26	3.13	4.15	5.63	4.85	1.43	3.72	3.40	.85	1.46	36.87	18
Iowa City	.73	1.00	2.16	2.96	4.04	4.92	1.19	3.34	4.01	3.00	1.55	1.03	35.57	20
Independence	1.56	1.80	1.89	2.63	3.94	5.81	4.09	3.52	4.31	2.53	2.00	1.68	35.20	16
Keokuk	1.04	1.00	2.29	2.63	3.66	4.96	5.41	3.91	4.72	1.80	1.34	1.35	36.74	35
Le Claire	1.64	2.04	2.78	2.50	3.66	4.86	3.33	3.67	3.33	3.04	2.06	3.04	39.56	13
Logan	1.61	1.04	1.20	2.00	4.10	5.86	6.06	3.57	3.71	3.12	1.45	1.80	45.58	16
Monticello	.81	1.18	1.20	2.03	4.61	4.91	4.33	3.12	4.91	3.03	1.78	1.20	31.80	11
Muscatine	1.51	2.64	2.20	2.65	3.66	4.48	6.05	5.43	4.03	3.04	2.20	1.80	41.80	19
McGregor	.86	1.25	1.29	2.65	1.43	4.41	5.11	3.35	2.71	2.50	1.90	1.96	33.06	12
Nashua	.96	1.11	1.46	2.65	4.51	5.04	4.05	3.12	4.04	3.06	1.30	.97	30.92	10
Oskaloosa	.67	.72	1.29	2.94	3.86	4.36	4.40	3.66	3.61	3.35	2.35	1.04	35.20	15
Omaha, Nebraska	1.25	1.18	1.52	2.03	4.36	4.74	3.71	3.36	2.56	1.93	.76	.54	39.76	16
Sac City	1.18	1.31	1.20	2.91	3.84	4.36	4.90	3.12	4.13	2.80	1.28	.73	35.29	16
Winterset	1.50	1.39	1.49	2.54	2.55	4.76	3.99	3.43	3.91	3.65	1.46	1.17	35.26	17
Waukon	1.14	1.21	1.12	2.39	3.34	3.74	3.30	2.75	3.85	3.37	1.12	.70	30.30	12
Wesley														10
AVERAGES	1.37	1.42	2.08	2.60	4.15	4.95	4.30	3.66	3.70	3.03	1.76	1.65	34.86	

Total for the six growing months, 23.47 inches.
Average per month of crop season, 3.90 inches.

SUNSHINE, CLOUDINESS, ETC.

Notwithstanding its copious rainfall and the abundant humidity of the air in the growing season, Iowa has a large average percentage of sunshine, and a correspondingly small amount of cloudiness. A little over fifty per cent of the days are clear, or partially obscured by clouds, and the average annual cloudiness is not over 47 per cent. The rainfall comes largely in the form of evening showers, and it may be stated that nearly one-third of the summer storms occur between the hours of six and ten p. m., and more than 65 per cent of the precipitation falls at evening or during the night. The rising sun, increasing heat and expanding air of the morning hours, and throughout the larger part of each day, serve to dissipate the clouds and rapidly dry the surface of the fields moistened by evening showers. Fogs are of rare occurrence, and usually of short duration. At Des Moines the average number of days on which there is a fall of rain or snow amounting to .01 of an inch or more is 117 per year, and the average number of cloudless days is 126 per year. Prof. Parvin's thirty-two years records at Muscatine and Iowa City show an annual average of 116 clear days, 169 variable and 80 cloudy. The average for the State is 115 clear days, 144 partly cloudy, and 105 cloudy days per year. For the three summer months the average is 30 clear, 41 partly cloudy, and 21 cloudy days. That shows a very large average amount of sunshine during the season of crop production. The maximum of cloudiness is in March and December, and the minimum in July, August and September.

TEMPERATURE.

In Iowa the summers are decidedly warmer, and the winters slightly colder than in the eastern States on the same parallels. The annual mean temperature is about 47 degrees, ranging from 42 at the more elevated northern points to 50 degrees near the southern line. The mean temperature of spring and autumn very nearly correspond to the yearly average. And the normals of April and October also approximate very closely to the spring, autumn and yearly means.

The temperature range of the State is quite high, averaging probably 120 degrees from the minimum of winter to the maximum of summer. But the winters are relatively of much shorter duration than on the same lines of latitude in the Atlantic states. And the transition from winter to summer temperature is usually very rapid, the average increase in April and May being a third of a degree per day. The average of the three summer months is as follows: June 69.2, July 74.1, August 71.0, giving a mean summer temperature of 71.4. The mean of the three winter months is 20.6; spring 46.5; autumn 48.5.

The charts issued by the Signal Service, showing the isothermal lines of the United States, furnish a basis of comparison of the temperature of Iowa and the eastern States. In January the State lies between the isotherms 15 and 25. The line of 20 passes diagonally through the northern half of the State from a point below Sioux City to the northeast corner, thence diagonally through Wisconsin to the northern part of Michigan; and eastward through Kingston, Canada; northern New York, Vermont and New Hampshire to Eastport, Maine. In February the 20° and 30° lines cut the northwestern and southeastern corners of the State, and the 25° isotherm crosses the State on a nearly direct line from Sioux City to Dubuque, curving slightly northward across Wisconsin through Milwaukee, thence eastward with slight curvatures through Michigan and Canada, and along the southern shore of Lake Ontario, through northern New York, ending in Portland, Maine. And for the three winter months the normal temperature of Iowa corresponds very nearly with that of the latitude of northern Michigan, northern New York, Vermont, New Hampshire and Maine. The Iowa winters, however, are much more endurable and enjoyable than the corresponding season in the regions above named, which have a much larger number of stormy days and heavier precipitation.

In March the isotherms touching Iowa follow more nearly the parallels of latitude, with sharp curvatures to the southward in crossing the Alleghanies. In April the temperature of Iowa corresponds nearly with that of central Ohio, southern Pennsylvania, Washington, Philadelphia and New York city. In May and through the summer months the isotherms curve sharply southward on nearing the Atlantic coast, and the temperature of Iowa is as high as that of central Ohio, southern Pennsylvania, West Virginia, Maryland and New Jersey.

These comparisons show the wide range between the winter and summer temperature of this portion of the Mississippi valley. In short, the winter temperature is like unto that of Montreal, and the summer heat is equal to that of Baltimore and Washington.

The marked extremes of temperature above noted give to this region its marvelous productiveness, the cold as well as the heat being an important factor in the growing of crops. The myriad plowshares of Jack Frost penetrate the earth to great depths, pulverizing the soil and preparing it to respond to the quickening influences of the gentle rains and almost tropical heat of the summer months. The winter campaign is usually short and sharp, and the clear, pure air tones up the systems of all who have the vitality to withstand extremes. It is not exactly an ideal climate for invalids who need an equable temperature, but the tables of vital statistics show that it is remarkably healthful.

THE SEASONS IN IOWA.

The calendar year is divided into four seasons of equal length, but in matter of fact in this latitude the seasons are of variable duration. In Iowa, summer is the longest season, averaging about four months, during which the mean temperature ranges above 60 degrees. The average duration of winter, during which the mean temperature is below 30 degrees, is a little over three and a half months. The balance of the year is divided about equally between spring and autumn, the mean temperature ranging between 30 and 60 degrees. On this basis the average dates of beginning and ending of the seasons in this State may be tabulated as follows :

Winter—November 28th to March 17th.
Spring—March 18th to May 20th.
Summer—May 21st to September 23d.
Autumn—September 24th to November 27th.

Spring and summer usually open from one to two weeks earlier in the extreme southern part of the State than in the northern and more elevated localities. There is, however, less difference in the opening of the winter season.

TEMPERATURE DATA.

The following table gives the average monthly and annual mean temperatures in degrees, at a number of stations in Iowa from records covering the number of years in the last column.

STATIONS.	J'N'RY	FEB'RY	MARCH	APRIL	MAY	JUNE	JULY	AUGUST	SEPT'R	OCT'R	NOV'R	DEC'R	ANNUAL	NO. OF YEARS
Amos	16.2	23.1	30.1	49.3	59.1	69.1	73.3	71.4	62.1	49.1	30.7	22.3	46.4	8
Amana	13.2	20.1	29.6	47.5	59.5	68.6	73.1	69.8	60.6	47.7	31.6	21.2	45.4	11
Algona	10.7	17.3	25.1	43.6	59.3	67.6	73.3	70.2	59.9	46.6	31.4	17.8	43.6	11
Brookside	12.8	20.9	29.1	45.1	59.0	65.6	71.3	69.9	61.0	46.8	31.4	17.5	41.2	9
Cedar Rapids	15.8	22.9	30.7	49.0	59.5	69.2	73.4	70.6	61.1	49.0	34.9	25.1	46.9	29
Clinton	19.1	27.1	32.2	47.8	56.4	66.1	70.6	68.5	62.5	49.2	35.5	55.0	47.2	19
Cresco	9.8	18.4	26.5	49.6	61.0	70.4	67.2	68.5	58.9	45.5	37.5	24.9	49.3	19
Davenport	20.8	25.1	34.5	48.6	61.8	64.9	73.6	71.2	63.6	52.1	35.8	24.9	47.7	14
Dubuque	18.1	23.3	32.7	46.6	60.9	69.9	74.9	69.9	61.0	50.8	33.8	35.0	48.3	13
Des Moines	17.9	19.0	34.7	50.6	60.6	69.2	74.9	71.5	61.8	47.0	31.8	25.0	45.6	11
Elkader	11.3	14.7	31.7	47.8	58.9	73.1	75.6	72.4	61.1	46.3	27.2	35.4	50.8	11
Fort Madison	22.7	29.0	31.5	51.2	63.0	72.7	75.6	71.5	59.5	48.5	34.8	25.3	50.4	11
Glenwood	11.2	14.3	31.1	46.6	57.8	68.1	73.6	67.7	63.3	46.3	34.7	31.3	47.5	16
Guttenberg	15.3	20.8	29.4	44.6	55.8	66.7	72.8	71.7	59.8	45.3	31.3	21.6	41.7	17
Independence	13.7	21.9	32.1	45.2	60.1	69.1	71.1	67.3	59.8	47.5	33.5	19.1	45.9	31
Iowa City	11.7	19.3	32.7	48.1	60.1	68.8	70.2	71.3	63.3	50.3	40.6	29.8	49.0	16
Keokuk	18.9	25.1	36.8	51.9	62.8	72.5	71.3	71.5	66.1	51.8	35.5	25.4	48.8	30
Logan	23.6	28.4	34.9	49.2	60.0	68.5	71.4	72.5	62.7	48.8	33.6	22.1	46.6	36
Monticello	18.0	22.1	31.8	48.3	59.1	70.4	71.5	72.5	61.0	50.4	35.8	31.8	46.0	35
Mount Vernon	15.1	21.6	31.9	48.5	60.5	68.1	72.9	71.2	61.1	49.1	34.8	24.4	46.1	13
Muscatine	17.2	21.3	34.7	46.9	58.8	64.1	73.6	70.5	62.1	50.2	35.1	34.8	43.9	26
Nashua	20.2	28.4	35.0	41.8	54.6	61.1	70.6	67.3	57.1	32.2	36.1	14.4	41.8	15
Omaha	8.5	15.1	26.9	50.5	62.3	71.1	71.0	66.4	62.7	49.1	36.1	25.4	49.4	9
Oskaloosa	18.9	25.6	35.4	49.6	59.1	69.6	70.9	68.2	62.2	49.4	36.4	27.2	48.0	13
Washington	16.8	23.7	32.2	50.9	61.1	72.5	73.6	71.0	63.8	51.0	35.4	25.1	49.0	10
AVERAGES	16.2	22.2	31.7	48.0	59.7	69.2	71.1	71.0	62.0	49.5	34.1	23.5	46.5	

Average for the six growing months of the year, 63.8

LATE AND EARLY FROSTS.

On an average there are 140 to 150 days between the latest damaging frost of spring and the first killing frost of autumn. The latest of spring occurs on an average, about the last week in April or the first week in May; and the earliest damaging frost of the fall is about the 25th of September. Light and comparatively harmless frosts occasionally occur between those dates, but as a rule there is in every season ample time to produce a well-matured crop of the best varieties of western dent corn, which with favoring conditions may be grown in 100 to 110 days after germination. Prof. Parvin's very complete records, covering the years from 1839 to 1869, show the mean dates to have been for the latest frost May 4, and for the earliest September 24. This would give an average exemption from hurtful frosts of 142 days. Prof. Parvin, writing in 1870 said:

"It has happened but once or twice in the last thirty years that the frost has, over a great extent, seriously injured the corn crop. When the spring is late, the fall is either quite hot or lengthened, so as to afford time for the crop to mature."

This has been the result of observation in the years since this paragraph was written. A careful study of all available records leads to the conclusion that Iowa has, on an average, as long a period of exemption from killing frosts in the crop season as any State within the same parallels of latitude in the eastern part of the United States, except possibly within a few miles of the coast.

DESTRUCTIVE STORMS.

In common with nearly all portions of the United States east of the Rocky Mountains, Iowa is subject to the occasional visitation of violent atmospheric disturbances, in form of wind-squalls, hail and thunder storms. The more destructive effects of these disturbances, however are purely local, and limited to small areas compared with the extent of territory benefitted by the storm. Being well watered, it cannot escape these almost universal conditions.

The Gulf is the great thermal fountain of humidity, and the boreal regions send down the valley the titanic forces which wring fertilizing moisture from the vapor-laden winds of the south. The Gulf and the Arctic sea are the positive and negative poles of the battery which propels the alternating life currents through this favored region. And the earth is watered and made fruitful by this conflict of elements, which at times becomes so intense and violent at local points as to cause destruction to life and property. But the more violent storms which occasionally sweep over small areas of the State are the incidental ills resulting from conditions which promote the general good. Hail-storms, thunder storms, tornadoes and wind-squalls are the exceptional products of the benign elements of heat and moisture which make this valley a paradise of abundance. If the course of this great valley had been east and west instead of north and south, with the mountain ranges at right angles with their present direction, the interior of the continent would be exempt from atmospheric disturbances of this character; but it would be an uninhabitable desert instead of the garden of the world. There are regions of wide extent which enjoy almost perfect immunity from the class of storms above referred to, but they are deserts or arid sections which must needs be irrigated to yield even a scanty support to their inhabitants. The climate of this State, with all its drawbacks and incidental disturbances is vastly to be preferred to the deserts or semi-arid regions, notwithstanding their exemption from destructive storms.

The reputation of Iowa's climate has been injured among people who are not well informed on the subject, by exaggerated descriptions of the occasional severe storms incident to this latitude ; and the idea has prevailed to some extent that this section is alternately plowed by tornadoes and harrowed by blizzards. This has resulted from the fact that newspaper reports of wind-storms are often highly over-wrought, from indulgence in the American passion for sensationalism. And, unfortunately, some of these exaggerated reports have been embodied in official records to the detriment of the State. Using these highly colored newspaper reports as a basis, there was published a few years ago in the American Meteorological Journal, a so-called "Iowa Tornado Chart," giving the tracks of alleged tornadoes for the period of fifty-two years. The total number charged to the account of this State was 128, and the year of greatest frequency was 1886, which year was credited with a crop of twenty-six veritable tornadoes raised on Iowa soil. A careful investigation showed that the bulk of these disturbances were merely wind-squalls accompanying thunder-storms of some local severity. The aggregate of damage from storms that year was very light. The tendency to exaggerate the importance or violence of local phenomena causes certain newspaper reporters to apply the term "cyclone" to every wind gust which is powerful enough to demolish some of the frail structures which were very common in this State in the pioneer era, and which are yet quite numerous. But the people who have resided in Iowa through good and evil report have learned that it is as safe as any other section within the temperate zone.

And despite the exaggerated reports it may be positively affirmed that veritable tornadoes are quite infrequent in this State. Since its settlement by the whites, there have been in Iowa two notably destructive tornadoes which are entitled to rank with the great disturbances of like nature at Lawrence, Mass., Reading, Pa., and Louisville, Ky.

Dr. Gustavus Hinrichs, in his annual report of the Iowa Weather Service for the year 1888, published a very complete refutation of the exaggerated statements that had been given currency relative to Iowa tornadoes. Gen. Greely, Chief Signal Officer, in his book on American Weather, says that three thousand persons have been killed in the United States by this class of storms, and the loss of life has been greatest in relative order in States as follows : Missouri, Mississippi, Iowa, Illinois, Minnesota, Wisconsin and Ohio. The loss of property aggregates several millions, and has been fixed in round numbers, as follows : Ohio, over eight millions of dollars ; Minnesota, six millions ; Missouri, three millions ; Mississippi, two millions ; Iowa, one and a half millions ; Wisconsin, over one million.

In his report for 1890, Gen. Greely gives a statement of the relation between the total area visited annually by violent storms of all classes to the area of the State, with the following result : In Alabama, one square mile of limited destruction to each 8,866 square miles ; Arkansas, one to 14,418 ; Georgia, one to 6,696 ; Illinois, one to 8,162 ; Indiana, one to 6,210 ; Iowa, one to 7,164 ; Kansas, one to 9,720 ; Missouri, one to 5,336 ; Ohio, one to 4,554 ; Wisconsin, one to 12.042. Gen. Greely adds :

"It appears that in no State may a destructive tornado be expected oftener, on an average, than once in two years, and the area over which the total destruction can be expected is exceedingly small, even in the States most liable to these violent storms."

And he further concludes that, dangerous as are tornadoes, they are not so destructive to life as thunderstorms. This accords with observations in Iowa, as it is evident that, in the aggregate, very many more deaths have been caused by lightning strokes than by any class of wind-storms.

WIND MOVEMENT.

The State is sufficiently well ventilated to make it healthful. On an average the wind movement is ample to secure immunity from malaria and the germs of disease which arise from decaying vegetation, and to furnish mechanical power for the pumping of stock water and the grinding of feed. The mean velocity of the wind over the State accords very closely with the average for the United States. The average hourly movement is 7 to 8 miles. At an early period, when the prairies were comparatively treeless, the effects of winds were more apparent than now, their force having been greatly modified in recent years by artificial groves, hedges and timber belts. The prevailing winds are southerly in summer and westerly at other seasons.

IS THE CLIMATE PERMANENT ?

All the recorded weather observations of the past fifty years answer affirmatively. In recent droughty seasons fears were expressed by certain writers that through tillage, ditching and tile drainage, and from the effects of clearing away extensive forests in the northwest, the climate of this portion of the Mississippi valley has been materially changed by decreasing the humidity and seasonal rainfall. But the records prove absolutely that there has been no diminution in the humidity and rainfall within the last decade as compared with any preceding decade, nor within the last twenty years as compared with any preceding score of years since the States was settled by civilized people. There have been seasons of excess and of deficiency all along the line of recorded observations, but the shortage has been no more serious in the eighties and nineties than in the fifties and sixties.

No, there has been no appreciable change in any essential feature of the climate. It is as stable as the everlasting hills, and as permanent as the inflow and outflow of the currents of the Gulf, by which it is so copiously watered.

In concluding this chapter the writer desires to acknowledge his indebtedness to the Chief of the Weather Bureau for voluminous records relating to the climate of this State, and to Dr. Geo. M. Chappel, Local Forecast Official and Assistant Director of the Iowa Weather and Crop Service, for very efficient aid in the arrangement and tabulation of meteorological data.

NATURAL RESOURCES.

Nature gave to Iowa a better dowry than mines of diamonds or mountains stored with silver and gold. Its more valuable resources consist in water, sands, rocks, coal and timber, and above all its deep, porous wonderful soil. Gold, silver, nickle, zinc, iron, aluminum, and natural gas have been found; but whether they exist in remunerative quantities is to be determined by future efforts for their development.

WATER.

We class water as one of the natural resources of this productive state. Go west—cross the continent to the Pacific—and you ask why those great deserts which you pass in your journey. They are desert because the rainfall, the natural irrigation essential to vegetable production, is withheld. Here fructifying showers nourish, invigorate and perpetuate vegetable life. In the three score years of our written history no pen has ever written of Iowa's fields being made barren by burning drouth, or of her people suffering the pangs of famine because the essential rainfall was withheld until crops were parched and starvation befell them. The beneficient Creator gave to Iowa a wealth of resources of more priceless value than mountains of the precious metals, in her ever duly recurring showers, and her numerous springs and perennial streams.

MEDICINAL WATERS.

We have valuable healing waters in Iowa. Streams flow from unfailing fountains that give strength to the weak, ease to the pain-ridden, and healing to the sick. We can speak only of a few of such fountains.

The Lake View Mineral Spring—This is a natural spring near the western shore of Wall Lake, a body of water lying in Sac county and furnishing fine opportunities for boating, fishing and pleasure driving in its vicinity. Circumstances have led to the improvement of the surroundings of this healing fountain that has now wide reputation for the cure of many of the ills to which mortal nature is subject. We give the following analysis of its water made by Prof. Walter J. Haines, of Rush Medical College August, 1888.

Each gallon of 231 inches contains:

	GRAINS.
Chloride of Sodium	1.124
Sulphate of Potassium	.285
Sulphate of Sodium	1.566
Bicarbonate of Calcium	18.111
Bicarbonate of Magnesium	9.479
Bicarbonate of Sodium	.336
Bicarbonate of Iron	.032
Phosphate of Sodium	Trace
Alumina	.150
Silica	1.180
Organic Matter	Trace
Total	32.284

THE SARATOGA OF THE WEST.

Who has not heard of Colfax, the famous health resort of Iowa, and its waters that have won a fame that has crossed oceans? This now famous health and pleasure resort is in Jasper county, on the main line of the Chicago, Rock Island and Pacific railroad.

Some fifteen years ago an enterprising citizen surmising that a paying vein of coal lay hidden under the high wooded hill east of the village, procured a drilling apparatus and started the tools downward in quest of the desired treasure. By slow, laborious process he put his drill down about four hundred and fifteen feet when a sudden bursting forth of a fine stream of water caused a stoppage of his work. He was not pleased with what he then considered ill luck, but his complaints interposed no check to the gushing stream. It continued its bright and abundant flow. The workmen and spectators sipped thereof to investigate its quality. Its taste at first peculiar, after a little use was not unpleasant; those who drank freely, however, were soon admonished that it possessed unusual qualities, and a quantity of the sparkling fluid was sent to an educated physician at Davenport for examination. Acting on his recommendation a quantity was forwarded to Prof. Heinrichs of the State University, who reported the following analysis of the fluid:

NAME OF COMPOUND.	GRAINS PER GALLON.		Millogrames per litre or parts per million
	American Gallon of 231 cubic inches.	Imperial Gallon of 70,000 Grains.	
Sodium chloride	3.85	4.62	66
Sodium sulphate	78.86	91.57	1,351
Potassium sulphate	.41	.49	7
Magnesian sulphate	31.87	38.22	546
Calcium sulphate	13.07	15.68	224
Calcium carbonate	17.51	21.00	300
Iron carbonate	.67	.81	11.5
Silica alumina	.29	.35	5
Lithia	Trace	Trace	Trace
Carbon dioxide	7.18	8.61	123
TOTAL	153.71	181.35	2,633.5

Other borings have been made and similar fountains have been reached in that locality. Their analysis varies but slightly from that above given. The "Colfax Springs" running "abundant, free and clear" are already of great value. Their healing virtues have been tested by thousands of visitors from our own and other states who came to them enfeebled by disease, but went from them with radiant cheek and buoyant step to proclaim their health restoring power.

DES MOINES MEDICINAL WELLS.

Several artesian flows of water have been struck in and near the city of Des Moines that are reputed to have medicinal value. The water from one in the central part of the city has been used quite extensively with great benefit to many persons.

At Cherokee, Lineville and other places in the state there are waters reported to be of considerable medicinal value.

THE CLINTON WELLS.

The city of Clinton is finely supplied with pure health giving water, obtained from artesian wells, drilled into the Potsdam sandstone. Of the source and abundance of the supply, Superintendent Highlands of the city water works reports as follows:

"It might not be amiss in this connection to say something about the source of this magnificent water supply. In this locality the Potsdam sandstone is reached by the drill at 1,475 feet, or about 1,400 feet below low water line in the river and this is the source from which the water is derived. This stratum of sandstone is covered over with 1,100 feet of limestone and 300 to 500 feet of shale. The 400 to 500 feet of limestone immediately over the sandstone was broken up by some convulsion of nature and whenever the drill strikes one of these crevices the water will flow to the surface, with the same pressure, but with less volume, as if the drill had penetrated the sandstone. In drilling well No. 3 the drill penetrated three such crevices. The pressure of water from each of those crevices or apparent veins was carefully tested by packing off the water above them and it was found exactly the same as when tested at the depth of 1,600 feet. The fact that the water will only raise 68 feet above the river, shows conclusively that the water does not come from any point near the head waters of the Mississippi river, and it is also equally plain that it could not enter the ground on the line of the river where it is only 68 feet above us, for the reason that in so short a distance it could not have penetrated through the shale and limestone into the sandstone. The only alternative is that it must come from the Lake Superior region where the sandstone crops out." The difference in levels between this and Lake Superior would seem to bear out this opinion.

Speaking of the city wells he says: "The rise and flow of our wells now are as follows:

"No. 1, eight inch bore, 1,450 feet deep; daily flow 700,000 gallons.
"No. 2, five inch bore, 1,235 feet deep; daily flow 400,000 gallons.
"No. 3, eight inch bore, 1,675 feet deep; daily flow 900,000 gallons."

These three wells are drilled within a radius of 200 feet and the flow and pressure seem to remain constant.

The city mains are connected with three other wells, one owned by the city of Lyons and the other by private parties, and the total supply at command is thus stated: "Our mains are also connected with the pumping stations of the Lyons water works, W. J. Young & Co., and C. Lamb & Sons' Chancy mills. The total pumping capacity for fire protection is as follows:

	GALLONS PER DAY.
Clinton station	9,000,000
Lyons station	3,000,000
W. J. Young & Co	6,000,000
C. Lamb & Sons	4,000,000
Total	22,000,000

"As our maximum daily consumption rarely reaches 2,500,000 gallons per day this would leave 19,500,000 gallons per day for fire protection, or water enough to supply eighty-one inch fire streams with 100 pounds of pressure through 400 feet of hose; or if any one of the stations were disabled it would be very easy for the other three to afford adequate fire protection."

The quality of this abundant supply is shown by the following analysis, made by E. G. Smith, Professor of Analytical Chemistry of Beloit College, Wisconsin:

NATURAL RESOURCES.

SOLID RESIDUE IN PARTS PER 1,000 OF WATER.

Silica	.0105
Sulphuric acid	.0640
Chlorine	.0692
Alumina	.0003
Ferric oxide	
Lime	.0663
Magnesia	.0345
Soda	.1499
Carbonic acid, etc	.1182
	.5129
Less Oxygen equivalent to chlorine	.0156
	.4973
Total solids from 1,000 parts of water actually weighed after drying at 140c	.4980

Or to state it in another manner as showing grains per gallon it would show thus:

GRAINS PER GALLON 231 CUBIC INCHES.

Sodium Sulphate	6.6266
Sodium Chloride	6.6616
Sodium bicarbonate	6.2824
Calcium Bicarbonate	11.2291
Magnesium Bicarbonate	7.4267
Alumina	.0174
Ferric acid	
Silica	.6124
	38.8552

At the city of McGregor there are two artesian flows from the same source. The largest one flows a large volume, the bore being put down 1,008 feet. The Potsdam stone here lies many hundred feet higher than the stratum lies at Clinton, the stratum cropping out at the former place. The water in the McGregor wells appears to be more highly medicinal than the Clinton water. We cannot give any reported measurement of the flow at McGregor, but the facts that we have given indicate that abundant supplies of the purest water can be obtained in the cities along the Mississippi wherever the Potsdam sandstone can be reached.

SOIL.

Soil, sunlight and water are the great essentials to the production of the bread, meats and fruits that feed our race. Iowa has world-wide fame for the depth and richness, the mellowness and productive quality of her soil. Prof. White, in his report as State Geologist, speaking of the soil of Iowa said:

"After careful consideration of the results of my examinations, I do not hesitate to thus publicly announce my estimate that 95 per cent. of the surface of Iowa is tillable land. The state being without mountain ranges, hills or other barren surfaces and everywhere covered with a soil of such fertility and depth, its agricultural capabilities are almost beyond computation."

The theory of geologists that the soil of Iowa is formed largely of decomposed rocks floated over the portion of the State the drift covers, may be true or not. Its depth and productive qualities are the matters of our chief concern. There are but few places in this remarkably productive state where a plow can turn up barren subsoil; the fertile soil is found through the state ranging in depth from one to one hundred feet. This is more fully described in the chapter on the Geology of Iowa, by Prof. Keyes.

One great advantage of our soil is its porousness. It is easily pulverized, is light and warm and the roots of growing crops easily penetrate it. This characteristic not only makes farm labor inviting on account of the crop produced, but doubly so by the ease with which the cultivation is done. We hear nothing in Iowa of soil being worn out. It cannot be worn out with any proper farming, hence there is wealth for the ages in its fertility and productive power, and there is perpetual comfort in the ease with which agricultural operations are performed.

CLAYS.

This species of earth is important in essential manufactures. The savage may build his wigwam frame of poles and cover it with grass or skins or barks. The pioneer will build his cabin of logs or sod, but by industry and economy he soon provides the means for better things. The brick maker and mason's services are soon needed and openings invite the pottery and the tile factory, and search is made for suitable clays for these manufactures.

In all parts of Iowa, clays suitable for the manufacture of excellent brick is easily obtained, hence the brick industry is obtaining large dimensions. The demand for building brick, paving brick and the finest quality of pressed brick is having yearly increase.

The day of building cheap, perishable shanties for residences, and structures of cheap combustible and perishable material for business uses is outgrown in this State. Three to eight story solid, stately business blocks now grace our cities, and solid brick and stone residences are found in our numerous thrifty villages. Our cities and towns now mostly have their "fire limits," and the indulgence of a false economy in the erection of cheap, unattractive, combustible structures in our business centers is largely prohibited. This wise provision encourages improved architecture and the use of building material of substantial quality, and so the brick makers art is encouraged and his business enlarged. No better clays can be found for the manufacture of the finest quality of pressed brick than are now obtained in numerous places in this state.

Superior clays for the manufacture of stoneware and finer forms of pottery are found in numerous places. During the year 1892 several hundred carloads of clay, for the manufacture of tableware were shipped from Hardin county to Sheboygan, Wisconsin, Milwaukee and elsewhere. Tests of this clay have been made at Liverpool, Paris, and Wellsville, Ohio, Terre Haute, Indiana, Perth Amboy, N. Y., and elsewhere with most satisfactory results in the manufacture of white ware. Large deposits of this quality of clay are found.

With the taking up of the wild lands and the consequent increased value of lands the demand for tile to drain springy, spouty places and waste sloughs is rapidly increasing, and the manufacture of tile for drainage purposes has already assumed large proportions. Excellent clays for this manufacture are found throughout the state.

The settlement of the country with its increasing population and wealth makes good roads more important and leads to road improvement. The growth of flourishing towns and cities, and care for their cleanliness and healthfulness provide enlarging markets for sewer pipe, and its manufacture is becoming an important and growing industry.

SAND.

According to slang phrase, is a valuable quality in the mental constitution. It is an essential element in our industries. Many important mechanical and manufacturing operations demand its use. The people of Iowa have rich endowment of the mental element expressed by the term, and nature has provided numerous banks of this material in suitable qualities and quantities for mechanical operations. The builder readily finds suitable sand. The brick maker and iron moulder find sands suitable for their operations, while glass factories and smelting furnaces export sands in quantities from our state for their work.

STONE.

Iowa is not a mountainous nor rocky State, but the exact reverse. Yet there is abundant supply of stone for building, the manufacture of lime and other uses. The general distribution of railroads throughout the state, makes these supplies, that the Creator liberally provided, everywhere available.

Census bulletin No. 78, Census of 1890, devoted to Mines and Mining, treating of limestone, gives important figures respecting this important natural commodity.

The whole number of limestone quarries reported in the country was 1,954. Of these 143 were in Iowa. These Iowa quarries had a reported value of $530,863.

The product of these 143 quarries in this state was reported as 6,280,727 cubic feet of stone for building purposes, valued at $236,792. Lime burned 365,394 barrels of 200 pounds each, of the value of $170,043. For street work 1,732,630 cubic feet of the value of $70,387 were produced. These products of the 143 limestone quarries of Iowa, having a reported value of $477,222. Relatively among the states of the Union Iowa has fair rank in the production of this useful and valuable stone. In the number of limestone quarries having fifth place; in the number of employees working such quarries seventh place; in amount of wages paid tenth place; in amount of stone produced, twelfth place; and in the aggregate value of the product of limestone quarries tenth place.

The limestone beds of Iowa are not found in one corner or in one locality of the State merely, but have quite general distribution over its area.

A further description of the rocks of the State is given in this chapter by Prof. Keyes.

GYPSUM.

Is found in large deposits in Webster county, along the Des Moines river. All the operators in its production in 1889 had their headquarters at Fort Dodge. All the deposits or beds of gypsum being found near that city.

To quite a large extent gypsum has been used in Fort Dodge for building purposes. When first quarried it is easily dressed with an axe or saw, hardens when in the wall and makes a solid structure. Prof. White, in his geographical report, wrote in 1870 of a residence built of this rock in 1861: "Its walls appear as unaffected by exposure and as beautiful as they were when first erected."

In the year named gypsum was produced in California, Colorado, Iowa, Kansas, Michigan, New York, Ohio, South Dakota, Utah, Virginia and Wyoming. Iowa ranking third in the quantity produced and third in the total value of the product. In that year the industry at Fort Dodge gave employment to 59 men.

Part of the product is sold and used as a fertilizer, 14,434 short tons of the Iowa product being sold in 1889 for that purpose 7,550 tons were calcined for stucco. The product of the mines and factories that year in Iowa was valued at $55,250.

The deposits are found in the bluffs of the Des Moines river, covering an extent of about seven miles along the river valley.

Prof. White gives the thickness of the deposit at Goss' Mill, then its known southern extremity, as ten feet. At the Cummins quarry, six miles northward from the Goss Mill, as twenty feet. The deposit is sufficiently large to be virtually inexhaustible, but is formed in somewhat irregular layers, Prof. White pronounces it of "as good quality as any in the country, even for the finest uses."

Iowa gypsum manufactured into stucco, was very largely used in the manufacture of "staff," the material used for the external covering of the exhibition buildings in Jackson Park.

COAL.

The coal product of the country is of the utmost importance to the public prosperity. While this statement is true in regard to the whole country it is energized when we apply it particularly to a prairie State. Iowa may not be far known as a mining State, yet the productions of her mines are no mean interest. Few suppose that she has place in the list of States near to the top in any mining production. But she has high rank in the production of bituminous coal. The United States census of 1890 reports twenty-seven coal producing States and their entire production as 95,729,026 tons. It reports the following five States as producing for the year 1889, the amounts given below, they being the five leading States:

STATES.	PRODUCTION.
Pennsylvania	36,174,089 tons
Illinois	12,104,272 "
Ohio	9,976,787 "
West Virginia	6,231,890 "
Iowa	6,095,358 "

Iowa ranges tenth in population but fifth in the production of bituminous coal, producing in 1890 one bushel in every twenty-two bushels of the product of the country.

The state mine inspectors in their last biennial report to the governor of the State, report production of coal in twenty-three counties. The State has three mining districts. We copy tables given by the several inspectors showing the number of mines, production and other interesting items relating to this business in each county named:

NATURAL RESOURCES.

Showing number of mines, annual output, number of miners and other employes, value of product, etc., in District No. 1, for the year ending June 30, 1891.

NAME OF COUNTY.	Number of mines.	Number of tons of coal produced.	Number of miners employed.	All other employes	Average price per ton paid for mining.	Total amount paid miners.	Total amount paid to all other employes.	Average selling price per ton at mine.	Total value of product at the mine.
Adams	15	14,872	80	11	$1.34	$20,031.42	$2,296.00	$2.01	$29,384.00
Appanoose	58	393,255	1,193	249	.95	368,924.61	60,356.98	1.37	540,767.10
Davis	6	3,272	17	7	.91	2,972.00	180.00	1.58	5,160.50
Lucas	6	136,722	187	20	.76	103,490.00	6,000.00	.26	172,190.00
Monroe	18	355,177	609	192	.72	255,773.84	95,508.05	1.23	536,172.58
Page	3	2,700	26	3	1.63	4,400.00	500.00	2.41	6,550.00
Taylor	12	13,120	62	34	1.37	18,105.00	4,013.00	2.02	27,120.00
Wapello	21	160,290	358	123	.75	120,376.27	44,104.11	1.30	217,737.28
Wayne	8	31,578	101	30	.90	28,252.00	10,875.00	1.40	41,172.00
Warren	22	15,604	80	15	1.04	16,303.61	2,797.23	1.80	27,809.60
Total	170	1,136,190	2,721	687	$ .83	$938,828.75	$227,130.37	$1.32	$1,507,012.06

DISTRICT NO. 2.

Jasper	16	116,091	283	70	$ .85	$125,134.25	$30,328.67	$1.43	$208,587.96
Jefferson	7	2,932	18	6	.98	2,714.49	556.36	1.80	5,217.20
Keokuk	20	363,617	665	240	.74	269,102.04	37,240.95	1.40	509,230.03
Mahaska	40	963,558	1,105	416	.75	719,976.14	214,140.06	1.25	1,207,090.08
Scott	7	10,534	17	4	.97	10,195.32	1,180.00	1.75	18,141.50
Van Buren	7	46,764	93	18	.85	39,596.00	6,940.00	1.31	61,288.00
Total	97	1,533,496	2,211	754	$ .76	$1,166,718.24	$290,715.04	$1.32	$2,009,916.77

DISTRICT NO. 3.

Boone	19	189,577	480	128	$ .94	$177,003.75	$69,364.11	$1.86	$351,826.31
Dallas	6	43,324	106	34	.93	10,278.40	14,150.00	1.78	76,133.40
Guthrie	10	11,983	87	15	1.48	17,770.00	2,360.00	2.50	29,982.50
Greene	4	74,544	158	32	.85	68,502.79	14,558.93	1.59	118,173.29
Marion	27	210,061	347	132	.75	158,679.22	13,311.19	1.31	275,300.31
Polk	18	397,833	652	217	.86	321,048.78	97,544.26	1.53	604,921.25
Webster	20	124,963	273	96	.84	104,360.09	44,628.17	1.61	200,328.50
Total	110	1,052,295	2,103	654	$ .81	$882,732.76	$277,116.06	1.57	$1,657,165.56

SUMMARY.

NUMBER OF DISTRICT.	Number of mines.	Number of tons of coal produced.	Number of miners employed.	All other employes	Average price per ton paid for mining.	Total amount paid miners.	Total amount paid all other employes.	Average selling price per ton at mine.	Total value of product at mine.
District No. 1	170	1,136,190	2,721	687	$ .83	$938,828.75	$227,130.37	$1.32	$1,507,012.06
District No. 2	97	1,533,496	2,211	754	.76	1,166,718.24	290,715.04	1.32	2,009,916.77
District No. 3	110	1,052,295	2,103	654	.84	882,732.76	277,116.06	1.57	1,657,165.56
Total	377	3,721,981	7,035	2,095	$ .81	$2,988,289.55	$795,291.47	$1.39	$5,171,394.39

This summary of the three mining districts of the State includes reports from 377 mines. It reports the production of 3,721,981 tons of bituminous coal, being 1.94 tons *per capita* to the population of the State. It shows that this industry gave employment to 9,130 persons, paying to those employes the sum of $3,783,572.02. That the coal produced was valued at upwards of five million dollars. No further elucidation is necessary to prove that Iowa has highly important and valuable mining interests. Her producers of "Black Diamonds" add greatly to her prosperity. It may be remarked that many mines operated only in the winter months are not reported by the inspectors, and coal is mined in six counties not included in the above tables. Hence the discrepancy between the census and state mine inspectors' reports.

Iowa coal is not anthracite. It may not be a fine quality of coking coal. It may not be renowned for its excellence as a gas coal, but it is an excellent fuel coal, a fine steam producer and is of great value to her people for household use, for locomotive consumption and for all industries using steam power.

Coal is found and mined in the following counties not named in the above tables, namely, Cass, Adair, Fremont, Lee, Hardin and Hamilton counties. It will doubtless be found by deeper prospecting in counties where it is not now known to exist. The field now as developed, extends from Scott county on the Mississippi on the east, to Fremont county on the Missouri on the west, a distance of upwards of 200 miles. While in the opposite direction it extends from the Missouri line into Hamilton and Hardin counties, a distance of 140 miles. Nature has stored away in the deep and hidden chambers of this vast field, supplies of fuel to furnish heat and light for Iowa's millions.

THE MINERAL RESOURCES OF ALLAMAKEE COUNTY, IOWA.

Iron Ore We know that it is not in accordance with the arrangement of geological strata as usually seen that a bed of iron ore should exist in this part of Iowa, and the imperfect surveys heretofore officially made of the State have either ignored, or unjustly misrepresented their existence. We know, also, from years of personal examination, the many test pits that have been dug, varying from a few to thirty-two feet deep, and the bottom of the ore not yet reached, all through an almost solid mass of iron ore, lying below one to four feet of surface soil, though cropping out above the ground in many places, and from the hundreds of tons of ore that have been mined, that it exists here in vast quantities. One bed about one and one-half miles northeast of Waukon, covers three hundred or more acres. It has been estimated that 500 tons daily could be taken out for 100 years. Its quality is a brown hematite, is quite porous, permitting heat to permeate the center of the mass, making its reduction easy. On the north and west sides it laps on Trenton limestone; on the south and east sides on St. Peter's sandstone. It lies on top of one of the highest points of land in the county, about 700 feet above the Mississippi, and about fourteen miles distant from that river. A railroad could be run right into its sides, and up a valley into its very center so that loading would be all down hill. Several analyses have been made ranging from 52 to 60 per cent. One analysis was as follows:

Sesquioxide of iron	52.751
Sesquioxide of magnese	8.054
Sesquioxide of cobalt	.230
Alumina	1.777
Lime	1.090
Magnesia	.374
Sulphuric acid	.047
Phosphoric acid	4.092
Water and organic matter	13.134
Silicious matter	10.631
	100.000

Another test made by Prof. Fisher, analytical chemist, of Milwaukee, Wis., from ore taken by himself from the mines, gave these results, as he reported to the writer:

	Black.	Yellow.	Constituents of average ore.
Metallic iron	58.59	54.79	
Oxide of iron			76.74
Silica	4.00	5.12	11.02
Water		11.92	11.92
Phosphorus (Phosphoric Acid)		.131	.30
Sulphur			
Lime		.70	.70
Total			100.68

Magnesia, trace. Alumina Trace. Manganese, trace.

These deposits were first discovered by Mr. C. Barnard about fourteen years ago, who soon after called the attention of the writer to them, who with him made personal and extensive examination of the same, though neither one ever has had, nor has to-day, a dollar's worth of interest in the lands in any form. Our aim has been to develop the resources of this county. These lands have been leased at three different times to outside parties. The changes in the tariff in 1883 caused a suspension of their development at that time. Again they were being opened and on the point of successful development when the principal capitalist and promoter interested, died. And since they have been leased by parties who seem to hold them in abeyance while they are devoting immediate, personal attention to the Lake Superior newly developing iron regions. There is not local capital to open and work them. It is not desirable that they should fall into the hands of speculators, because we believe that we have the quantity and the quality here for the development of a great industry on a solid foundation. It advertises itself best by a personal examination by experts and competent judges.

Other extensive beds of iron ore exist in the county.

Lead also is profitably mined in large quantities five or six miles northwest of Lansing, and is also believed to exist in paying quantities near Dorchester in the northern part of the county.

ZINC.

This metal is mined in the vicinity of Dubuque and quite extensive works are being erected in that city for the preparation of the metal for commerce.

While Iowa has mineral interests that are of great value, and give promise of enlarged development and commercial importance in the near future, the tools of the farm more than the mine have been the chief instruments used in her great wealth production. It may be conceded that this State will never lead some others as a mining State, but her mining and manufacturing interests are becoming important factors in her industrial enterprises, and will hereafter add largely to wealth acquisition.

COMMERCIAL FACILITIES.

We have already intimated something of the commercial opportunities and facilities of Iowa. We find the state situated in a position to command the advantages of 20,000 miles of inland water navigation. No transportation can be so cheap as that carried on the great water channels formed by the Creator.

Our great rivers are permanent fixtures; the lakes and springs pouring their flows into the Mississippi and the snows of the mountains sending their streams into the Missouri must ever maintain these great rivers as navigable thoroughfares. As the years roll on and population and wealth increase, public interest will demand still greater outlays to perfect those great channels of interior communication and transportation, and their benefit to this commonwealth will increase with each succeeding generation. Those divinely formed channels of trade and transportation are indispensible to Iowa. They will yet bear a large proportion of the products of her farms, orchards, dairies, mines and shops to distant markets, and bring in return immense supplies of commodities and material that her industries and her people will demand, and by their competitive position will keep the cost of transportation to the lowest figure possible. The vast development of wealth in the country will yet be interested in providing for the safety, enlarged capacity and consequently cheaper transportation on those channels that must ever be free as air to commercial interests. The country is moving in behalf of cheap transportation, and the people of Iowa are in position to gain great commercial advantages from the consummation of these movements.

We have spoken of the development of steam as a motive power on the rivers of the country. That success led to experimenting as to the application of steam as a motive power on land, and at the time of the commencement of the settlement of Iowa, the invention of railways and transportation thereon by steam power was, though yet in crude condition, proving successful. It was not until twenty years after the founding of the firs permanent settlement in Iowa that a locomotive reached the Mississippi river.

THE RAILROAD FACILITIES OF IOWA.

The first settlers of Iowa came from the east by teams. The first movement in the interest of railroad construction culminated in a convention at Iowa City in the winter of 1848. It projected two roads, one from Keokuk to Dubuque, the other to span the state from Davenport via Iowa City to some point on the Missouri at or near Council Bluffs. The first organization of a company to construct a railroad in this state was organized to build the proposed road from Davenport to Council Bluffs. Petitions were sent to Congress asking for grants of land to aid in the construction of the projected road, but soon there was heated contention respecting the lines on which the projected roads should be located. The petitioners of that day could not foresee the Iowa they were making, ribboned with tracks of steel as it is now. The road from Keokuk to Dubuque was never built.

In February. 1854, the Chicago & Rock Island reached the Mississippi and the enthusiasm for railroad building was intensified. In May, 1856, the national Congress made its first grant of land in aid of railroad building in this state. That act was approved by President Pierce the fifteenth day of that month. It made grants to four roads as follows. We quote from the act:

"Sec. 1. Be it enacted by the Senate and House of Representatives of the United States in Congress assembled, that there be and is hereby granted to the State of Iowa for the purpose of aiding in the construction of railroads from Burlington on the Mississippi river to a point on the Missouri river near the mouth of the Platte river, from the city of Davenport via Iowa City and Ft. Des Moines to Council Bluffs, from Lyons City northwestwardly to a point of intersection with the main line of the Iowa Central Air Line Railroad near Maquoketa, thence on said main line of the Iowa Central Air Line as near as practicable to the 42d parallel across the State of Iowa to the Missouri river. From the city of Dubuque to a point on the Missouri river near Sioux City, with a branch from the Tete des Mortes to the nearest point on said main line, to be completed as soon as the main line is completed to that point, every alternate section of land designated by odd numbers for six sections in width on each side of said road."

This legislation further provided that when the lines of these roads should be definitely fixed, if it should appear that the United States had sold any section or part thereof, granted as aforesaid, or the right of preemption had attached to the same, then the roads, by agents duly appointed by the governor, might select, subject to the approval of the Secretary of the Interior, from the lands of the United States nearest to the tiers of sections above specified, so much land in alternate sections or parts of sections as shall be equal to such lands as the United States have sold or otherwise appropriated or to which the rights of pre-emption have attached as aforesaid. The lands so located to be in no case farther than fifteen miles from the line of said road.

Some other grants of land for internal improvements in Iowa followed this first grant. Under these land grant acts the several aided roads in Iowa received land as follows:

	ACRES.
Burlington & Missouri River (now C. B. & Q.)	287,095.24
Mississippi & Missouri River (now the C., R. I. P.)	550,193.57
Iowa Central Air Line (now C. & N. W.)	775,454.19
Dubuque & Pacific (now Illinois Central)	1,226,558.32
McGregor & Missouri (now C., M. & St. Paul)	372,293.27
Sioux City & St. Paul	407,879.31
Des Moines River Improvement Company	1,105,967.88

The grand total of land bestowed by these grants aggregated 4,674,744.88 acres. It is true the gift was princely but it is equally true that the benefits sought in return were commensurate. Iowa was then without railroads, its interior unsettled and unless railroad advantages were secured it would largely remain unsettled. The reader should remember that these grants were made forty years ago. Then much of the land entered or pre-empted in the interior of the State had been taken by speculators. The few settlers in those interior counties who were trying to improve homes were laboring in privation, difficulty and poverty. The surplus they raised had to be wagoned over unbridged sloughs and streams to far away markets. Millions of acres about them were in market to the first taker at $1.25 per acre, but were taken slowly at that price. There was no wealth in the State to provide the transportation facilities that every settler desired, and those pioneer settlers far out from market, in great breadths of sparsely settled prairie were willing that Congress should give out of its immense domain what seemed to them at that time a mere pittance, in order that they might secure facilities of transportation that were absolutely essential

HIGHWAY AND C. & N. W. RY. BRIDGES AT CLINTON, IA.

alike to their prosperity and happiness. They figured the value of the land, not as we figure it now, with daily railroad trains speeding through every neighborhood, but as they figured it when the nearest railroad yet lingered by the Mississippi, one or two hundred miles from them, and the millions of acres of this seemingly boundless west were awaiting purchasers at the government price. But though the land was granted and railroad surveys were made the railroads did not come. The financial crash of 1857, prostrating business all over the country, followed. Before the country fully recovered from that disaster the civil war broke out and its horrors engrossed the thoughts of the people. It was not possible to proceed with the building of these great lines of road until the pageant of the laurel crowning of the victors in that terrible conflict was made possible by the supremacy of the olive branch through the surrender at Appomattox. Soon thereafter work was begun to push the construction of railroads across Iowa.

The Chicago & Northwestern, first to cross the State, reached Council Bluffs in 1867. The Chicago, Rock Island & Pacific and the Chicago, Burlington & Quincy reached that city early in 1869, and connection was made to the Pacific coast. Then the commerce and travel of the Orient heard of a shorter route to Occidental Europe and the great highway of travel between the empires of the far away east and the Kingdoms of Europe turned across this grandeur of vale and hill the world soon learned to know as Iowa.

We will not ask what Iowa would be now had no railroads been built in her territory, we will rather endeavor to comprehend what she is today with her lacework of railroads that has brought to her every neighborhood commercial advantages unsurpassed, and now secure grace to her homes and wealth to her people.

The report of her railroad commissioners for 1892 publishes the fact that Iowa now has 8,513.76 miles of railroad within her boundaries or one mile of railroad to every 6.46 square miles of her area. There is not a county in Iowa without railroad facilities, and but one county seat of her 99 without a railroad, and yet that county—Pocahontas—has four lines of railroad within its borders and seven railroad towns. If we estimate these 8,513.76 miles of railroad with their rolling stock, side trackage, depots and other terminal facilities, to have cost but $25,000 per mile, then we have an expenditure of $212,844,000.00 for this great property interest. The expenditure of this sum of millions in Iowa in railroad construction with the general distribution of market facilities brought to every locality in the State, with the development of mines, quarries and other interests made possible by their construction and the encouragement thereby given to agriculture, has been a potent factor in the material development made in Iowa in the last two decades, and the wonderful advance in property values that have been effected.

The advantages of railroad transportation are equally distributed and farmers in all parts of the State have easy access to railroad markets. Five of Iowa's ninety-nine counties have within their area from 150 to 172 miles of railroad, twenty-six have from 100 to 150 miles, fifty-three have from 50 to 100 miles, while there are now only fifteen Iowa counties that have less than 50 miles of railroad and but six that have less than 40 miles of railroad line, and but two counties having fewer than five railroad stations, namely, Ida, four and Emmet, five.

There are 1,150 railroad stations in the State. The railroads are divided into three classes for taxation and charges for freightage and railroad fares. They are under the supervision of a board of three commissioners elected by the people and are being wisely controlled.

A glance at the State map found in this volume will reveal that all our farmers are within easy range of railroad markets. We doubt the possibility of a farm being now found in Iowa, the occupant of which in fair weather and with fairly good roads, cannot start with his team from his home in the daylight hour of the morning and returning from his market reach his home ere the twilight of the evening has declined into the darkness of the night. While the majority of Iowa farmers are so situated that with their teams they can haul off at least two loads of produce in a day. We have heard it said "no farmer is so far from market as he who has nothing to sell." The farmers of Iowa do have produce to sell and have market places and good markets of easy access.

TONNAGE CARRIED.

The total tonnage carried by the railroads of commodities moved from place to place in Iowa is difficult to obtain. Last year the two great roads, the Chicago, Rock Island & Pacific and the Chicago, Burlington & Quincy made no report in this matter. The roads reporting their business to the Board of R. R. Commissioners moved the following tonnage:

	TONS.
Grain	3,457,688
Flour	369,064
Live stock	1,208,271
Coal	2,783,965
Lumber	1,476,902

For the two great roads failing to report, alike for their main line and numerous important branches, the mileage controlled by these two roads aggregating nearly one-fourth of the mileage of the State, the commissioners estimated an addition of one-fourth to the above tonnage in the five items named. This would make a total of upwards of eleven millions tons of those five commodities for the year, largely produced or consumed by the agricultural population of the state. Facilities furnished for the rapid and cheap movement of such a mass of commodities are a solid factor to our business prosperity.

EARNINGS.

The total earnings of the roads of Iowa for passenger service in the state for the year ending June 30, 1892, was $10,387,247.89. The total freight earnings of Iowa business was $26,359,095.00. Total earnings on Iowa business $37,405,473.32. Total operating expenses $25,076,828.00, leaving as net earnings the sum of $12,328,645.22

EMPLOYES AND SALARIES.

The whole number of employes in this service was 30,192, salaries paid, $17,807,915.89. Nature made it possible to bring those great aids to agricultural, mining, manufacturing and commercial pursuits into every locality and community in the State, and the enterprise and liberal spirit of our people has so encouraged the improvement of these favoring opportunities that in the grand threadwork of iron track-ways now flecking the state, every business pursuit and every community enjoys those facilities absolutely vital to its prosperity. No state of the Union can show these essential advantages more general and equably distributed than they are now in Iowa. But the work of railroad building is not complete. Some localities yet need better railroad facilities, and the work of railroad building will go on till the demands of all for the best possible railroad advantages are met.

POSTAL FACILITIES.

In this age postal conveniences are important to the business interests and social life of every community. No agricultural state in the central portion of the country has more complete and convenient postal facilities than the people of Iowa enjoy.

We have shown that there are 1,150 railroad stations in Iowa. These places all have daily mail facilities. Many country postoffices have also daily mail. Postoffices in Iowa with only a weekly mail are obsolete.

Under date of January 17th, 1893, the First Assistant Postmaster General informed us that January 1st, 1893, there were 1835 postoffices in the state. That of this number 179 were presidential offices namely: 1st class 7; 2nd class 23; 3rd class 149; other postoffices 1,556.

The whole number of mail routes in the State was then 834. Their total length being 13,484 miles. Number of miles of travel required yearly to carry the mails 13,229,678.

The gross amount of postal receipts in this State for the year ending June 30, 1792, was $1,949,847.05.

These figures show that the people of Iowa are large patrons of the postal department. Her people read newspapers and write letters.

TELEGRAPHS AND TELEPHONES.

These modern inventions for the speedy conveyance of intellegence are established throughout this State and are largely patronized by the people aiding business transactions and facilitating communication.

BANKING.

The growth of wealth in Iowa has brought enlargement of business, has developed new lines of business pursuit and incited the founding of new and important business enterprises.

The banking business is an essential to commercial transaction and accommodation in this age of quickened activity and communication. The interests of commerce and security of the patrons of banking institutions incorporated under our State legislation demand a careful, legal supervision to secure their wise management. This is provided by our banking laws.

Provisions are made by our laws for the incorporation of two classes of banking institutions denominated severally, State banks and Savings banks, both classes being banks of exchange and deposit; National banks being the only banks of issue. Hon. J. A. Lyons, Auditor of State, in his annual bank report, June 30, 1892, returned 104 Savings banks, and 141 State banks. The Savings banks having a capital of $5,304,000.00, and holding deposits to the amount of $26,115,384.25. The 141 State banks were reported as having a capital of $7,430,000.00, holding on deposit $16,361,011.34. The total capital of these two classes of banks being $12,734,200. The total deposits held by them $42,476,395.79.

PRIVATE INSTITUTIONS.

The Comptroller of the Treasury, Hon. A. B. Hepburn, reported June 30, 1892, eight incorporated loan and trust companies doing business in Iowa. These had a capital stock of $2,122,028 and held deposits amounting to $1,001,399.

At the same date the same officer reported 185 private banks in the State with a capital of $5,404,914.00. Individual deposits $10,928,893.

NATIONAL BANKS.

In the same document that officer reported 154 National banks in this State, having a capital stock of $14,325,000, and holding on deposit $30,491,755.68.

That officer estimated the population of the State June 1, 1892, at 1,964,000 persons. He reported the total banking capital in the State at $44,586,152. Individual deposits held by the several classes of banks above named, $84,899,443.227.

The total sum of deposits in the several institutions enumerated averaged $43.22 per capita, to the estimated population. Surely a people with such an amount of cash per capita at command in banks if not rich are at least in that happy condition desired by Agur: "Give me neither poverty nor riches, feed me with convenient food for me, lest I be full and deny thee and say who is the Lord? Or lest I be poor and steal and take the name of my God in vain."

INSURANCE.

The insurance business has assumed large dimensions and like the banking business it is placed under strict legal supervision. It is operated under two lines, namely, stock and mutual companies, all subjected to the same strict supervision.

There were in the State 141 Co-operative or Farmers' Insurance companies, carrying December 31, 1891, risks to the amount of $93,291,790. They paid for losses during the year 1890, $103,912.75, doing their business at an average cost of $1.57 per $1,000 of insurance. Insuring nothing but farm property or what are strictly detached dwellings in towns their losses are light, and doing business strictly on the mutual plan and without expensive agencies their expenses are very low and insurance is carried in them at the lowest possible rate.

There are nineteen other companies incorporated under the laws of Iowa, doing general fire insurance business. Of these eleven are joint stock companies holding a paid up capital of $875,000. Seven are mutual companies. The eighteen companies have a total of gross assets of $3,890,463. Their total income in 1891 was $1,883,461.25. They wrote risks during that year to the grand total of $97,785,403.87, and paid in losses $784,386.31.

FOREIGN COMPANIES.

All foreign companies before they can do business in Iowa must make satisfactory showing of their condition to the Auditor of State. There were 108 of such companies doing business in Iowa in 1890, namely, 1 German company, 2 Scotch, 14 English, 2 Canadian, 7 Connecticut, 27 New York, 6 Massachusetts, 4 New Jersey, 1 Maryland, 1 Pennsylvania, 14 Wisconsin, 4 Colorado, 1 Michigan, 3 Rhode Island, 3 Illinois, 5 Tennessee, 1 New Hampshire and 2 Minnesota. Three foreign countries and fifteen other states are represented in the fire insurance business in this State. These do a large business.

LIFE INSURANCE.

The life insurance business is carried on by home and foreign companies. Including both classes twenty-nine life insurance companies were authorized to do business in this State in 1892. Of these companies four were home incorporations and twenty-five were foreign, namely, five Connecticut, nine New York, one each Massachusetts, Michigan, New Jersey, Vermont, Wisconsin, California, Nebraska, Ohio and Maine and two Pennsylvania incorporations.

The total number of life policies in force December 31, 1892, was 38,302. The total amount of life insurance in force at that date was $78,356,022. The total premiums received during the year 1891 was $2,237,425.99. Amount of losses paid, $659,922.69.

DEVELOPMENT OF WEALTH.

Iowa, in regard to her rank in the accumulation of wealth, occupies a position of which her citizens may well be proud. In the census of 1850 thirty-two of the thirty-three States then forming the Union exceeded her in wealth, *per capita*; a fact that at once proves that her pioneers were men in very moderate circumstances. In the census returns of 1860 thirty of the thirty-six States of the Union exceeded Iowa in *per capita* wealth. In 1870 Iowa had reduced the gap between her place in 1860 and the head of the list by passing ten of the thirty states that had outranked her in this particular in 1860. In 1880 she had surpassed others until by the census of that year, but six states east of the Rocky Mountains exceeded her; and but five in the Union, namely, New York, Pennsylvania, Ohio, Illinois and Massachusetts outranked her in aggregate wealth. In this respect Iowa is still gaining, and in the past twelve years has outstripped others of her sister states in the development of wealth, *per capita*. That Iowa has enjoyed such material prosperity and that her people are in thriving condition are facts which we gladly record.

A HISTORIC RESUME.

Sixty years ago, a space of time embraced in the life of men yet active in business, Iowa was devoid of the essentials of a civilized State. There was not a charitable institution, public building, postoffice, church, school, mill, bridge, orchard, farm, or scarcely a squatter's cabin or barn within its boundaries. The whole region was then traversed only by Indians. The only dwellings, save a few cabins in Lee county, being the tepee or wigwam. The means of interior transportation in aid of trade, were the shoulders of the squaw, the Indian pony or canoe, or the pack horse of an occasional venturesome hunter.

Consider further the greatness of the change made in these three score years, a mere hand-breadth of time in the life of a nation. Look at the 110,000 miles of broad, largely well constructed, open highways, with their innumerable culverts and thousands of substantial bridges which now carry those highways across our streams, furnishing ready means of communication and transportation to all. Look at the 215,000 grand farms in Iowa, with their barns and other outbuildings, many of them costly structures; the grand pastures flecked with feeding herds and flocks of noblest blood and finest form; the spacious orchards and gardens of fruit, the stately artificial groves which grace those fine farm homes. View the 370,000 family dwellings, the homes of comfort and elegance of our two millions of intelligent, Christian citizens, thousands of those homes being spacious dwelling places, palatial in architecture, luxurious in furniture, and royal in their surroundings. Then view the beautiful prosperous towns and cities which have sprung up as though thrown forth by magic all over our broad prairies; and the shops, the mills, the mines, the manufacturing plants, the bazaars of trade, teeming with life and activity, the halls of art, the public schools, with their 13,275 fine school houses, the private and parochial schools, the academies, seminaries, normal schools, colleges, technical and professional schools and the universities which now give grace and culture to our social life. Extend your vision and take in the 4,500 church edifices many of them majestic temples, standing everywhere with open doors, inviting all to enjoy their sanctifying associations. Then look further at the noble charitable and reformatory institutions, the great schools and asylums for our unfortunate classes, our homes for the maimed, the infirm and the poor. View these and consider that all have been constructed and are maintained either by means voluntarily donated or by taxation which has been generously and freely voted. Then consider that in addition to the outlays essential to the construction, maintenance and improvement of the institutions mentioned our people have made a large accumulation of private wealth. Surely such gains attest not only that Iowa has an industrious, economical citizenship, but also that her generous soil has great wealth producing power.

THE DEMONSTRATION OF FIGURES

We are not left merely to rhetorical statement to express the growth of wealth in this inland State. The rapid increase in valuation of taxable property in Iowa shows an almost incomprehensible growth of wealth. In 1850, 13,732,000 acres of land were assessed for taxation. Its average assessed value was but $3.54 per acre, and the aggregate valuation $48,611,230, the total valuation for the purpose of taxation that year being $58,007,121. This was only two score and three years.

In 1860, 24,386,217 acres were assessed for taxation, their aggregate value being $123,447,181 or $5.06 per acre. The valuation of personal property assessed that year was $30,147,858. The total aggregate assessed valuation in 1860 was $153,539,116.

A HISTORIC RESUME.

In 1870, 33,018,604 acres of land were assessed for taxation. Of this amount only 9,369,467 were reported as improved land. The average assessed value per acre was $5.50, and the aggregate valuation $181,881,953, while the total taxable valuation that year had reached $294,532,250, the real wealth in the State had according to the United States census, grown to the sum of $717,644,750.

In 1880 the aggregate value of taxable property within the State had grown to the sum of $409,819,020, the area of assessed lands being 34,- 569,858 acres. Only 19,866,514 acres, or little more than one-half the area of the State, were reported as improved lands, but the average taxable valuation of the lands that year was $7.11 per acre.

In 1890 the taxable lands had increased to 34,734,579 acres, and their valuation to $272,847,509, which was an average of $7.85 per acre, the total taxable valuation in the State that year being $523,862,858.

But these remarkable figures fall far short of showing the true growth of wealth in this prosperous State. The flight of time has not been more rapid than has been the advance in all lines of improvement, in labor saving machinery, modes of transportation, and business facilities. Railways, telegraphs and telephones have extended their conveniences and industrial inspiration through every county. Hamlets have grown into thriving towns and thrifty towns have developed into large and prosperous cities. Yet as wealth has grown the ratio of the taxable to the true value of property has been reduced. The assessments in 1850 and 1880 were nearer the true value of property than were the assessed values of 1890. We give a few instances in support of this statement.

In 1870 cattle were assessed at an average of $12.67 per head, in 1890 at only $7.11.

In 1870 horses were assessed at an average value of $42.67 per head, in 1890 at $25.64.

In 1870 swine were assessed at an average value of $3.09 per head, in 1890 at $1.64.

Nearly the same reduction in ratios of the assessed, to the true values, has obtained in all lines of property. As shown above, the average assessed value of lands throughout the State was $5.50 per acre in 1870. Then there were but 9,369,467 acres of land, or only one-fourth of the area of the State, reported as improved lands. In 1880 the improved land had more than doubled in area, being that year reported as 19,866,541 acres. The value of the improvements on the land had largely increased. In 1870 we had but 2,683 miles of railroad, in 1890 there were 8,436 miles, traversing every county in the State. While land has increased several times (a hundred per cent.) in value, its assessed valuation has only increased from an average of $5.50 to $7.85.

Well informed judges of property-value in this State believe that the present taxable valuation does not exceed twenty per cent. of the real value of the property of the people. Taking this figure as a factor in the calculation, it will be seen that the real value of property is now in excess of $2,700,000,000. In the brief period of sixty years property values have grown from nothing to the immense sum named.

It is worthy of mention in this place that this vast aggregate of wealth has been developed from the soil of Iowa. None of these thousands of millions have been washed from glittering river beds. Iowa has scores of "sunny fountains" but none of them

"Roll down their golden sands."

Nor have any of these millions been mined from argentiferous or auriferous rocks, in which hundreds of golden millions lie, awaiting the workman with his picks and drills; they have been won almost solely in agricultural pursuits. The tillers of the soil and herdsmen have been their chief producers, and the plow, the harrow and the corn cultivator, the mower and the reaper the chief implements used in their acquisition.

The healthfulness of Iowa for man and beast, through the earlier as well as the later years of its settlement has had important bearing on this gain of wealth. Iowa has ever been rightfully recognized as a healthy State.

COMPARATIVE GROWTH OF POPULATION AND WEALTH.

We take the following figures from the returns of the several enumerations of population and wealth made in Iowa by the National Census authorities, placing the same in concisely tabulated form, not only to present still more clearly, if posssble, the fact of the great development of wealth, but also to show how the growth of wealth has outran the growth of population in the history of the State.

The first national census in Iowa was the sixth of the country. It was taken in 1840. The population of the territory was then returned as 43,113 persons. Of the real wealth of the territory at the time of that census we are not informed.

COMPARATIVE GROWTH OF POPULATION AND WEALTH.

YEARS.	POPULATION.	PER CT. INCREASE.	TRUE WEALTH.	WEALTH PER CAPITA
1850	192,214	288.	$ 23,714,638	$ 123.39
1860	674,913	251.	247,338,265	366.46
1870	1,194,752	96.91	717,644,750	640.89
1880	1,624,615	36.	1,724,000,000	1,059.00
1890	1,911,826	17.	2,700,000,000	1,412.00

The fact that this development of wealth has come from the areable fields, the pastures and meadows of Iowa, and that it has been developed while large areas of the State have been but sparsely settled, and while but little more than one-half of its area has been "tickled with the plow," unmistakably demonstrates the excellence of her soil, the richness and healthfulness of her sunshine, the fertilizing potency of the rains that fall upon her lands, and its pre-eminence as a field for successful agricultural industry. Such vast development of wealth in a State of the population, area and age of Iowa, having neither ocean commerce, nor great fisheries, nor forests, nor rich bonanzas of precious metals, will ever be one of the marvels of history.

FINANCE AND TAXATION.

Iowa is in happy financial condition. The State has an elegant, commodious, solid Capitol of stately proportions, located in the city of Des Moines on a commanding site. It has numerous other public buildings providing accommodations and educational advantages for unfortunate classes, as the blind, deaf and dumb, the feeble minded; reformatory schools for the unruly of both sexes, insane asylums, orphans home, a home for aged and needy veterans, penitentiaries for the punishment of criminals, the Normal school, Agricultural college and State university. All these great properties have been built up and millions paid for their maintenance. All expenses for State government have been met, yet taxation has been low— the assessed valuation has ever been far below the cash value of property. Taxation for all purposes has been less than one per cent. on the true value of property; and yet Iowa occupies the proud position occupied by only three other States in the American Union, of having no State debt either bonded or floating. According to the figures given in Census Bulletin No. 64, its total debt, State and county, in 1890 was but $1.91 *per capita*. In 1880 it was $2.10; a pleasing reduction for the ten years. On the ninth page that bulletin shows that only three of the States of the Union have a less State and county indebtedness *per capita*, namely Vermont, $.46; Rhode Island, $1.22 and West Virginia $1.81, while the State and county indebtedness of the States adjoining Iowa range from $2.21 to $10.04 *per capita*. The average State and county indebtedness for the States of the Union is $5.83. Although the cry, that the farmers of Iowa are overwhelmed by a mortgage indebtedness, is raised by uninformed persons, there are but few farmers in Iowa distressed on that account. It cannot be expected that in a new State, in which within the twenty years last past so great an area has been improved and such great improvements in farm homes, schools, roads, business structures and machinery have been made, that there would be no debt contracted, but that there has in the ten years last past, been a rapid reduction of the mortgage indebtedness against the people of Iowa, is a fact not only shown by the census of 1890, but one well known to all intelligent observers. The reduction in the three years that have elapsed since the taking of the last census has been very large. The prosperity of the people during those years has been unequaled in any previous period in the history of this, or any other State.

On page 7, Census Bulletin No. 16, census of 1890, the mortgage indebtedness on the farms of Iowa is given at $149,457,144. The total mortgage indebtedness on the entire reality within the State being $199,774,171. The whole number of mortgages on farms was 171,441. Considering each as a first mortgage, then the figures indicate the number of farms mortgaged. The average amount of these mortgages was $876. The records however do not show the fact that many of them were nearly paid, and that on others the debt secured was largely reduced by payment made thereon, but not shown on the record. Nor do they show the fact that the major part of these mortgages were given for purchase money on lands, or to raise money to buy more lands, to improve lands or to purchase stock where-by more money might be made on lands occupied. Estimating the farms covered by those 171,441 mortgages at eighty acres each, then we have 13,715,220 acres of mortgaged land. Further estimating their average value at $25 per acre, a moderate estimate, and we have for their total value the sum of $342,882,- 000,—certainly a good security for the sums owed; while there remains 22,000,000 acres of farm lands free from mortgage with upwards of $208,- 000,000 of live stock, the increase of which is applicable to the reduction of this indebtedness. It should not be forgotten that the dairy and poultry products alone would wipe out the mortgage indebtedness on Iowa farms within two years. The farmers of Iowa may not do all of their business on a cash basis but they certainly do it on a very safe one. The large sums held on deposit by the banks, as shown in the chapter on "Banks and Banking," much of which is money made on Iowa farms and subject to check by Iowa farmers, shows that very many of the farmers are money lenders rather than borrowers.

The assessments of real and personal property for purposes of taxation are made by local authorities, each civil township and incorporated town and the several wards in cities electing the assessors. Personal property is assessed each year and real property biennially. The township trustees and town and city councils, the country boards of supervisors and the Executive Council of the State constitute boards of equalization. The Executive Council assesses the railroads, telegraph and telephone lines.

Taxes are low when compared with the true value of property. The valuations of property for taxation as equalized by the several boards for the year 1890 were reported by Hon. J. A. Lyons, State Auditor, as follows :

Lands, 34,734,579 acres and town lots	$374,753,112
Personal property	105,543,264
Railroad property	42,962,264
Telegraph companies	502,874
Telephone companies	162,000
Total taxable valuation	$523,862,858

The lands within the State were assessed at $8.18 per acre; cattle at $7.11 per head; horses $26.46; mules $28.80; sheep $1.18, and swine at $1.64. Cattle, horses and mules under one year old and sheep and swine under six months are not listed or valued for taxation.

The taxes levied for the year 1890 were reported by the State Auditor as follows :

For purposes of State government	$1,207,872.85
For county purposes	5,107,000.27
For insane fund	348,098.27
For support of common schools	6,021,758.68
For municipal government	2,405,156.65
For special purposes	384,098.27
Total	$15,563,974.04

Taking the estimate of the real value of property within the State at the moderate figure of $2,700,000,000, the taxes levied for the year for all purposes aggregated the small figure of .71 of one per cent. The interest on county and municipal indebtedness, and provisions for sinking funds are provided for in the taxes levied as above given. In no State in the Union are the people less burdened with taxation.

AGRICULTURAL PRODUCTIVENESS.

Iowa has world wide fame for its agricultural productiveness. Its soil produces all the standard grains, grasses, vegetables and fruits, successfully grown north of the Ohio river. The figures required to express the vast production of grains, vegetables, meats and fruits within this region are of surprising magnitude, but the capabilities of Iowa's thirty-five millions of acres to produce foods are yet uncomprehended. With the cultivation of her yet unimproved acres, better drainage of her wet lands and the more perfect cultivation of her areable fields, meadows and orchards the products of this superlatively fine farming region will have a wonderful increase.

Iowa does not owe the greatness of her food productiveness to the extent of her area. In this regard she has but 20th place in the list of the States of the Union. Michigan, Minnesota, the Dakotas, Nebraska, Kansas, Missouri and Illinois, her near kin in locality and climate, all outrank her in this particular. Compared with Texas and California, she ranks respectively as one to five and three. In respect to population Iowa has but tenth

FLAX PALACE, FOREST CITY, IOWA.

place in the rank of States. She also held the tenth place in 1880, in respect to persons engaged in agricultural occupation, so that her larger agricultural productiveness is to be found in other causes than the greater number of her agricultural laborers or her larger area. In the census just referred to, this State ranked fifth in the number of farms, sixth in the production of wheat, sixth in the production of potatoes, fourth in the production of barley, second in the production of Indian corn, second in the production of oats, second in the production of hay, second in the production of all grains, third in respect to the number of horses, second in respect to the number of cattle, and first in respect to the number of swine. Although this State then ranked second in the production of all grains, second in the production of beef animals, and first in the production of swine, only 19,866,541, or a trifle more than one-half of her thirty-five million acres were reported as being improved. Iowa, then largely unimproved, was outranked by only three other States in the total value of her agricultural productions. The four leading States compared then as follows:

STATES.	VALUE OF AGRICULTURAL PRODUCT.
Illinois	$203,980,137.90
New York	178,025,695.00
Ohio	156,737,152.00
Iowa	136,103,473.00

The above schedule clearly establishes the fact that an agricultural laborer in Iowa's climate and working Iowa soil effects larger production than an agricultural laborer in any other climate and any other State of the Union. This one fact accounts for its unequalled development of wealth.

In the annual report of the National Department of Agriculture for 1888, Iowa is placed second in the list of States in the production of potatoes, her production that year being over 16,000,000 bushels. New York alone led Iowa in this important crop; but the reported yield per acre in Iowa, largely exceeded that of New York.

The same high authority gave Iowa for the same year second place in the production of hay, her production being 5,972,783 tons. The crop of New York, the only State then leading Iowa was 5,462,667 tons, or only 143,984 tons more than the product of Iowa.

The National Department of Agriculture reported that 9,506,716 acres of Iowa farms in 1891 were cultivated in "corn," and reported their aggregate products at 350,878,000—an excess of over 115,993,000 bushels over our neighboring State on the east, then the second in rank in the corn producing states. If corn is "king" then surely Iowa is the prime province of his kingdom.

Since 1886 Iowa has been the largest corn producing State in the Union. No region on this earth of the same area furnishes such vast production of this most important cereal. The production of corn in Iowa for the years 1888, 1889, 1890 and 1891, according to the report of the National Department of Agriculture, aggregated 1,221,305,000 bushels, or an average of 34,963,753 acres. This is an average production for the four years of 33.4 bushels per acre. A few special yields of this cereal in this famous corn State may properly be mentioned in this connection.

In the winter of 1890-1 Mr. Henry Wallace, editor of the Homestead, an agricultural paper published in Des Moines, offered three prizes for the best three acres of corn grown within the State in the season of 1891. It will be noticed that the competitors came from nine counties, these counties covering one-half of the State from south to north.

Wm. M. Husted, Des Moines, Polk County		364 bu.,	and	65 lbs
James Pemble, Wapello, Louisa	"	315	"	65 lbs
J. W. Ryncarson, Yorktown, Page	"	300	"	5 lbs
A. F. White, DeWitt, Clinton	"	291	"	
Frank Wright, Anamosa, Jones	"	285	"	34 lbs
A. D. Belknap, Amber, Jones	"	217	"	55 lbs
A. D. Zimmerman, Avoca, Pottawattamie County		277	"	20 lbs
A. D. Irving, Madrid, Boone	"	270	"	3 lbs
J. H. DeFord, Mt. Sterling, Van Buren	"	269	"	30 lbs
J. C. Frazey, Shelby, Shelby	"	262	"	14 lbs

AGRICULTURAL PRODUCTIVENESS.

The largest yield was 115 bushels and 45 pounds per acre, the smallest 87 bushels and 18 pounds per acre, for the three acres.

The immense importance of the corn crop in Iowa agriculture is evident to all. Secretary Shaffer of the State Agricultural Society in the report for 1891 said: "Iowa's single product of corn is worth more than the entire output of all the gold and silver mines of all the states combined."

President Harrison in returning from his journey to the Pacific coast, having seen the land of "the orange and the palm," and having reached on that return the great fields of "golden ears," in his address at Omaha, said: "I have seen the orange groves and all the fruits which enrich and characterize the state of California. I have seen the summit cities whose mining camps are on the peaks where the men are delving into the earth to bring out the rich stores there; but I return again to the land of the corn stalk with an affection that I cannot describe. I am sure those friends who have delighted us with visions of loveliness and prosperity will excuse me if my birth and earlier training in Ohio and Indiana leads me to the conclusion that the states that grow corn are the greatest states in the world."

The directors of the Iowa State Agricultural Society in their report for 1891, by their Secretary, Hon. Jno. R. Shaffer, present the following table estimating the agricultural products for Iowa for that year and their values:

AGRICULTURAL PRODUCT OF IOWA FOR 1891.

KIND.	PRODUCT.	VALUE.
Corn, bushels	325,031,598	$100,509,479
Wheat, bushels	33,151,488	25,741,039
Oats, bushels	115,810,800	26,436,184
Rye, bushels	2,051,400	1,333,110
Barley, bushels	4,528,069	1,811,167
Buckwheat, bushels	414,000	276,000
Potatoes, Irish, bushels	25,620,350	5,380,271
Potatoes, sweet, bushels	207,900	207,900
Grass seeds, estimated		1,750,000
Flax seed, bushels	3,154,016	2,523,212
Hay, tame, tons	5,582,800	33,497,310
Hay, prairie, estimated		6,800,000
Broom-corn, tons	3,480	270,570
Sorghum, gallons	2,092,485	904,718
Butter, pounds	168,630,715	33,738,158
Cheese, pounds	5,000,000	450,000
Wool		300,000
Horses, number	1,312,079	91,911,133
Mules, number	41,648	2,459,928
Sheep, number	152,000	1,430,750
Hogs, number	5,921,100	29,475,236
Milch cows, number	1,278,612	23,973,975
Other cattle, number	2,680,247	47,098,317
Orchard and vine products		3,000,000
Hive products		550,000
Poultry products		5,600,000
Small fruits		750,000
Timber		3,000,000
Miscellaneous		10,000,000
Total		$ 464,219,308

In Iowa in 1892 there were 565,031 head of sheep, 4,011,233 head of cattle, and 7,105,320 head of swine and flocks innumerable of turkeys, geese, ducks and other barn yard fowls. At least 5,000,000 head of finely fatted swine were supplied for slaughter, furnishing fifteen pounds, *per capita*, of the best pork to the whole country, while at least 400,000,000 pounds of finest beef was furnished to the markets of the world. These figures of moderate estimate, are given to convey some idea of the abundance that is found in this most fertile region. Iowa farmers not only feed well all of Iowa's people, but feed also millions in other states and countries. In grain and meat production Iowa, but sixty years removed from a absolute wilderness State, now stands without an equal.

THE OLDEST LEGENDS OF THE ORIGIN OF MAIZE.

Maize (zea mays—L) derives its name from a Greek word zea, meaning *spelt*. There are many varying opinions as to its first home. It never occurs naturally, but is a native of all tropical America, and probably indigenous there. Humboldt says it is an American Plant. Some older writers, however, claim that it originally came from Asia, going thence to America, from which country it was first brought into Europe. Gerard in the "Herbal" written in 1597, calls it "Turkey Corn," and says, "This kind of grain was first brought into Spain, and thence into other provinces of Europe, out of Asia, which is in the Turke's Dominions, as also out of America." No corn is found in Egyptian tombs, but the plant is represented in an ancient Chinese Book in the French Library at Paris. There is a variety known in Chili, (Zea Curagua) which has small grains, some of which are often found in tombs. The Chilians are superstitious about these, as they split so as to image a cross on their inner surface. This corn is called *Curu* in Quichua, and it is to the kind suggestion of the great Americanist, Count de Charencey, that I owe the statement that many similar names are given to rice in various Asiatic tongues, probably referring to the small eared corn, (Cha-rang, among the Kodougs of Nepaul, *Chasrak* in Chungthangy, *Sila* in Nachhereng, *Sera* in Chourasya, and *Seri* in Kolungya.) These facts, heretofore unnoticed, so far as I know, would seem to indicate the Asiatic origin of the grain. Several tribes of the Nepaul hills call Sorghum, *Mazyi*.

But we may find a legend of Asiatic origin to account for maize, which, however foolish it may seem in its details, is significant, as indicating a knowledge of this plant at an early period. The legend is from the *Manek Maya*, a Javanese legendary poem of unknown date. It relates that the body of a certain maiden who died from the too ardent embrace of her pursuing lover, *Sang Yang Guru*, (the personification of man) was buried in a wood; from the head, sprang the cocoanut; from the hands, the plantain tree; and from the teeth, Indian corn or Maize.

This legend, referring the origin of corn to the teeth of the buried woman, carries us back to the antique fable of the armed men springing from the dragon's teeth, and it is a curious fact that in central Illinois the sharp kernelled variety is popularly known as "Horse-tooth corn."

We may, however, find legends among the American Indians which bear a close resemblance to the old Javanese story of the origin of corn. Dr. Brinton relates an Iroquois myth of Ioshkea, the dawn-hero, one of the great American culture-heroes, which accounts for the appearance of Maize among the Indian tribes. The heavens are here said to have been peopled by a race of supernatural beings, and one of these a woman, *Atalensic*, fell through the sky. As a result of her fall, being pregnant, she died, after one of her twins Ioshkea, had burst from her arm pit into the world. Her body was buried, and from it sprang the vegetables; from the head, the pumpkin; from the breast, maize, (hence the milk;) and from the limbs, the bean.

We may also have a key to both of these myths, which seem to express the operations of nature in promoting the growth of so beneficial a plant. As Dr. Brinton says, plainly expressed, "The sense of the story is that the orb of light moves daily over the water (*Atalensic*, sea, water) preceeded by its child, Ioshkea, (light, dawn.)

Still another legend, from a different tribe, ascribes the origin of corn to the body of a woman. This Cherokee myth is reported by James Mooney. Two boys, one the child of a hunter living at Looking Glass Mountain (Tsuwaklda) in North Carolina, the other issuing from the water, from the blood poured into it by the hunter, kill the hunter's wife because she was a witch, they having seen her rub corn out of her body. She tells them: "When you have killed me, clear a large piece of ground in front of the house, and drag my body seven times around the circle. Then drag me seven times over the ground inside of the circle, and stay up all night and watch, and in the morning you will have plenty of corn." They kill her with clubs, cut off her head, and set it on the tent-pole, then clear away the ground. Instead of all of it, they only clear seven little spots, and this is why corn only grows in certain parts of the world. Then they drag the body of Nela around the circle, and where her blood falls, corn springs up. Instead of dragging it about seven times, they do so twice, and this is why the Indian only works his crop twice. In the morning, the crop is ripe.

Instead of the body of a mortal, the body of an animal has been substituted in an Osage legend, reported by Rev. J. O. Dorsey. In this tradition, four Buffalo bulls came by, and as each rolls upon the ground he dropped from his left hind leg an ear of corn and a pumpkin: red corn came from the first, spotted from the second, black from the third, and white from the fourth. Therefore, when a child is named in the *Tsicu* Gens, the head man of that Gens takes a grain of each kind of corn, and a slice of each variety of pumpkin, which he puts into the mouth of the infant.

The early Spanish conquerers found the native tribes here in possession of this esculent vegetable, which sustains life among so many indigenous tribes of our Hemisphere. They endeavored to find the history of its origin. As might be expected, they found nothing but legends to account for this, as well as other plants. One of them is given by Brasseur de Bourbourg, from a Caqciquel manuscript of Mexico. It is a legend of the creation. The primitive Gods of Mexico and the world becoming discouraged for lack of food, Queatzalcoatl, the culture hero, decided to visit the interior of the country and of distant lands, to find some alimentary food. The legend relates that he found some of the people of a distant country bearing stalks of maize, which he received from them, and brought back to the Mexican valley. The region was called "Paxil Calaya", the place of divided waters, to a hill known as "Tonacatapetl", "or the hill of our Subsistence." It has been named as a sort of Terrestrial paradise, says the Abbe, throughout all antique America.

Another Mexican myth reported by Sahagun, relates not to the origin, but to the mysterious connection of maize with the Gods. Tezcatlipoca, disguised as an old woman, parches maize, and the odor of the savory corn attracts the Toltecs, whom she then destroys. One of the names of Quetzalcoatl was Ce-acatl, "one reed", a corn stalk (possibly phallic also). A day in the Mexican calendar was named after him, and this day, Ce-acatl, was a most unlucky one, as he was the God of Storms. Persons born on this corn-stalk day would lose their possessions by having them blown away.

In Aztec, *elotl* is milky corn, *mumnehtl* ripe corn in the ear, *tlaxcaeli* corn cakes, and *atoeli* hasty-pudding. Centestl is the Mexican Maize Goddess, and sometimes bears a corn-stalk in her hand. A stalk of grain carried by a bird headed Deity, signified the winds. South American Indians, and those of Central America, also know the value of maize. Many of them use it as food, but more ferment it as a sort of beer. Sometimes it is mixed with other substances, such as quinoa seeds, to make a fermented drink. D'Orbigny says the Guarany Indians of Brazil attribute the discovery of maize to Tamaui, a Culture hero.

A Quichua legend, according to Comara, relates that *Con*, son of the Sun and the Moon, gave maize to man.

One of the four Maya Gods (Bacubs) was *Hobnil*, the Belly. His habitat was the South, and he was of the color of ripe yellow corn, and was favorable and propitious to man. Stalks of maize-colored red were expressive of generative force. The spirit of the South brought maize to the Iriquois.

Mr. A. M. Stephens relates the following curious legend of the Snake order of the Moquis Indians. Many years ago, several bachelor brothers lived together in a house. Their names were, in the order of their ages, Red Corn, Blue Corn, Yellow Corn, Green Corn, Spotted Corn, and Black Corn. When the last attained his majority, the others told him to find a bride. He was dissatisfied at this, not knowing where to find a suitable one. He started out on a journey with four feather plume sticks and a bag of sand meal. He finally came to a stream by a lake, where he was told by Dawa, the sun-chief, to throw his plume sticks into the water. They immediately grew into a raft on which he embarked. He came to Napa Teua (Big Rattlesnake) after a four days sail, his raft again becoming plume sticks, after wafting him ashore. A snake fiend approached him, and gave him a bag and stick. His name here changes suddenly to Kueteat-ri-yi (White Corn), without any assignable cause. Finally, after many miracles have been performed by the aid of the bag and stick, he arrived in the presence of the Snake King, where he obtained a beautiful bride, first obtaining a snake skin dress for himself. He then learned the many songs and ritual still practiced by this gens of the tribe. After this, he returned to the South, with his wife Teua-wati.

Among all the Indian tribes of the Southwest, corn has a peculiar significance. Its connection with their religious ceremonials will be alluded to again.

Schoolcraft, who chronicaled many Indian legends now unattainable, relates the following "Algic" story of the advent of maize.

Kitchimonedo (the Creator) first made men who looked like men, but were really worthless. He put them and the world into a great lake, and drowned them. From the water he then made a very handsome young man and afterwards he sent a sister to live with him, as he was lonesome. After some years, this young man had a dream, after which he told his sister "Five young men will come to your lodge door this night to visit you. The Great Spirit forbids you to answer or even look up and smile on the first four, but when the fifth comes, you may speak and laugh, and show that you are pleased." She acted accordingly. The first of the five strangers who called was *Ilsaman*, meaning tobacco, and on being repulsed, he fell down and died. *Wapako*, or pumpkin, was next. *Eshkorsini*, the melon, third, and fourth *Kokseels*, the bean. All these perished, but when *Tamin*, or Montanin (Maize), presented himself he was admitted. From the union of the maiden and Montanin sprang the Indian race. This legend, however, is not so well known, as another related by Schoolcraft, which, through

its being utilized by Longfellow, in his poem "Hiawatha", has been widespread. The legend is here given, condensed from the diffuse story as published.

The son of a poor Indian hunter (in another version it is Massmamium, or Manalozho, the magican), on attaining the age of fifteen, built a fasting lodge in the forest, and set about his task of fasting for several days, as all young Indians did at that age. He was a serious young man, and got to thinking how he could be of service to his people. On the third day, he became too weak to walk, and kept his bed. He fancied as he lay there that he saw approaching a handsome young man dressed in green with green plumes on his head.

> "And he saw a youth approaching
> Dressed in garments green and yellow,
> Coming through the purple twilight,
> Through the splendor of the sun-set,
> Plumes of green bent o'er his forehead
> And his hair was soft and golden."

This young man bade him arise, weak as he was, and wrestle with him, telling him that he might benefit his whole race. After three trials, each resulting in failure, the seventh and last day of his fast came, and the stranger returned to a final struggle. He told the young man that he would prevail, and then instructed him what to do. Let the poet again speak:

> "Make a bed for me to lie in,
> Where the rain may fall upon me,
> Where the sun may shine and warm me:
> Strip the garments, green and yellow,
> Strip this nodding plumage from me:
> Lay me in the earth and make it
> Soft and loose and light above me,
> Let no hand disturb my slumber,
> Let no weed nor worm molest me.
> Let not Kahgahgee, the raven,
> Come to haunt me and molest me."

The young man, as the story goes, obeyed this injunction and carefully buried his opponent after he had conquered him. He still kept the secret, partook sparingly of food, and tended the grave, keeping it inviolate:

> "Till at length a small green feather
> From the earth shot slowly upward,
> Then another and another,
> And, before the Summer ended,
> Stood the Maize in all its beauty,
> With its shining robes about it,
> And the long, soft yellow tresses,
> And in rapture Hiawatha
> Cried aloud, It is Mondamin,
> Yes, the friend of man, Mondamin."

Schoolcraft, who gives in this beautiful tale in prose-guise, almost as the poet has made it, says of Mon-da-min, "It is the spirit grain." I cannot forbear quoting the closing lines of the poem which appeals to every Western man from the Corn Belt:

> "And still later, when the Autumn
> Changed the long green leaves to yellow,
> And the soft and juicy kernels
> Grew like wampum hard and yellow,
> Then the ripened ears he gathered,
> Stripped the withered husks from off them
> As he once had stripped the wrestler,
> Gave the first feast of Mondamin
> And made known unto the people
> This new gift of the Great Spirit."

Many of the Indian tribes had, and some still have, extended religious ceremonies connected with corn. Several have a Green Corn Dance, some a dance at corn planting, and others at the harvest time, while corn or its products are used in nearly all the ceremonies of some of the tribes of the Southwest.

The Chahta-Muscogees of Florida held their Busk or Green Corn Dance when the corn was just old enough to use. They then held a feast of several days.

Hawkins, an early traveler, describes it. Several purging plants were used, and an elaborate dance was held.

Among the Iroquois, the Green Corn Dance was preceeded by a four day's hunt, during which the corn was parched by the squaws. At the end of this time, a feast was held, and the especial feature was that of gambling, in which all indulged, as well as partaking of the pudding of corn, beans and bear's meat.

Seven days were given up to the corn planting feast: the first four were spent in council, all the chiefs making boastful speeches in turn. On the fifth day, the chiefs took hold of a belt of wampum, and made a sort of a lame confession of their sins. On the sixth day the other warriors did the same, and on the seventh, there was a feather dance—quite an elaborate ceremonial—and a feast of dog-meat.

At Corn gathering, the last public feast of the year, corn tassels, silks, and leaves were worn as ornaments by the dancers.

Among the Seminoles, and other Southern tribes, the Green Corn Dance was a great event.

The Omahas have a Hunting Feast in which, after a Buffalo hunt, they have a certain formula of songs, which reproduce in mimicry the growth of maize. These songs are called: 1. I clear the land. 2. I put in corn. 3. The corn comes up. 4. It has blades. 5. The ears appear. 6. The ears have hair on. 7. At length we try the corn to see if it is ripe. 8. At length it is ripe. 9. At length we pull the ear from the stalk. 10. At length we husk the ear. 11. At length we shell the corn. 12. At length we eat the corn. A feast follows these songs.

All the various colors and kinds of corn have different names among these and other Indian tribes. The Omaha names are, Wata zi-ska, white corn; Wata-zi-sko, blue corn; Wata-zi-zi, yellow corn; Wata-zi yscije, spotted corn; Wata-zi-tsijde, reddish blue; Wata-zi-jiveghi, red; Wata-nyaan, figured yellow and red stripes; Wachstya, sweet corn.

The Hopi, or Moqui Indians of Arizona, in making certain rounds, required by their religious ceremonies, use corn-meal, which is sacred in the Southwest among many tribes, sprinkling it on the sand. Ears of corn are also placed at the extremities of lines drawn to the four points of the compass, with the tips pointing in. Meal is also sprinkled to these cardinal points. The corn is afterward washed by the priest.

Among the Tusayans, in the same neighborhood, corn is even more extensively used in religious observances. Corn husks fillets are worn on the heads of the novices and meal plentifully scattered on the shrines. The novices carry corn in their hands at certain times during a dance, and a quantity of corn is shelled, the kernels being stuck all over clay images. The standard of one of the clans has corn plumes at the top, and the helmets of two of these men are made of a mosaic of split corn ears. A magic altar was made and at its six corners and sides, corn, feathers, and pebbles were laid, always keeping the colors as here indicated for the corn:

1. Northwest, yellow corn.
2. North, black corn.
3. Northeast, white corn.
4. Southeast, red corn.
5. South, sweet corn.
6. Southwest, blue corn.

Among the Navajos, corn meal is also used in sacred ceremonies. It is sprinkled on the sand-pictures made in these ceremonies, carried in fawn skin bags by carriers of sacred heralds, and used by them in incantations. The priest who instructs them says, "Sprinkle meal across a little valley, across a big arroyo, across the roots of a tree sprinkle meal, and then you may step over. Sprinkle meal on a flat rock."

In the mythical journey taken by the ancestors of these Indians, they came to the first Corn Palace—a house built of corn pillars, with a door of daylight, a ceiling supported by four spruce trees, and rainbows over the house. Corn meal and pollen formed their food here. The account of this is given by Dr. Washington Matthews.

In the ceremony commemorative of this journey, some sick person is usually introduced, to be cured by the rites of the Hoshkamn dance. This sick person carries corn meal, and sits in a sand picture, where a corn stalk is drawn. This corn stalk is in the hands of a white bodied figure, representing the Southeast—the symbolism of color always being carefully preserved. A corn cake baked in a hole in the heated earth is given to the attendant priests during the ceremonies. The white bodied figure alluded to above is accompanied by three others typifying the bean, the pumpkin and the tobacco, the four sacred plants. Among the Zunies, meal is also sacred in many ceremonies. A pinch of it forms the heart of a dummy rabbit used in the Kok-ko iniation, as described by Mrs. Stephenson.

The novices, as they come from the north, present yellow corn to the priests. Those from the West, blue corn. Those from the South, red, and those from the East, white.

In the Navajo prayer to the Gods, the priest says, "I give to you food of corn pollen, etc."

One of the Tusayan Gens is the corn Gens. The 4th Gens of the Moquis, the 7th of the Zunis, the 5th of the San Felipe Puebloes, the 6th of the Santana Pueblo, the 9th of the Cochiti, the 1st of the Isleta, the 3rd of the Jemez and the 4th of the Zia Pueblo, are all Corn Gentes, according to Capt. Bourke's list.

Tradition says that corn was planted by the Navajo Chiefs in the primitive migrations, and that it would grow by night of the same day. The stem, roots, leaves and ears are all used in the ceremonials of certain Gentes.

A line of meal is spread upon the floor of the house in the dance Hasjalia Daljis, also on the debris from it, while the soles of the feet, the hands the knees, the breast, the shoulders and the head of the officiating priest. A deer is smothered to death as a sacrifice, and in its mouth corn pollen is put and a line drawn from mouth to tail along the breast. Corn pollen is sprinkled on little balls, and on blankets used in other parts of the ceremony. Meal is sprinkled in the water used on the second day of these ceremonies. Corn husks containing beads are placed on blankets on the east side of the house on the third day. Medicine tubes of corn husks, sprinkled with meal and pollen are also used.

One of the mythical sand figures is composed of five grains of corn put on a sand bed, one white, one yellow, one blue, and two variegated ones arranged in quincunx order.

Corn pollen is put on the soap suds used in purification by the priests, and the waters are sprinkled with pollen. Dried and ground as gruel it is given as medicine. In the sand paintings, which are a part of these extended ceremonies, the stalk appears frequently. The red of the bodies means red corn. The goddess is clothed in corn husks, and ten ears of yellow corn wrapped in pinion leaves are placed at the girl's feet in certain ceremonies.

Superstitious usages with reference to planting or harvesting corn, or caring for the crop, among our farmers are not abundant. The old custom of corn huskings celebrated by Longfellow in Evangeline and Hiawatha, is almost entirely in abeyance. As these lines may not be in sight, it will not be amiss to quote them:

"And whene'er some lucky maiden
Found a red ear in the husking,
Found a maize ear red as blood is,
Nushka cried they altogether,
Nushka, you shall have a sweetheart,
You shall have a handsome husband"

"And when e'er a youth or maiden
Found a crooked ear in husking,
Blighted, mildewed or mis-shapen,
Then they laughed and sang together,
Crept and limped about the corn fields,
Mimiced in their gait and gestures.
Some old man bent almost double,
Singing singly or together:
Wagemin, the thief of corn fields,
Pancosaid, who steals the maize ear!"

These scenes are also borrowed from Schoolcraft who describes them in much the same terms. Wagemin means "crooked," and Pamosaid, "He who walks", both being taken as meaning a thief in the corn field. These words, he said, from the basis of the cereal song, which, however, is not repeated. In the same song is a description of blessing the corn field based on these lines of Schoolcraft. "It was the practice of the hunter's wife, when the field of corn had been planted, to choose the first dark or over-clouded evening to perform a secret circuit *sans habiliments* around the field. For this purpose, she slipped out of the lodge in the evening, unobserved, to some obscure nook where she completely disrobed, then taking her malchecota, or principal garment, in her hands she dragged it around the field. This was thought to insure a prolific crop and to prevent the assaults of insects and worms upon the grain."

Among Pennsylvania Germans, Dr. Hoffman tells us when corn and beans are reserved for the next year's planting, the cob, husks and stalk must be carried out into a field or highway and quickly destroyed. Should they be burned, the next crop would be attacked by the black fungus (Brant).

Contributed by Lieutenant Fletcher S. Bassett, U. S. Navy, Sec'y Chicago Folk Lore Society, author of "Legends and Superstitions of the Sea" "Folk Lore Manual", etc., etc. A former resident of Burlington, Iowa.

THE LIVE STOCK INDUSTRY.

To show the growth and present magnitude of the live stock industry in Iowa we present the following table which we compile from the United

States Census Reports and the report of the secretary of Agriculture, the figures for 1892 being given from the report last named:

Year.	No. Horses	No. Mules.	No. Neat Cattle.	No. Swine.	No. Sheep.	Value.
1850	38,568	754	136,621	323,247	149,960	$ 3,689,275.00
1860	175,088	5,734	540,088	934,820	259,040	22,476,293.00
1870	433,642	25,425	1,006,235	1,353,908	855,493	82,987,133.00
1880	792,322	44,224	2,612,036	6,034,316	455,329	124,715,103.00
1892	1,314,360	41,029	4,011,233	7,105,320	565,031	208,768,191.00

In 1891, according to the report of Hon. J. M. Rusk, Secretary of Agriculture, the total value of the wheat, oats and corn products and the live stock of the six leading states of the Union were as follows:

IOWA.
Grain products..$154,269,430
Live stock..181,967,670

Total...$336,237,100

ILLINOIS.
Grain products..$147,843,414
Live stock..169,151,563

Total...$316,994,977

MISSOURI.
Grain products..$105,800,269
Live stock..121,217,095

Total...$227,017,364

OHIO.
Grain products..$ 89,878,403
Live stock..109,516,961

Total...$199,395,364

KANSAS.
Grain products..$ 98,321,629
Live stock..109,516,961

Total...$207,838,590

INDIANA.
Grain products..$ 99,121,446
Live Stock...103,255,029

Total...$202,376,475

These figures gleaned from the high authority named, establish the fact that these central prairie States are the great food producing States of the country, and in this respect Iowa, though but fourth in area—Illinois, Missouri and Kansas all being larger—leads all in the value of her grain production, and exceeds all in the value of her live stock. With such permanent agricultural productiveness, Iowa must ever be one of the wealthiest States of the Union.

In 1892 Illinois ranked first of the States in the number and value of its horses, and Iowa second. In the number and value of milch cows New York ranked first, and Iowa second. In the number and value of work oxen and other cattle Texas ranked first, and Iowa second. In the number and value of swine Iowa ranked first and Illinois second. In the total value of live stock Iowa stands at the head, leading Illinois, the next in rank, by the grand sum of $22,000,386.

But the superior quality of the live stock of Iowa may be seen by an examination of the values reported by Commissioner Rusk. Kentucky, with her famed blue grass and her generations of fleet horses, leads Iowa in the average value of her horse stock only in the ratio of 69 to 66, while Iowa leads Texas in this matter in the ratio of 66 to 41. Iowa farmers have not given so much attention to breeding fleet animals for sport on the track as they have given to the breeding of animals for service on the road and farm; yet Iowa's pastures, grain and atmosphere have produced Axtel and Allerton to win world-wide fame by their speed qualities, and thousands of massive Percherons, Clydesdales, Belgians, Shires and Cleveland Bays of noble form, fine stylish coach animals and fleet standard-breds are found in every locality. No country nor State need desire finer horses than are seen at our county fairs, or are shown in the great displays at Iowa's famous State fairs.

CATTLE.

In this department of the live stock industry Iowa knows no superior. The best beef and milk breeds are all encouraged by the votaries of these different interests, so that all the improved breeds, as Shorthorns, Herefords, Galloways, Polled Angus, Polled Durhams, Dutch Belted, Swiss, Devons, Holsteins, and the butter producing Alderneys, Guernseys, and Jerseys are all bred in Iowa to perfection. In her pastures thousands of full-bloods thrive and add wealth to their fortunate owners, while herds of fine grades are seen on every farm. The longhorned rangers of the wilderness and the bony, coarse and scrawny "scrubs" no longer waste Iowa grass unless in some chance way such a bovine specimen is imported from some distant State.

SHEEP.

By the table given above it is shown that the sheep husbandry in Iowa declined largely from 1870 to 1880. Formerly, for various reasons, sheep were found to be inconvenient stock. But Iowa farmers are now enclosing and subdividing their farms with good fences, and more attention is given to sheep raising and wool growing and flocks are rapidly increasing in numbers. Animals of the fine and long wooled breeds are being largely imported. Iowa's climate, soil, pure waters and nourishing pastures are finely suited to this industry, and the State in the near future will become as famous for her wool and mutton production as she is now for her corn, butter and pork.

SWINE.

Iowa excels, not only in the number of swine yearly produced and marketed, but also has no superior in the quality of the blood and breeding of her herds. Swine production has been a potent factor in Iowa's development of wealth, and will long remain so. Iowa soil, from the richest spot in the flood plain by the river's brink to the summit of her highest "divides," will grow corn; and corn fed to Poland Chinas, Chester Whites, Berkshires, Durocs and Victorias, is turned into pork of as superb a quality as ever graced the board of Norman or Saxon lord. The markets of the world are own open to pork and lard from this interior west, and the farms of Iowa

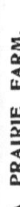

A PRAIRIE FARM.

can furnish supplies in quantities which the world will almost deem incredible.

THE GRASSES.

Grass is a natural product of Iowa prairies. Kentucky's blue grass pastures have world-wide fame, but Iowa farmers now enjoy as rich, abundant, healthful, nourishing and beautiful blue grass pasturage as was ever found in Kentucky or any other State. Everywhere in Iowa blue grass has become a spontaneous product.

Timothy, the clovers, millet and other grasses thrive luxuriantly in Iowa sunshine and soil. In all parts of the State great clover fields are plentiful. Timothy meadows produce surprising crops, and large quantities of grass seeds are annually exported. The power of Iowa soil to produce grass will ever make stock raising a highly remunerative industry in Iowa husbandry.

FLAX.

But little attention was devoted to this crop in the early years. It was ever found to be productive, but the absence of machinery or mills for working up and giving value to the fiber, precluded its being largely remunerative to its producers, yet its production has increased until Iowa has attained second place in the rank of States in the production of flax seed—her product aggregating in 1891, (according to the returns of the Department of Agriculture) 2,898,596 bushels.

Lately, considerable attention has been given to the fiber in Winnebago and other northern counties of the state, and it has been found that the fiber, there produced, is unexcelled in quality for linen fabric. There are inviting openings in Iowa for the manufacture of linen and other flax products.

THE DAIRY INDUSTRY.

Butter and cheese are important items upon the table and also in the markets of the country. The reports of the Department of Agriculture for 1891, show that there are in the United States 16,416,351 milch cows, of the aggregate value of $351,378,132. In the following table we give the number of milch cows, their aggregate and average value in each of the five states leading in this respect:

STATES.	NO. OF MILCH COWS.	AGGREGATE VALUE.	VALUE PER HEAD.
New York	1,552,217	$40,637,041	$26.18
Iowa	1,304,181	24,179,534	18.76
Illinois	1,104,861	23,561,060	21.27
Pennsylvania	929,091	23,459,518	25.25
Missouri	869,726	15,220,205	17.50

The dairy industry, as a distinct business, is comparatively new in Iowa. Having no great cities or manufacturing centers within our area, we had to seek markets for our dairy products abroad. These products were without reputation in the East prior to the Centennial Exhibition of 1876. The awards received there opened markets in the east for Iowa creamery butter.

The plans for an Iowa exhibit in that exposition were made, and the work of providing exhibits therefor was largely done, and the expense therefor met by private organizations before any provision was made for State aid. In February, but three months before the opening of the

Exposition, the Iowa General Assembly passed an act providing for State supervision and the encouragement of an Iowa exhibit, and appropriated $20,000 therefor.

This was our first effort for an exhibition in a "World's Fair." Intelligent, patriotic citizens saw that it was a prime opportunity to promote the interests of Iowa and made earnest effort to improve it.

The managers of that Exposition made no reservation of space in the agricultural department for the dairy interest, and the dairymen of the country found their industry without place for display. The American Dairymen's Association arranged with the managers of the Exposition for the erection of a building at the expense of the dairymen of the country, to provide a place for the exhibition of dairy products. The dairymen of Iowa were assessed by the American Dairymen's Association $1,000 for this purpose.

On the 14th day of April, 1876, John Stewart, of the firm of John Stewart & Co., manufacturers of "fine creamery butter," Manchester, Iowa, addressed a letter to Governor Kirkwood in which he stated the facts outlined above, and urged him to favor the dairy interests and said :

"If we can exhibit our butter side by side with the eastern dairymen, we can succeed in breaking down the prejudice that has been so prevalent in the minds of eastern people ; and if so, we will get one million dollars more, annually, for our dairy products than we do now. If it is not asking too much of you in your official position, we would ask you to urge the executive committee to appropriate this amount or so much of it as is possible out of the $20,000. We do not ask the State to transport our goods, but simply to give us a place to exhibit them."

But the State authorities did not appropriate $1,000 or any other sum out of the $20,000 or any other fund, for a dairy exhibit, but John Stewart & Co., and other creamery men exhibited twenty-nine packages of their butter, having a total weight of 9,150 pounds and won for Iowa butter the following award—gaining a first prize.

"Creamery 859, Stewart & Mellen, Manchester, Iowa, Creamery Butter. Commended for its clear sweet flavor, firm texture and superior excellence."

That award gave Iowa butter an entrance into eastern markets in which it soon won a reputation that has been worth scores of millions of dollars to the State. The dairy business has become of vast importance in Iowa agriculture.

State Dairy Commissioner Tupper, in his report to the Governor, December, 1892, said :

"The total shipments of butter billed out of the State for the year ending September 30, were 71,563,013 pounds. The best authorities estimate the home consumption of butter to be fifty pounds, *per capita*, or 100,000,-000. This would bring the total product of the State up to 171,563,013 pounds. Estimating it at 20 cents per pound, the value of Iowa's product for the year would be $34,312,602."

As the amount shipped out of the State was ascertained by correspondence with the several railroad authorities and getting reports of their actual shipments to points in other States, the report of shipment is practically correct. The Commissioner reports the ninety-nine counties in detail. The amount consumed at home of course is estimated. Iowa people live well and the estimate is reasonable.

The butter production of the State is most largely in its northeastern portions. In Delaware county there are 38 creameries, in Linn 29, in Bremer 24, and Fayette 23. Mr. Tupper reports 729 creameries in ninety-seven counties.

The Dairy Commissioner's report for 1892 is the sixth annual report from that office. The dairy business, furnishing an export of 71,536,013 pounds of butter to go into the great markets of the country, and in addition furnishing 50 pounds, *per capita*, for 1,911,896 people, is an industry of large importance. Only 1.4 cents, per pound, on the amount exported, would raise John Stewart's $1,000,000 to the creamery men of Iowa. This business may appear to have immense proportions, but it may be said of the dairy industry of Iowa, "There yet is room," —the dairy business is still growing.

Dairy Commissioner Tupper reported one hundred and eleven cheese factories in operation in Iowa in 1891, twenty new ones having been established that year. In 1892 he reported one hundred and fourteen cheese factories operated in fifty-one counties. He made no report of the production as he had been unable to collect full statistics.

HORTICULTURE.

The culture of the garden is a higher form of agriculture than that of the common field. It is the tilling of the soil to produce things more delicate, beautiful and valuable than the common grains, grasses or coarser root crops. It includes the culture of garden vegetables, seeds, nursery stock, fruits and flowers. Floriculture, being a higher type of horticultural industry; may be classed as a lighter form of labor, requiring greater intelligence and care than common farm operations. Having no place nor part in a savage state, it is only when some degree of wealth is developed, taste incited, and culture takes the place of barbarous conditions that the interests of horticulture prosper.

Common gardening is the first branch of horticultural industry pursued in the settlement of new countries, the nursery business being the next in order. The latter has now become of great importance. The number of established nurseries in the State was reported, in the census of 1890, as 183, employing 1,193 persons, and occupying 12,049 acres of land devoted to the growth of apple, crab, pear, quince, peach, apricot, plum and cherry trees for orchard planting; various nut bearing trees, evergreens and flowering shrubs. Thirteen and a half acres were devoted to the propagation of the rose; 427 acres to the propagation of the grape, and numerous acres to strawberries, raspberries, blackberries, currants, gooseberries and other fruit bearing plants. The total value of these 183 nurseries was reported at $1,276,379.

Of these 183 nurseries so far as information could be gained, eight were established between 1850 and 1860; thirteen between 1860 and 1870, twenty-six between 1870 and 1880, and sixty-seven between 1880 and 1890. While these figures do not give full data in the matter, they show that this business has rapidly increased in the State as wealth and improvement have developed.

But twenty years ago large quantities of apples were imported into Iowa from States farther east. Then orchardists in Indiana, Ohio and

Michigan imagined that apples could not be successfully grown on Iowa's prairie soil, and that this State would ever afford a great market for the products of their orchards. The fine exhibits of Iowa-grown pears at the Centennial Exposition in 1876, by Messrs. C. B. Brackett, of Lee county and W. T. Smith of Mahaska, with the exhibit of forty varieties of Iowa-grown apples by W. S. Willett of Malcolm, of seventy-five by L. Hollingsworth, of Montrose, and 160 varieties by James Smith of Des Moines, dispelled that idea forever. Iowa won, by those exhibits, high encomiums for the superior size and quality of her fruit. At the New Orleans Exposition, ten years later, her apples again won high honors, and thereby opened the markets of all the great cities alike on the Atlantic, the Gulf and the Pacific coasts for the products of Iowa orchards. Under these inspirations pomological industry in Iowa has been greatly increased, immense orchards have been planted and great attention has been given to their culture, and the exportation of apples from Iowa is becoming a business of large volume. Our apples find profitable markets in both our own and foreign countries.

In the fall of 1891, the shipments of apples from Iowa reached large figures. The "Red Oak Sun" gathered the amounts shipped from a few counties in the southwestern part of the State. We copy its reported shipments from the five counties named below:

COUNTIES.	BBLS. SHIPPED.
Freemont	43,144
Mills	41,309
Page	26,115
Montgomery	17,384
Adams	14,574
Total	142,526

Peaches, plums, apricots, quinces, cherries, and pears are successfully grown. Many varieties of these fruits specially adapted to our climate and soil have been produced. The production of grapes is becoming immense. It is now known by all that Iowa produces fruits of finest size and appearance, abundant in variety and unexcelled in quality and flavor, in quantities not only to supply her own population, but also to meet the large demands that come from other States. Fifteen carloads of Iowa grapes were shipped from Council Bluffs in one month the past season. The small fruits, as raspberries, blackberries, gooseberries, currants and strawberries all grow in this State to superlative perfection in size, appearance and flavor. The tables of Iowa farmers throughout the season abound with those luxuries grown in their own gardens.

VEGETABLES.

Iowa's soil, climate and rainfall all combine to promote the growth of vegetation. Its depth and mellowness make gardening a pleasure. In no country is the labor of the gardener more abundantly repaid. Every kind of vegetable grown in the country east of the Rocky Mountains and north of Mason and Dixon's line is cultivated with success in the gardens of Iowa.

FLORICULTURE.

Iowa is a land of flowers. The Violet, the Crimson Phlox, the Lily, the Helianthus, the Rose, the Aster and the Golden Rod in many varieties are native to the prairies; and, in grand profusion in their season, waved their magnificent welcome to the pioneer who delighted in beautiful surroundings. Iowa homes, from the occupancy of the first cabin, have ever been adorned with Flora's magnificent handi-work. The early settler brought in the cultivated annuals and perennials common to the home surroundings in the States from which they came; and no country produces flowers of richer hue or grander magnificence in form and fragrance than are grown about the homes of Iowa.

COMMERCIAL FLORICULTURE.

The enumerators of the census of 1890 report for the whole country 4,659 floral establishments. Idaho, Nevada, Indian Territory and Oklahoma were the only portions of the country in which such establishments were not found. Three hundred and twelve were owned and conducted by women. These four thousand and more establishments, including fixtures and heating apparatus were of the value of $38,823,547, and gave employment to 16,847 men and 1,958 women.

Such an industry is an important one. Its most favorable field of operation is in the vicinity of the great cities, the centers of wealth and luxurious living. Iowa has a respected place in this esthetic industry. The number of florists establishments, reported for Iowa in that census, was sixty-nine. Of forty-four reporting the date of their establishment, twenty-four were started between 1880 and 1890. In this business that census reported for Iowa the employment of 166 men and 49 women, and $66,234 paid the male employees in wages and $13,818 were paid female employees. It further reported the propagation of 255,330 roses, 1,109,037 hardy plants and of 1,838,850 other plants. The value of the plants sold was $125,164.55; of cut flowers sold, $107,638.29; the total for sales reaching the sum of $232,808.34. There is not only pleasure but profit in the florist's occupation.

With the increase of wealth floriculture is encouraged as taste is gratified, and the love of the beautiful ever strengthens with the development of the finer elements of our nature. In this State this business receives great encouragment, not only in our large and prosperous growing cities, but in the scores of beautiful, thrifty and progressive towns which offer inviting openings to persons of taste and enterprise, who desire to engage in this pleasant industry. The people of Iowa, lovers of the beautiful in nature as well as in morals and social culture, have taste for floral decorations and are liberal patrons of floral production.

SEED FARMS.

This branch of horticultural industry has been rapidly enlarged in the State during the last decade.

In the census of 1890 attention was given for the first time to gathering the statistics of this industry. The enumerators found that there were then in the country 596 farms with a total of 169,851 acres of land devoted exclusively to seed growing. This was an average of 284 acres to the farm. The total value of farms, implements and buildings reported was $18,325,935.86. Those farms employed in that census year 13,590 men and 1,541 women.

Of these 596 seed farms, eighteen were located in Iowa. Such farms are found in thirty-six of the forty-four States, and one of 120 acres in the District of Columbia. The eighteen seed farms in this State embrace 11,152 acres of land valued at $27.75 per acre. The total value of farms, implements and buildings being $633,823.67. The average acreage of such farms in Iowa is 620 acres. Of course considerable portions of these farms are devoted to meadow and pasturage. Ten of these were established in the last decade. Those eighteen farms gave employment to 354 men.

Of the seeds cultivated on Iowa seed farms we notice the following varieties named in the census report: Asparagus, beans, beets, cabbage, carrot, corn (sweet), corn (field), cucumber (to which 472 acres of Iowa farms were devoted), egg plant, lettuce, melon (musk), melon (water), okra, onion (seed), onion (sets), parsnip, pease, potatoes, pumpkin, radish, rhubarb, salsify, spinach, squash, tomato turnip, and flower seeds, fourteen acres of land being devoted to the latter production. One man in Poweshiek county raised last year forty acres of sunflowers for their seed.

Prior to 1850 this industry was confined almost exclusively to the New England States.

The extensive and very rapid settlement of the northwest since 1870 created an immense demand for garden seeds, and led to the establishment of this industry on quite a large scale in the central western States.

SORGHUM.

This saccharine plant is cultivated successfully in Iowa. Our light, deep prairie soil and moist, warm summer months are favorable to its development. In the table given elsewhere, from the report of the Secretary of the State Agricultural Society, the value of the sorghum product for 1892 was estimated at $1,000,000, the product being over 2,000,000 gallons of syrup. This plant is grown in all parts of the State and is an important adjunct to family supplies. But little effort has been made to grow this cane as a source from which to manufacture sugar, but its cultivation and the manufacture of syrup therefrom reduces sugar consumption in many households. Years of experience in its cultivation has proved that a cane very rich in saccharine matter can be grown almost as cheaply as corn.

BEETS.

Experiments have proven that beets, very rich in saccharine substance, can be easily grown, and no soil produces a more vigorous growth of the beet. No plant has yet been erected for the manufacture of sugar in this State. With large coal fields, cheap fuel, cheap lands and suitable soil for beet culture; with our rapidly increasing population that each year furnishes a larger supply of labor for the better cultivation of our fields and the raising of crops that involve large labor, Iowa offers inviting opportunities for the profitable employment of capital in the beet sugar industry.

STATE ENCOURAGEMENT.

State Legislation has extended wise encouragement to agricultural and horticultural interests.

THE STATE AGRICULTURAL SOCIETY.

This is an efficient, well officered and ably managed State organization. It owns very fine, extensive and conveniently located grounds lying immediately east of the city of Des Moines, and of easy access by railroad and

STATE AGRICULTURAL COLLEGE, AMES, IOWA

electric car lines from the capital city. These grounds are now well improved and a State fair is held annually thereon. The Iowa State Fair is becoming widely known as one of the most successful Agricultural Fairs of the country. The grounds embrace several hundred acres, afford fine camping grounds, fine shade and are well supplied with pure water. No intoxicating drinks are sold on the grounds and all gambling schemes are excluded from them, and yet most interesting and successful fairs are annually held.

COUNTY AND DISTRICT FAIRS.

These are provided for by law, and are encouraged by annual financial aid. There are now few counties in the State without a duly organized County Agricultural Society and its annual County Fair. Where no County Organization exists, there are District Fairs. These cover parts of two or more counties. Our County and District Fairs are excellent educators of our people in agricultural interests, presenting the newest features in agricultural progress and affording pleasant opportunities for enlarging acquaintance and mutual interchange of ideas, and the enlargement of agricultural knowledge.

THE STATE HORTICULTURAL SOCIETY.

This is an important and highly serviceable organization to the people of the State. It is financially aided by the State and holds an annual meeting at the State Capital in which it has rooms. At its meetings horticultural matters are discussed, the leading horticulturalists of the State interchange thought and compare experiences. Its proceedings are published and freely circulated and so most useful horticultural information is thereby freely disseminated.

In addition to the parent State society there are several auxilliary district and county societies which hold frequent meetings, and render valuable service in the spread of horticultural knowledge.

LIVE STOCK BREEDERS ASSOCIATIONS.

We have various organizations in the interest of breeders and farmers interested in the improvement of the live stock and poultry of the State. Almost each particular breed of live stock having an organization of its friends working earnestly to set forth its merits. They are doing successful work in improving the several varieties of domestic animals kept on farms.

POULTRY.

The poultry interests of Iowa are worthy of consideration. Hon. J. R. Schaffer, Secretary of the State Agricultural Society in a late report estimated the poultry products of the State to have an annual value of $5,000,000. The flocks of "biddies," geese, ducks, turkeys, guineas, and pea fowls that grace our farm yards and furnish dainty luxuries for our daily meals and holiday feasts, add millions yearly to the profits of Iowa farms and by their valuable production the managing, industrious housewife multiplies the family comforts.

The traveler everywhere in the agricultural portions of Iowa sees numerous flocks of the finest fowls, all the improved breeds being found in every locality. Hundreds of men using large capital are engaged in the poultry and egg business. Could we gather the true figures representing the extent of this business they would present a startling sum. This business is a growing one because the production of poultry is found to be profitable on the farms of Iowa. The shipment of live fowls is becoming a large business and the exhibit of patent cars in the Transportation Building at the Columbian Exposition for their transportation shows that the inventors as well as the transportation companies of the country are awake to the fact that this to some seemingly trifling "chicken business" is one of such magnitude as to be worth caring for.

NATIVE FLORA OF IOWA.

By Prof. L. H. Pammel, Iowa Agricultural College.

The climate and physical features of the State have not favored a very large number of flowering plants compared with some of the States within our borders, and yet we have a good many species. We have few mountain forms as the conditions favoring the perpetuation of these species are absent. A few are maintained along our streams, especially in the eastern and northeastern parts of the State. The Red Berried Elder, with its bright red fruit, is a conspicuous object along the Mississippi above Dubuque. Here too may be found the Mountain Maple overhanging the rocks; an occasional Paper Birch stands in strong contrast to the southern Kentucky Coffee tree. An occasional Sycamore or Honey Locust in the bottoms indicate that we have here a commingling of northern and southern forms. Our Oaks in central, eastern and western Iowa are those common to the north. The White Oak and the tall, majestic Red Oak, large and handsome but less valuable than the White Oak are common. The swamp White Oak, a southern species, may be found in the southern part of the State. Another common Oak in this State is the Burr Oak with its sweet acorns, also a valuable tree for its wood. Common throughout Iowa is the Soft Maple, the Cottonwood, and the American Basswood. The Elms are familiar objects; the most graceful of the family is the American or White Elm. The Slippery or Red Elm is common and is a valuable tree.

NUT BEARING TREES.

In this class the widely known Black Walnut is the most valuable; then there is the White Walnut or Butternut, a species growing on high grounds. The Black Walnut prefers lower grounds, and is a southern tree which gradually diminishes northward; the Butternut being a northern tree. The most valuable of the Hickory family is the Shag or Shell Bark. It is so by reason of its wide distribution as well as for the superior value of its wood. The Mocker-nut Hickory occurs in the southern part of the State bordering on Missouri. The Pecan is also a southern species extending northwardly along the Mississippi and Missouri rivers. The Butternut is quite common in many parts of the State.

CONIFEROUS TREES.

There are some coniferous trees found in Iowa, the White Pine and the more widely distributed Red Cedar.

THE ASH.

There are several species of the Ash in this State. The White Ash, on account of its beauty strength and value should not be overlooked. It is a valuable tree for cultivation, being easily propagated and a rapid grower. It grows naturally along our streams and as an ornamental tree along fence rows, roads or lawns and in parks is worthy of attention. Its wood, especially the young growth, is of great value in many lines of manufacture.

SHRUBS.

Of smaller trees and shrubs which lend beauty to our landscapes, there are many. Conspicuous among them is the Wild Crab. Its shape is symmetrical and when in flower the sweet perfume fills the air. Nothing excels it in beauty when in flower. The Wild Plum is found in all parts of the State. When in bloom the plum groves are masses of creamy beauty and the fruit is of great value, but was especially valuable to the early settlers. Many of our most valuable cultivated plums have been developed from a wild parentage. The Flat Topped Thorn, with its masses of flowers is especially striking in June. The Red Bud is limited in its distribution, yet its purple flowers coming out before the leaves, makes it an interesting object. It is found as far north as Muscatine. In the month of May, before the forests are clothed with their green leaves, a white flowering shrub dots the forests here and there; it is the Shad Bush, or Service Berry. It bears an inviting fruit. We should also mention the primitive form of the Snow Ball, commonly called High Bush Cranberry, which occurs in wet grounds in the northern part of the State. In this connection we may also speak of the Red Root, a common low shrub on the prairies, well known to prairie breakers for its hard, strong root. Its red stems, rich green leaves and cream colored tufts of flowers in June and July make it conspicuous.

HERBACEOUS PLANTS.

Of these we have many striking forms. Our flora on the prairies partakes largely of the western type. We have also many species that are common in the eastern states. Some of these are introduced and some are woodland species that have been kept in close contact with our forest trees. In early spring soon after the snow disappears, in shaded banks, the little (Hepatica L.) Liverwort makes its appearance, soon followed by the Spring Beauty, the Blue Violet, the Dutchman's Breeches with delicate white flowers, and the Dog Toothed Violet. These are early flowering woodland species and common further east. In the open prairies we find the Pasqueflower, its flowers are pale blue, coming out long before the fields are green. There are also several species of Crowsfoot. Several varieties of the Phlox family give beauty to our prairies by their brilliant colors. The common American Columbine should be remembered, a beautiful flower in different colors, easily transplanted and worthy of cultivation for the long season of its bloom and beauty. There is nothing common about it either in its color or form. Of the same family, but growing on the prairies the Azure Larkspur should be mentioned. In the southern part of the state another species occurs, a woodland species, but like the former its flowers show a tendency to vary in color.

In June, July and August the prairies are bright with various flowers of the Composite Family. Some of the species are coarse, yet many are very showy. There is the Cone-flower. The tall Compass-plant, Pilot Weed or Prairie Burdock, a resinous plant, and its near relative the Cup-plant. These bear showy yellow flowers. In July we have the purple Cone-flower or Comb-flower, the upright Lily and, later, two varieties of Lilies with pendant flowers. But few cultivated flowers are more beautiful than the Lilies of our prairies.

There are several pretty members of the Orchis family, the fringed Orchis, with its long spur containing nectar and fringes to its petals is an interesting plant. Several species of Ladies Tresses occur. I have not mentioned the Moccasin-flower, two species of which are not uncommon in Iowa. The Large White Moccasin-flower also occurs. The Larger Yellow Moccasin-flower, or Ladies' Slipper, is an early flowering species in our moist woods.

September is the month for Asters, Golden Rod, Sunflowers, Wild Artichoke, Boneset, and members of that family. The Lobelia (Greater Blue) and the Cardinal-flower, growing in moist places, the latter especially growing near streams where the alluvial deposits occur, some river bottoms being fairly red with them in their season. The writer remembers the first impression made on his mind when he first saw this species in flower. The Missouri river valley has some most striking plants. The Yuccas, so distinctively American, are represented by the Yucca angustifolia, to be appreciated this plant should be studied as it is a most remarkable plant as regards its pollination. The Wild Licorice is distinctively western. The Mint family is also represented on our prairies by a few western species.

The grasses are numerous. Blue Grass (*Poa pratensis*) has become naturalized everywhere in Iowa. The Wild Ryes are common. But more than any other grass the Blue Joint was found everywhere in Iowa on its rich dry prairie lands. The Beard Grass is also a native variety. These are typical prairie species and in the autumn add to the beauty of our extended prairie landscapes.

The Ferns are rare except in certain sheltered and isolated places. Muscatine county has, perhaps, more species than any other county. The Brake, Maidenhair Fern, Sensitive Fern, and one Spleenwort are widely distributed. The rocky hills of the east support several interesting species. The Walking Leaf Fern and other varieties are interesting plants.

The chief feature of our native flora is its diversity. It lacks species of trees which may truly be called grand, but our trees may be characterized as vigorous and sturdy.

I would call attention to several catalogues of the Flora of the State. One of the earliest accounts of plants in this State was by the late Dr. C. C. Parry, in David Dale Owens' Geological Survey. Prof. C. E. Bessey published an account in one of the early Bi-ennial Reports of the Iowa Agricultural College. Dr. J. C. Arthur published a list of Iowa plants for the Centennial Exposition which was nearly complete. Later Prof. A. S. Hitchcock published a catalogue of the Anthophyta and Pteridophyta of Ames. The writer also published a short list in Proceedings of Iowa Academy of Sciences for 1892.

FORESTS AND ARTIFICIAL GROVES.

Iowa is rightly classed as a prairie State. It has never had forest nor timber resources to give it fame as a lumbering State, yet its surface at the time of its discovery and settlement was flecked with groves of timber that were serviceable to its early settlers. In all parts of the State there were found groves that yielded supplies for fuel, building and fencing purposes in advance of railroad construction. In many localities there are yet extensive and valuable bodies of native timber.

In the valleys and along the acclivities bordering the Mississippi, Des Moines, Cedar, Iowa, and other rivers and many of the smaller streams in the eastern portions of the State, there were many considerable bodies of timber, some of which yet furnish large supplies for manufacturing purposes.

Along the Cedar, before the settlement of the country bordering it, there were valuable groves of Red Cedar. These attracted the forest pirate and ere immigration came, these groves were mostly cut off and rafted to St. Louis.

No county in Iowa was entirely destitute of timber. Many counties had comparatively small supplies, yet there were native groves which were central places in the early settlement, and gave names to places and postoffices which are still retained. Some were important land marks to the traveler before the roads were distinctly marked. The changes resulting from settlement and the construction of railroads have rendered the names of many of these once widely known groves obsolete.

There were many valuable varieties of timber native to those groves; the black and white walnut, the white oak, burr oak, red oak, the maples, the white ash, the hickories, the elms, the honey locust, and many others. The hard maple in some localities was found in quantities to be of service to the pioneers in sugar production.

With the stoppage of the annual destructive prairie fires the acreage of young timber has been greatly enlarged. But the people are not dependent upon their native groves for supplies of lumber. Railroads now transport fencing and building lumber from the timbered states at reasonable rates, and a few acres of prairie cultivated in corn settles the fuel and lumber matter. It is easy to buy the lumber and coal needed for the farm and family with the money the corn brings. Timber lands are now of less value than corn growing lands.

ARTIFICIAL GROVES.

The settlers on the prairies soon planted groves. Some on a liberal scale, which soon became, not only objects of convenience and beauty, but of usefulness and value for the shelter they afforded. In half a dozen years from such planting, with careful cultivation, the settler had a beautiful grove. For a few years the soft maple would make more rapid growth than the black walnut. After ten years the walnut would be the faster grower and make the stronger and more valuable timber tree. Many groves were planted of the white ash, the honey locust, and oak. Young elms could be had in almost every fringe of native timber. The law gave exemption from a certain amount of taxation for planting groves and orchards, and thus timber and fruit growing were encouraged. Pines, Cedars, Firs and Spruces have been numerously planted for wind breaks and ornamentation; and the broad prairies have been relieved of their wild magnificence by intelligent industry, and have been made more beautiful by these serviceable ornamentations—the handi-work of industrious settlers.

IOWA AND MANUFACTURES.

People living in different portions of the country, generally regard Iowa as exclusively an agricultural State. Very few even of those who are resident here have just conceptions of the extent and value of our mineral resources or our possibilities for success in manufacturing industries. All know that in this famous wealth producing region we have unequalled advantages of soil and climate for great success in the industries common to the orchard, the garden and the field. It is equally true that we have here most inviting openings for the establishment of great and profitable manufacturing enterprises. Two millions of intelligent people possessing the wealth producing power for which this State has now wide fame will ever assure an immense and constant market for the vast supplies of manufactured commodities demanded in their industrial and social life.

This portion of the country having unequalled possibilities to produce foods, the laborer will ever find here, at reasonable prices, the essential articles of human subsistence; the best social and moral surroundings, and clothing as cheap as it is obtainable in other markets. These desirable circumstances combined with our healthful climate, and excellent educational opportunities will invite the most intelligent and desirable class of citizens. Our ever-flowing rivers furnish valuable water powers that may be cheaply harnessed to drive manufacturing machinery. As we have shown elsewhere almost one-third of our ninety-nine counties produce coal, and excellent fuel to produce steam is cheaply obtained. The facts we present are worthy of consideration by all who are seeking opportunities for the investment of capital in manufacturing enterprises.

Supplies of raw material for important manufactures are readily obtainable. In convenient and readily accessible localities there are large deposits of metallic ores; as lead, zinc, and iron. Alluminous clays, rich in that valuable and now largely used metal, exist in many places. Clays of quality suited for the manufacture of the best qualities of stoneware and finer qualities of pottery are found in heavy deposits in the State, while clays for the manufacture of building, and the best qualities of paving brick, articles now in very large demand in Iowa towns and cities are common. Timber is found, in valuable varieties and abundant quantity in the eastern and southeastern counties, of large value in many lines of manufacture. Straw and flax fibre suitable for the manufacture of paper and other commodities is grown abundantly. The vegetable productions and summer fruits suitable for canning are easily produced. For starch and glucose manufacture, the raw material is produced throughout the State in larger quantities than in any other equal area on earth. For the packing house industry most finely fed cattle and swine everywhere await the buyer. The vast improvements being constantly made in the building of new bridges, large, fine, and solid buildings, the construction of waterworks, electric light plants, and other improvements in our growing towns and cities, create a large and constantly growing demand for the products of the foundry and machine shop. The common use of all lines of labor-saving machines, alike in the homes and shops, and on the farms throughout the State makes Iowa a most inviting field for the manufacture of such machines. The use of buggies and fine carriages will ever be large in this center of wealth and pleasure. Our citizens enjoy the good things possible in earthly state and live in a style of luxury not excelled in the life of any agricultural population anywhere. They enjoy the best of literature in their homes, and fine furniture in their parlors; they cultivate music in their families and are esthetic in their tastes. Such a people dwelling in such surroundings and possessing such ample means of enjoyment, will ever offer a vast home market for the products of the factory, and Iowa must ever be an inviting field for the operation of manufacturing capabilities and the employment of capital therein.

The pioneer settlers came not here to mine gold, to gain wealth by lumbering pursuits or to make their living by quest of game with the gun, or fish with rod or net. They came here for higher purpose; namely, to build homes, to turn our then barbarous wilds into a fruitful country and to found a Christian common-wealth that would secure to its every citizen equal privilege to work out the best and happiest conditions possible in their surroundings. Their first concern was to provide shelter, their second to provide for the cultivation of the soil. The first manufacturing plants for which they had concern were grist and saw mills. The streams flowing in their surroundings furnished them ample power to run the simple machinery their needs then required.

The national census of 1840 found in the Iowa territory only 1,629 persons engaged in what was then reported as manufacturing industries. When the census of 1850 was taken the count showed that the number of persons engaged in such industries had increased during the decade to but 1,707. Only 522 establishments were in the latter census reported as being engaged in manufacturing and mining pursuits, employing the nominal capital of $1,292,875. One woolen mill was then found in operation in the then new State. Three small iron foundries were reported that employed the trivial force of seventeen men. Four distilleries were then operated that employed sixteen hands, consumed 51,150 bushels of corn, and 7,200 bushels of rye, producing 67,600 gallons of high-wines and whisky. Such were the chief manufacturing industries found in Iowa forty-three years ago.

The census of 1860 showed that increased attention was being given to manufacturing interests in the State. It reported 1,939 establishments, employing a capital of $7,247,130 and 6,307 men, their products being valued at $13,971,325.

The census of 1870 revealed a very great increase in these important industrial interests, reporting 6,566 establishments in the State, in which 899 steam engines, and 726 water wheels were employed to furnish power. Those establishments employed 25,032 persons to whom were paid $6,892,292 in wages. The value of their products aggregated $46,534,322. Our manufacturing interests were then becoming of consequence in our industrial system.

DUBUQUE AND THE HIGH BRIDGE FROM THE ILLINOIS SHORE.

These interests made still further material increase in the decade extending from 1870 to 1880. That advance would have been still greater but for the severe financial depression that existed throughout the country during a considerable part of the period. The census of 1880 enumerated 6,921 establishments, employing a capital of $33,987,886 and 28,364 persons. The wages paid during the year 1879 aggregated $9,725,962, the value of products aggregating $71,045,926. That enumeration reported 1,516 water wheels and 1,668 steam engines employed to furnish motive power.

The manufactures reported for the latter period named, embraced agricultural implements, bakery products, brick and tile, bridges, carriages, wagons, butter and cheese, clothing, cooperage, flouring and grist mill products, foundry and machine shop products. (These being of the reported value of $1,594,349,) furniture, liquors, (distilled,) liquors, (malt,) lumber, marble and stone work, linseed oil, printing and publishing, saddlery and harness, sash, doors, and blinds, slaughtering and meat products, soap, candles, tinware. copperware, sheet-iron ware, tobacco, cigars, woolen goods, and miscellaneous productions.

We have been unable to obtain the census enumeration of Iowa manufactures for 1890, the figures not yet being in form to be given to the public.

The woolen industry may however be excepted from this statement as the returns for it have been made. The number of woolen mills in the State were reduced in the period, but production was increased. The number of establishments reported were twenty-four, sets of cards twenty-six, spindles 10,828, looms 158, knitting machines 19, capital employed in woolen manufacture, $901,900, value of lands and buildings, $500,150, number of hands employed, 387, amount paid in wages, $135,790, value of production, $700,981. There is room in Iowa for a large increase in this important industry.

We have before us partial returns of the manufacturing interests in several cities of the State as made by the census of 1890. These, while far from complete, are sufficiently so to show a large increase in the manufacturing industries in those cities during the decade. Agents of the census authorities have recently been in the State collecting more complete returns of those interests.

From census bulletins numbered 224, 274, 315 and 317 we gather these facts regarding manufacturers in the cities of Des Moines, Davenport, Sioux City and Burlington, the enumeration published covering only the industries in which three or more establishments were engaged. These four cities in 1890 reported 1,176 of such establishments, employing $19,-359,547 of capital and 14,910 hands to whom were paid as wages $7,057,831. The value of their products reached the sum of 36,111,831, being about one-half of the reported value of the products of the manufacturing industries of the entire State in the preceding census. These facts although meager are sufficient to show an important increase of our manufacturing industries during the last census period. In the three subsequent years the increase has been proportionately much greater. The following lines of manufacture were reported in the cities named. Brick and tile, carriages and wagons, confectionery, druggists preparations not including prescriptions, flouring and gristmill products, marble and stone work, foundry and machine shop products, iron work (architectural and ornamental work), planing mill products, printing and publishing, saddlery and harness, lumber, clothing, cooperage, malt liquors, slaughtering meat and packing, tobacco, cigars and cigarettes; of lumber the production was large in Clinton and other river cities.

The report of the Secretary of Agriculture shows that the beet sugar belt is located in the very heart of this State. All the requisites for growing the beets and manufacturing the sugar are here. The climate, the rainfall, the sunshine, the soil exactly suited to the cultivation of the sugar beet, are Iowa's proposed contribution to the people's sugar bowl, it only requires a little more education to give to capital the necessary confidence to establish factories and make it desirable for our farmers to engage in growing the beets.

In the manufacture of cotton this State offers inviting openings.

The rapid denudation of the forests of the country creates an extensive demand for metallic material for fencing purposes. Barbed wire is found to be the most efficient and enduring material for farm fences. With iron and steel easily procured, and with the advantages we have shown Iowa to possess, there is reason to believe that in the near future the manufacture of iron fencing material will become a great industry in the State.

Start at the Mississippi river and extend the line of the southern boundary of Missouri to the Pacific Ocean, and all the territory north of

AN OLD TIME IOWA BUSINESS BLOCK.

that line and west of the Mississippi river belonging to the United States may be made contributory to a large extent to the prosperity of Iowa manufacturers. A grand empire is there traversed by railroads and inhabited by thrifty, prosperous people, numbering millions, who are consumers of articles that can be manufactured in Iowa in competition with the manufacturing communities of the east.

The territory thus bounded contains 53,376 miles of railroad, one-third of the railroad system of the country. It has an area of 1,429,185 square miles, or nearly one-third of the territory of the Union. It numbers in its population 12,000,000 persons, nearly one-fifth of the population of the country. The growth of this great country for the next quarter of a century will be very largely confined to the area we have described. With public attention properly called to our advantages as a manufacturing State, capital will do the rest. Iowa manufacturers will in the near future enter this vast territory and find profitable market therein for the goods it is peculiarly within their province to provide.

No State in the Union offers more complete transportation facilities than does ours. The two great rivers on its borders offer conveniences for moving heavy or bulky commodities over extended regions of the country at the cheapest possible rates. Steam navigation is still and will doubtless be for ages successfully prosecuted along their channels with great advantage to the river cities and communities. But Iowa is netted with railroads, great arteries of commerce, along which moves its throbbing currents, giving life and vital force to business and animating industry at every point reached by them. There is now scarcely a spot of Iowa soil but what the man who stirs it hears the inspiring sound of the locomotive's rumble as it hurries the commodities he needs almost to his door. These everywhere present transportation facilities in our State, secure incalculable advantages for the employment of capital in manufacturing enterprises within its bounds. With the superior advantages it possesses, Iowa must inevitably in the near future become as noted for its manufacturing production as it is now for its agricultural superiority.

We are indebted to Hon. E. H. Thayer, of Clinton, for very valuable aid in the preparation of this chapter.

THE IOWA FISH COMMISSION AND ITS WORK.

By T. J. Griggs, Fish Commissioner of Iowa.

In the early days of Fish Commissions the chief efforts of those engaged in the work were directed toward the propagation and distribution of the brook trout, and the work was mainly in the interest of the angler. As the years wore on, the attention of the people generally was drawn to the subject by the gradual depletion of the public waters, and the necessity became apparent of taking active measures toward stocking the streams, and protecting their product. As the outgrowth of such public sentiment, nearly all the States established Fish Commissions, and through their legislatures enacted a code of laws for the protection of fish.

The waters of many of the western States were not adapted to the culture of brook trout, and some method of re-stocking the streams with fish indigenous to them was a necessity. Mr. Shaw, of Cedar Rapids, Iowa, conceived the idea of utilizing the fish that annually went to waste along the rivers, taking them from the ponds and sloughs where they were left by the spring overflow, and transporting them to inland streams and lakes. This plan was taken up by the Illinois Commission and carried into practical effect. Their work in this direction attracting the attention of the United States Fish Commission, they adopted the method, and inaugurated a system of work in the benefits of which all the western States were to share. Iowa, as well as other States, has been thus cared for, and during the last year I have induced them to distribute in our State about ten car loads of indigenous fish, which have been distributed as equally as possible throughout the State.

Iowa has great natural resources as a fish producing State. Filled as it is with beautiful lakes and streams, it presents a magnificent opportunity for becoming the first in the list of States engaged in this work. Aside from the food so produced, there is the advantage to be gained in adding to the attractions of our magnificent lakes and streams, so popular as summer resorts, by furnishing a plentiful supply of fish for the pleasure-seeking angler.

Some of these lakes are well worthy of special mention. Spirit Lake and its connections have a shore line of fifty miles. Clear Lake twenty miles; Wall Lake twelve miles; and Twin Lakes fifteen miles.

All of these lakes are especially adapted to native fish, and all have been carefully stocked the present season.

The work of the Commission has not been alone the stocking of the waters, but the enforcement of the laws for the protection of the fish, as well. This latter work has been, for the greater part, of a thankless nature, not only attended by personal risks but incurring, for those engaged in it, the enmity of the fisherman and citizen alike whenever the operation of the laws interfered with what they had come to consider their vested rights. It has been an uphill fight to try to bring public sentiment into line with the laws, but we feel that something at least has been accomplished.

Our output last season was as follows:
400,000 black bass fry; 300,000 crappie fry; 50,000 wall-eyed pike fry; 100,000 lake trout fry.

These have been distributed throughout the State as generally and equably as our limited appropriation would permit, and are exclusive of those mentioned before as distributed by the United States Fish Commission cars.

Our property consists of nearly four acres of land situated on the isthmus dividing the waters of Spirit Lake and Lake Okoboji, in Dickinson county, near the tracks of the Burlington, Cedar Rapids & Northern Railroad. The grounds of the plant are surrounded by a wide fence, and the improvements thereon consist of a barn and a frame building 20x40 feet, with a stone foundation, having a cemented floor. The apparatus consists of hatching troughs and screens sufficient to handle a half million trout eggs, and jars sufficient to handle from five to six million pike eggs, with all other necessary appliances, such as tools, nets, etc., to carry on the work.

There are six winter ponds, properly walled, for storage purposes. The ponds are properly connected with a supply pipe extending out into Spirit Lake about 200 feet.

Iowa should, from its natural advantages, become the home of thousands of pleasure seekers every season, and there could be no more effective means of securing this end than to make our waters teem with fish. Angling is the favorite sport of a large majority of those who seek an outing during the warm months. We have the water, beautifully located and fairly stocked, and its product should be carefully protected by a rigid enforcement of the law, and the supply frequently renewed. As our State fills up these same waters will furnish a supply of food at small cost.

EDUCATION IN IOWA.

EARLY HISTORY.

The time when Iowa was an almost uninhabited region is within the vivid memory of those surviving citizens who were among the earliest settlers. No longer ago than half a century the larger part of its area, so richly stored with Nature's gifts, was still untenanted by the white man. Over broad stretches of fertile prairie the bright flowers of each returning spring and summer blossomed unheeded. The dancing leaves of her woodlands and the rippling waters of hundreds of streamlets awaited patiently the coming of the industrious pioneer, ambitious to establish anew under more favorable opportunities, the advantages of a superior civilization.

The first school in what is now Iowa was held in the three closing months of 1830, at Nashville, Lee county, Berryman Jennings, teacher. On the present site of Keokuk, I. K. Robinson taught a school commencing in December, 1830. These two teachers and many of their scholars are living at this time. Geo. Cubbage taught a school in a log church in Dubuque, in the winter of 1833-4. The first woman to teach in Iowa was Mrs. Rebecca Palmer, at Fort Madison, in 1834. A school for young ladies was opened in Dubuque in 1837, by Louisa King, and conducted for several years. In 1839, Alonzo P. Phelps established in the same city a classical school for both sexes, afterwards continued by Thos. H. Benton, Jr.

The first building to be used chiefly as a public school-house, was erected at Burlington in 1833, of roughly hewed logs, while to Dubuque must be accorded the credit of erecting the first school-house by taxation under the law of January 1, 1839, which granted the voters of any school district the power to levy a tax, select a place, and build a school-house. This was in 1844.

The constitution under which Iowa entered the Union in 1836 declared: "The General Assembly shall encourage by all suitable means the promotion of intellectual, scientific, moral and agricultural improvement." This constitution also required that every school district support a school for at least three months in each year. The right and duty of the State to maintain a general system of popular education, and generously to support the same by a uniform levy of taxes, became thus clearly recognized and permanently established as the policy of the new State.

The school law of 1849 authorized the electors of any district to determine whether a school of higher grade should be maintained. Several of the more populous districts availed themselves of this favorable enactment, and very early began to classify and grade their schools.

During the fifties the increase in population was very rapid and there was a corresponding development of school facilities. Rural communities and hamlets multiplied as if by magic, towns and villages in many cases put on the air of cities, larger school-houses were demanded and supplied, and the need of graded and high schools became more keenly felt. A few cities made provision before 1860 for a complete system or organization and the selection of a city superintendent, notably Dubuque, Davenport, and Tipton.

The statistics collected in Iowa in 1857 gave Iowa 3,265 school districts 2,708 schools, 2,996 teachers, and 195,285 children and youth between five and twenty-one.

Up to this time the money raised by general taxation had been insufficient to maintain the schools for as long a period in each year as the people desired, and the term of school had been supplemented by subscription, usually assessed upon the scholars attending. An enlightened public sentiment was demanding that the schools be wholly free, and supported by general taxation.

THE LAW OF 1858.

This comprehensive enactment, the first adopted by the General Assembly and afterwards with slight amendments, by the board of education, made a radical change for the better in our school system. Small districts were replaced by the civil township as the unit of organization, and adequate provision was made for sustaining the schools for at least six months in each year, and as much longer as the board of any district might desire, by public funds alone. The office of County Superintendent was created, and provision made for the thorough examination of teachers, the supervision of the schools, and the easier establishment and more generous support of graded and high schools. The management of the permanent school fund was removed from the school authorities. By the new law, the County Teachers' Institute was made a part of the school system. In many other ways the former laws were greatly simplified and improved upon. In its essential features the present school law differs but slightly from the Statute popularly known as The Law of 1858.

THE SYSTEM DESCRIBED.—ORGANIZATION.

There are two districts provided for in the law, district townships and independent districts. The district township usually agrees in boundaries with the civil township. Of independent districts there are two leading varieties, the village, town, or city district, and the rural independent district, the latter in size resembling the division in district townships known as the sub-district. All directors are chosen for a term of three years. Women are eligible to any school office. Boards determine the amount to be raised by tax for teachers' and contingent funds, fix the additional months of school over the legal requirement of six, establish graded schools and adopt courses of study, locate sites and build school houses, the money having been voted by the electors, and in general have full control over school matters.

Other school officers are the Superintendent of Public Instruction, and the several County Superintendents. These officers are elected for a term of two years. The Superintendent of Public Instruction has general supervision of the County Superintendents and the common schools. He may meet County Superintendents in convention, and as far as able must attend and lecture before teachers' institutes, must give written opinions in explanation of the school laws, decide appeals from decisions made by County Superintendents, and compile the school laws and decisions. He is president of the board of the State Normal School, president of the Board of Educational Examiners, and a regent of the State University. He makes a bi-ennial report of the condition and progress of the public schools, with plans for their more perfect organization and efficiency. Each County Superintendent has general control over schools and teachers in his county. He visits schools, holds a normal institute, examines teachers and issues certificates for a period of not more than one year, hears and decides appeals from orders made by boards of directors, and makes a complete annual report to the Superintendent of Public Instruction.

SCHOOL HOUSES.

The pioneer log school house increased in numbers until 1861, when 893 were reported, out of a total of 3,479. As population and wealth increased, larger school houses were built, of better material, more inviting in appearance, and more frequently well supplied with the many facilities required in order that the highest success in school work might be attained.

In 1849, the average value of each of the 387 school houses was about $100; in 1860 the average of the 3,208 was $376; in 1874 of 9,228, $892; and in 1892 of 13,275, $1,040. The gradual and continued improvement in school houses and their surroundings is an index of the great advancement in all valuable and desirable particulars. Our State furnishes for the constant use of her people school-houses of fine architecture, commodious and well furnished, having good sanitary provisions, thoroughly well equipped with the best apparatus, libraries, and other needed accessories. And these school-houses are supplied in abundance, one for each 4.14 square miles of the State, including all river and lake surface in the distribution.

TEACHERS.

In 1850 seventy teachers out of every hundred employed were men. This difference gradually diminished, until 1862, when the number of the gentler sex employed became the greater. The eminent fitness of women for the office of teacher has ever been favorably recognized in Iowa. As the number of women employed has increased in 1892 to 22,275 against 4,978 men, the relative difference in wages paid has decreased. And this apparent difference in monthly salary is really in most cases much less than shown, because of the higher salaries paid a larger number of men as superintendents and principals, which has the effect materially to increase the average paid men, while as a rule the larger number of the men receive only the same wages as the women teachers of the same grade doing the same work.

SCHOOL FINANCES.

The constant and rapid increase in the amount of money expended for educational purposes is indisputable evidence that the public schools are appreciated by the people. In many communities, the amounts paid for the support of free instruction aggregate more than one-half of the total taxes. This condition could continue only because there is a settled conviction in the minds of those voting and paying such taxes, that the money given for popular education is after all the wisest expenditure possible.

The total amount paid in 1892 for school purposes was $7,490,191, all raised by voluntary taxation, excepting the semi-annual apportionment, $789,040, a part of which is derived from the interest on the permanent school fund.

THE STATE BOARD OF EDUCATIONAL EXAMINERS

grants State certificates good for five years, and State diplomas valid for life. This official recognition of professional teachers of merit has become very popular, and many hold one of these credentials.

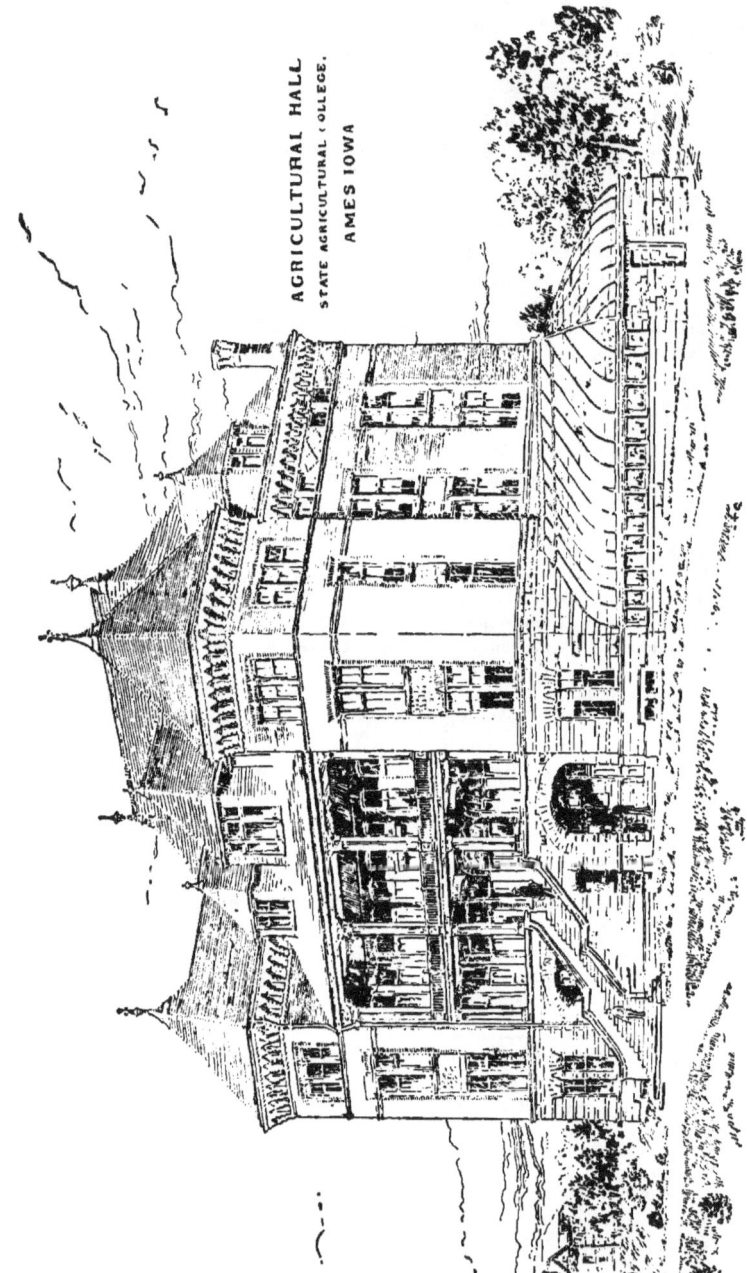

AGRICULTURAL HALL
STATE AGRICULTURAL COLLEGE.
AMES IOWA

TEACHERS' INSTITUTES.

The development of the institute cannot well be considered apart from the grand services of the pioneers in education. The early fathers laid the foundations of our school system broad and deep. Early in the fifties associations of teachers for consultation and instruction were frequently held. Several volunteer county institutes were held prior to 1858. The law of 1858 required the institute to be in session at least one week and a donation of $50 to its support was made from State funds. From this time institutes multiplied, and their usefulness increased greatly. The normal institute law of 1874 extended the term, and enlarged the opportunities for instruction in methods of teaching and in the principles of education. In many counties the session is now three weeks, and as a rule the very ablest educators to be secured are selected as conductors and instructors. In 1892 an institute was held in every one of the ninety-nine counties, 18,955 teachers were in attendance for an average of 2.4 weeks, and $52,934 were disbursed for expenses.

THE IOWA STATE TEACHERS' ASSOCIATION

has been in continuous existence since 1854. A general meeting of several days is held every year, in connection with which special sections or divisions apart from the others to discuss portions of the work more particularly related to themselves as engaged in a single line of school work. This yearly gathering of the prominent educators of the State is productive of great good to all attending.

COUNTY TEACHERS' ASSOCIATIONS AND ROUND TABLES.

In 1892 eighty counties reported a live teachers' association. These meetings usually begin on Friday evening with a lecture or some entertainment likely to interest patrons and school officers, and are continued through Saturday. Frequently city superintendents and principals of high schools join the teachers of the ungraded schools, in a meeting which may include several counties, their deliberations being conducted under the name of a teachers' round table. In some cases only the teachers in graded and high schools in several counties meet in a round table for high school teachers. These informal gatherings are always entertaining and profitable.

TEACHERS' READING CIRCLE.

Since 1889 a course of professional reading has been followed by a large number of teachers. A board chosen by the County Superintendents from their own number, selects books and gives advisory direction to the course of reading, and each County Superintendent is *ex-officio* manager of the circle in his county. More than nine-tenths of the counties are co-operating in this excellent work.

PUPILS' READING CIRCLE.

This organization commends itself by helping to direct the children in the reading of good books. The very best works for those of different ages are recommended by the board of directors and arrangements are completed by which the books chosen may be secured at a low cost. Teachers find that the circle brings new interest into the school work. In 1893 about 22,000 school children are reading the books selected for them.

COURSES OF STUDY.

The State University offers instruction in advanced subjects, and affords special preparation for the work of teaching, for the law, medicine, dentistry, and pharmacy. The courses of study for a very large number of the high schools connect directly with the course of study in the University, the Normal School, the Agricultural College, and many of the colleges of the State. For the ungraded schools of the rural districts a uniform course of study for country schools has received almost universal adoption, and is in very general use, with the most beneficial results. The value of a carefully outlined course of study in unifying and harmonizing the work and securing the wisest working plans for the schools, is conceded by all teachers and school officers who desire to avail themselves of the best means of advancing the interests of the schools.

ARBOR DAY.

In general a school-house contains an acre of ground. If natural shade

STATE NORMAL SCHOOL, CEDAR FALLS.

does not already exits the law directs that trees for shade and ornament shall be planted and cared for. This enactment led the way for the State-wide observation of tree-planting, and since 1887 a day has been designated for this annual spring festival. An Arbor Day pamphlet containing suitable lessons on nature, with choice selections about trees, birds, and flowers has been sent out from the Department of Public Instruction each year in numbers sufficient to secure uniform exercises in all the schools. Emulation and a just pride in local surroundings have been stimulated by the naming of trees planted, and the floating of a school flag on Arbor Day, making this the children's own day of patriotic celebration. Thus it has come to pass that though not legally established, Arbor Day has found such favor with the people that its continuance is assured.

STATE UNIVERSITY.

This grand institution stands at the head of the educational system. It is intended that the work of instruction shall commence where that of the best high schools ends. The ungraded rural schools are the large and massive base, the graded schools of the towns and villages and the high schools of the cities, the intermediate blocks, and the State University is the crown of an enduring monument, our system of free public schools.

Both sexes have been admitted to all departments of the University on an equal footing since 1859. The first class in the collegiate department graduated in 1863. The law department was established in 1868, the medical in 1870, and the homeopathic medical in 1876. A dental and a pharmaceutical department have since been added. Seventy-nine persons are employed in the work of instruction, and 950 students are in attendance.

STATE NORMAL SCHOOL.

This important factor in the school work of Iowa was established in 1876. From the first the school has enjoyed the greatest prosperity Enlarged several times by the addition of increased facilities, the school has always been patronized to the utmost limit of its capacity. Its students are everywhere sought for as teachers and their work in the schools has proven clearly the wisdom of the State in affording to those about to teach, an opportunity to fit themselves in a superior manner for this important work.

THE AGRICULTURAL COLLEGE

offers six courses of study. It is designed that instruction shall be furnished in all the arts and sciences that have any bearing upon agriculture. Of the large income a goodly amount is expended each year directly upon investigations and experiments, and in practical instruction in agriculture and horticulture.

CHARITABLE SCHOOLS.

Iowa provides bountifully for those prevented by infirmity from receiving instruction in schools for other children. The College for the blind, the School for the Deaf, and the Institution for the Feeble Minded, supply for these wards of the State the very best facilities that can be secured. The Soldiers' Orphans' Home and Home for Indigent Children furnishes care and instruction for many who otherwise would be homeless.

CLOSING SUMMARY.

Attendance on the schools is voluntary. The school population, 5 to 21, in 1892 was 675,024. The enrollment in public schools was 509,830. It should be noted that this number does not include the many of school age in attendance upon private schools, colleges, and other institutions of learning than the public schools.

The average monthly salary paid males was $37.76, paid females, $30.78. The schools were continued for an average of 158 days during the year, at an average cost of tuition for each pupil of $1.81 per month.

The census of 1880 credited Iowa with a lower percentage of illiteracy than any other State of the Union. In the results of the census of 1890 no doubt this exalted position will be maintained easily. This is indeed a high honor and an enviable distinction.

The school facilities of Iowa are being improved every year, better buildings are erected, teachers are paid a higher monthly compensation and relatively the attendance upon the schools is higher than at any time in the previous history of the State. The public schools are open to all residents, the children of poor parentage equally with those born to affluence, to persons of color as well as those of lighter skin, the idea being free, universal education. From the humblest rural school to the highest

WASHINGTON HIGH SCHOOL BUILDING, CEDAR RAPIDS, IOWA.

class-room in the State University, equal freedom of access is offered and all are invited to the fullest enjoyment of the invaluable privileges so liberally provided for the fortunate youth of this noble State. The interest which the people of Iowa have always manifested in all that pertains to education furnishes abundant ground for confidence in the continued growth and development of their matchless system of free schools.

In 1876 at the Centennial Exhibition, the schools of Iowa made a very creditable showing. At the Exposition in New Orleans in 1884 and 1885, Iowa received a diploma of honor for her collective educational display, and certificates of special merit were given to individual schools. The enviable distinction conferred upon Iowa by the award of first honors at the Paris Exhibition of 1889, and the bestowal of a gold medal and a handsome diploma, gave our proud State added reasons for self-congratulation, and increased the zeal of its people in the cause of education.

It requires no gift of prophecy to trace out the future path of Iowa. An observing eye need but take the past for a precedent, the present for an earnest, to draw a vast panorama of prosperity, such as our Union has never witnessed, and yet one which Iowa will not fail herself to excel.

PUBLIC LIBRARIES.

The people of Iowa are concerned to provide and disseminate sound reading and have given earnest attention to the establishment of public libraries; not only to their establishment in connection with State and city schools but also by generous contributions to establish such institutions in our chief cities and also in connection with secular and denominational schools and Universities. The State Library founded in 1840 contains now 42,637 volumes and has become one of the great Libraries of the country. The State Historical Library at Iowa City, founded in 1857, contains 15,000 volumes. The library of the State University embraces 28,344 volumes, the library of its law school 15,000 volumes. The Iowa State Agricultural College 9,500 volumes. The Library of the Grand Lodge of Free and Accepted Masons is the largest known collection of Masonic literature in the country, containing 12,000 volumes, gathered since its establishment in 1844. The Library of the Davenport Academy of Sciences contained at latest report 27,416 volumes. The Burlington Free Public Library catalogues 12,954 volumes. The Council Bluffs Free Library 14,894 volumes. The Iowa Official Register for 1893 reports one hundred and seven libraries in the State. Thirteen of the number belonging to State schools, or are State property; twenty-one belong to denominational schools; three to Young Mens' Christian Associations; and eight to secular colleges or academies. The whole number of volumes reported in the several libraries being 493,820. The report as published was not complete, there being many parochial and other school libraries not reported. There are in the State many large and valuable professional and other private libraries of which no enumeration is made.

CHURCHES AND CHURCH WORK IN IOWA.

We have shown elsewhere that the people of Iowa spend upwards of seven million dollars yearly in support of their common or public schools; they spend other large sums each year in support of parochial and other private schools, secular and denominational colleges and professional and technical schools. They show large interest in securing for their young people the means of an intellectual culture essential to useful and honorable life. They recognize also the importance of the proper culture of the moral faculties and desiring the predominance of sobriety, piety and good order, they not only tax themselves to provide facilities for public education but they contribute voluntarily large gifts to promote religious instruction and moral culture. No tax is or can be levied in this State for the building of churches or the support of the institutions of religion.

Devoted Christian men and women came in with the first immigration in the permanent settlement of the territory. Loyal alike to their God, their Christian profession and the moral interests of the communities they were establishing, they soon invited the services of the ministers of religion, and in their humble circumstances generously planned and labored to secure this beautiful region to the dominion of their Lord. They endured privations, worshiped in lowly cabins, often in "Gods first Temples," the shading grove, and by their fidelity to Christian principles, made the religious freedom, privileges and moral excellence we now enjoy a gracious possibility.

Enthusiasm in religious work led to the discovery of Iowa. The settlement of the territory did not immediately follow its discovery. One hundred and sixty years passed before the first settlers came to found homes in the area now constituting this State. In that flight of time, through the leadings of Divine Providence, great intellectual, moral and political changes occurred. Inventive genius evolved new agencies of moral, as well as intellectual, mechanical and military power, that resulted in vast changes, not only in their geography, but also in the social condition and the religious ideas pervading Christian nations. Under divine guidance this fertile and divinely favored region was reserved for settlement until these forces were in effective operation and an intelligent, liberal, Christian citizenship, hating oppression and loving righteousness, should bring to this "beautiful land" the highest type of Christian civilization ever enjoyed by men.

When the permanent settlement of Iowa began in 1833, the first emigrants were attracted to the vicinity of Dubuque and that place was founded. Galena, on the east side of the river, by its lead mining had become an active frontier town, and ministers of religion soon crossed to the new settlement west of the river. On the 8th day of August of the year named, a Congregational minister visited the new place and held religious services at the dwelling of a Mrs. Willoughby, the first religious service, so far as now known, ever held within the boundaries of the State. Soon thereafter Father McMahon, a Catholic clergyman, celebrated mass at the house of Patrick Quigley, in the new village. On the 6th of November the same year the Rev. Barton Randle, a missionary of the M. E. Church visited it and held services in a private house. Early in the following summer he organized a class in the town, the first religious society, so far as history shows, formed in Iowa. During that season the Methodists built a small church of logs, 20x26 feet, it being the first religious structure erected in the State. From these small beginnings, then offering but dim prospect of rapid or great enlargement, have grown the great religious plants that now cover the State with richness of blessing and yield their rich fruitage of cultured, Christian beneficence now sent forth, to carry the tidings of grace from this to other peoples.

It will be noticed that in this brief period, of fifty-nine years, this great work of building up our Christian societies, with their conferences, associations, yearly meetings, synods, Presbyteries, elderships, and assemblies, with their beautiful Christian temples, parochial schools, seminaries, colleges and universities has been organized and accomplished, and the millions raised that were required for their support and endowment. In those fifty-nine years there were crosses borne and privations endured but,

A WESTERN IOWA PIONEER CHURCH.

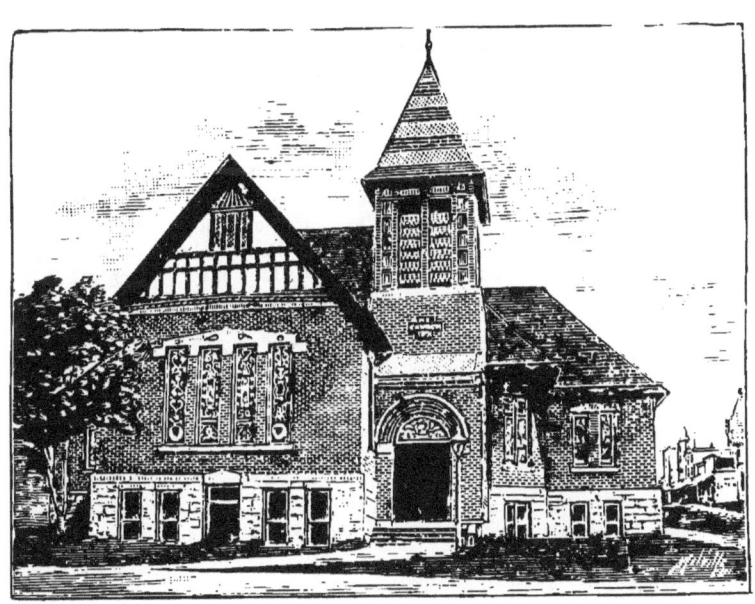

ITS LINEAL DESCENDANT.

there were wonderful accomplishments. Thousands, of liberal devisers of liberal things in Christian work, "crossed the flood," but their godly devotion won increasing thousands to take their places, and so as the workmen fell the work progressed with the results we present.

CHURCH STRENGTH IN 1850.

The census of 1850, taken but seventeen years after the settlement of the State began, presented many interesting facts regarding church work in the young State. It enumerated 207 church edifices, of the value of $177,425, an average value for each edifice of $809; they having a seating capacity of 43,529 persons, a small fraction less than one-fourth of the entire population. The total number of edifices then averaged seven to each of the twenty-nine settled counties. They were divided among thirteen denominations, as follows: Baptists 23, Christians 11, Congregationalists 14, Episcopalian 5, Friends 5, German Reformed 4, Lutheran 5, Methodist 76, Moravian 3, Presbyterian 38, Roman Catholic 18, Union 3, Universalist 1, Minor Sects 1. The total value of Church property reported in that census being $235,112.

CHURCH STRENGTH IN 1870.

Passing over two decades we reach the census year of 1870. Though the rebellion of 1861, with its awful cost of life and treasure had involved Iowa as it had involved every other State, immense progress was made during that trying period in all lines of church work. This census, the fourth national enumeration made in the State, reported 1,446 church edifices with seating capacity for 431,709 persons, being 38 in each 100 of the population. The value of church property had increased during the period to $5,730,352, an increase during the twenty years of $5,484,841, a gain of more than twenty fold, a sum larger than the original amount being added for each year of the period. The Baptists then had 165 church edifices, a gain of 142; the Disciple body 48, a gain of 37; the Episcopalian church 36, a gain of 31; the Congregational church 125, a gain of 111; the Evangelical Association 11; the Friends 60, a gain of 55; the Lutheran body 45, a gain of 40; The Methodist Episcopal church 492, a gain of 416; the Presbyterian body 222, a gain of 184; the Reformed Church in the U. S. 13; the Reformed Church in America 4; the Roman Catholic church 165, a gain of 147; the Adventists 10; the Unitarian body 2, Universalist 15, United Brethren in Christ 28. The total increase of church edifices during the period being 1,239. Surely the devoted Christian men and women in those years of trial, made great sacrifices to promote religious interests in the State.

Religious work in all communities is a vital factor to their truest prosperity. The work done by those devoted godly men and women who worked out these grand results in Christian work in the formative years of our commonwealth did much to accomplish its permanent prosperity. The census of religious work here presented, reveals not only the religious devotion of our people but also the general diffusion of religious privileges throughout the State.

DENOMINATIONAL ORGANIZATION.

In our researches regarding denominational organization in Iowa, we found in 1850 thirteen denominations existing and owning church edifices. The early settlers coming here to found homes brought with them their distinctive religious ideas, and sought to establish them. In 1870 a larger number of denominational organizations were reported. In the exercise of the freedom of religious opinion, secured to every citizen by our laws denominational organizations had multiplied.

The figures we herein present reveal a very great advance in this important interest since 1870, and yet great as they appear they fall far short of presenting the real accomplishment. The returns for many of the churches named being the statistics for 1889, they being the latest possible to obtain, we having to take their statistics from the last national census. Some denominations decline for "conscience sake" to furnish the information desired, others do not gather their statistics in such form as to enable them to furnish the information sought, respecting their work within this State. In a few cases the church officials addressed were not willing to take the time necessary to compile or gather the items we desired, the work requiring extensive correspondence. Our school statistics are gathered under legal authority. The reporting of church statistics is entirely voluntary. Many ministers and other church officials however aided us most kindly in the matter.

Only three denominations have organized existence in every county of the State, namely, Methodist Episcopal, Baptist and Roman Catholic. The Presbyterian church by a mutual arrangement with the Congregational churches have no organization in several counties, but in seven of the eight counties in which the Presbyterian church is unorganized the Congregationalists have organized churches, so that only Worth county is without a Congregational or Presbyterian church. In the counties of Davis, Decatur Madison, Monroe, Ringgold, Taylor and Warren there are no Lutheran organizations reported by the United States Census. We have tabulated eighty distinct denominational organizations in the State. Many of these however are divisions of general bodies, as the Methodist, Presbyterian and Lutheran. In some cases difference in language or nationality is the cause of separate organization. In others differences in the construction of expressions in their articles of faith. Other divisions have grown out of matters relating to social state, as dress or secrecy. Some of the Plymouth brethren, and the body we have denominated Christ's Church, deny being a sect or separate denomination, yet they are bound together by such ties of affiliation as constitute them separate and distinct bodies. We have not given any figures in connection with the latter named body as there are no means of obtaining any statistics regarding it. They deny having any officiary or leadership. The editor of "The Tumbling Stone," Toledo, Ohio, who may be regarded as their chief minister informs us that he is acquainted with them in forty-four towns in this State.

DENOMINATIONS.	No. of Counties in which Denomination exists.	No. of Church Edifices.	No. of Parsonages.	Value of Church Property.	No. of Church Members.	No. of Sunday Schools.	Amount raised during year for Church Work and Benevolences.
The New Church, (Swedenborgian)	6	3		$ 6,000	128	4	
The Salvation Army	15				387		
ADVENTIST CHURCHES—							
Life and Advent Christian Union	1				48		
Church of God (Adventist)	1	1		2,000	121		
Seventh Day Adventist Church	51	18		65,000	2,323	125	
Advent Christian Church	21	11		17,300	1,272		
The Theosophical Society	3				20		
Brethren in Christ (River Brethren)	2	2			40		
Moravian Church	3	3		4,500	100		
Plymouth Brethren	9				163		
Christ's Church (Come-outers)							
THE MENNONITE CHURCHES—							
The Mennonite Church	3	10		10,000	1,000	8	
The Amish Mennonite Church	4	5		6,700	903		
General Conference Mennonite Church	3	5		5,950	509	4	
Mennonite Brethren in Christ	1	1		500	14		
THE REFORMED CHURCHES—							
The Reformed Church in America	11	28		90,900	2,605		
The Reformed Church in the United States	34	30		68,350	2,513	19	
The Christian Reformed Church	3	6		18,000	623		
THE BAPTIST CHURCHES—							
The German Baptist (Conservative)	11	38		49,505	2,769		
The German Baptist (Progressive)	6	4		6,850	601		
The German Baptist (Old Order)	8	2		2,600	100		
Old Two Seed Baptist	1				10		
Seventh Day Baptist Church	3	2		4,300	169		
Primitive Baptist Church	25	16		9,950	853		
Free Will Baptist Church	24	36	7	65,820	2,029	42	
Regular Baptist Church	99	383	76	1,277,435	32,323	336	$ 365,856
German Evangelical Synod of N. America	25	43		110,300	6,902		
Roman Catholic Church	99	439		3,843,400	161,684		
JEWISH CONGREGATIONS—							
Orthodox Jewish Congregation	1				50		
Reformed Jewish Congregation	4	4		58,000	487		
SOCIETY OF FRIENDS—							
Friends (Orthodox)	27	73		102,682	9,760		
Friends (Hicksite)	4	4		3,800	440		
Friends (Wilburite)	9	13		12,350	1,539		
Re-Organized Church of Jesus Christ of Latter Day Saints	32	30		50,500	5,683	42	
Independent Churches of Christ in Christian Union	11	20		21,500	1,259		
Church of God (Winebrennarian)	16	21		25,000	1,200	15	7,000
Evangelical Association	49	83		178,135	5,069		
United Brethren in Christ	73	173		326,300	10,591	224	94,161
United Brethren in Christ (Old Consti'tion)	14	20		19,200	272		
Spiritualists	10			23,075	2,613		
Christadelphians	5				67		
Congregationalists	87	244		1,231,886	24,262	288	337,529
Universalists	19	25	20	218,300	987	18	
Unitarian Churches	10	9	1	78,500	1,575	11	20,780
THE PRESBYTERIAN CHURCHES—							
The United Presbyterian Church of North America	44	101	25	314,801	7,793	60	121,494
The Cumberland Presbyterian Church in the United States of America	17	25		34,550	1,167		
Reformed Presbyterian Church in the United States of America	7	9		21,900	984		
General Synod of the Reformed Presbyterian Church	2	1		1,000	33		
Associate Presbyterian Church of N. A.	4	5		5,800	233		
Welsh Calvanistic Methodist Church	5	7		7,650	349		
Presbyterian Church of the U. S. of N. A.	91	347		1,552,800	30,170	387	384,899

CHURCHES AND CHURCH WORK IN IOWA.

DENOMINATIONS.	No. of Counties in which Denomination exists.	No. of Church Edifices.	No. of Parsonages.	Value of Church Property.	No. of Church Members.	No. of Sunday Schools.	Amount raised during year for Church Work and Benevolences.
THE METHODIST CHURCHES—							
The Primitive Methodist Church	3	3	3	$ 5,000	100	5	
The Wesleyan Methodist Church	20	21	5	25,000	750		$ 6,567
The Free Methodist Church	41	62	17	56,153	2,230	63	
The Methodist Protestant Church	22	65	23	105,000	5,645	70	15,430
The African Methodist-Episcopal Church	24	29		87,361	1,820		
The Methodist Episcopal Church, South	2	7		9,200	730		
The Methodist-Episcopal Church	99	965	486	3,669,306	111,389	1294	1,076,133
THE LUTHERAN CHURCHES—							
General Synod Evangelical Lutheran Church	19	28		173,100	2,043	22	
Synodical Conference Evang'lic'l Lutheran Church	61	82		194,715	18,452		
General Council Evangelical Lutheran Church	62	132		420,689	20,009		
Joint Synod of Ohio and other States	3	8		10,500	650		
Hagues Synod Norwegian Lutheran Church	10	14		27,200	1,593		
Danish Evangelical Lutheran Church in America	16	14		24,800	2,211		
Norwegian Evangelical Lutheran Church in America	19	26		97,800	7,059		
German Augsburg Synod Evangelical Lutheran Church	1	1		1,000	70		
Danish Lutheran Church Association in America	6	2		3,800	413		
United Norwegian Lutheran Church of America	36	85		230,100	14,819	58	
Independent Lutheran Congregations	2	4		11,400	694		
Protestant Episcopal Church	68	77		1,359,720	6,260		146,876
Reformed Episcopal Church	1				27	1	366
Disciples of Christ or Christians	82	309		708,100	30,988		
The Christian Church or Bible Christians	33	32		32,775	2,555		
Independent Churches of Christ in Christian Union	11	20		21,500	1,253		
Christian Scientist	20	1		5,200	640		
Congregational Churches	87	211		1,231,886	23,733		337,529
Community of True Inspiration Society	1	7		20,000	1,700		
Icarian Community	1				21		
Plymouth Brethren II	2				48		
Plymouth Brethren III	6				106		
Independent Congregations	1	1		1,000	75		
TOTALS		4520		$ 18,485,639	579,960		

J. D. Roth, of Catasaqua, Pennsylvania, a leading statistician of the Lutheran churches in this country, estimates the expenditures of the several divisions of that body for church support and benevolent work in 1892 at $586,944. Accepting this estimate then the twenty-four denominational bodies which we report on this item raised and expended in their work in 1892 the grand sum of $3,174,055. These twenty-four bodies raising this princely sum by generous donation, contributed voluntarily for the maintenance and propagation of their religious convictions the sum of $9.49 for each of their 323,728 members. Taking the above average for the 578,756 church members, we find that the people of Iowa voluntarily paid that year $5,492,394.44 for the support and advancement of religion. Not a very small sum to be annually voluntarily assumed and paid. Such liberality demonstrates, not only that the Christian people of Iowa are of generous disposition, but also that they are in prosperous circumstances, and have high regard for their religious convictions and privileges.

The census for 1890 enumerated 4,482 church edifices in this State, of the reported value of $16,901,061, an average value of $3,771, furnishing seating room for 1,175,768 persons, or 60.9 per cent. of our population. It enumerated and named sixty-nine denominational organizations having existence within Iowa. Comparing these figures with the census enumeration of the churches for 1870, they show an increase that borders on the marvelous, the increase in the number of church edifices being 3,058 within the period of twenty years, equal to one new church edifice for each 2.39 days of the period. Surely, glorious things may truly be spoken of the lengthening of the "cords" and the strengthening of the stakes of "Zion" in this fair, beautiful and prosperous prairie State.

SABBATH SCHOOL WORK.

Iowa has an active, working State Sabbath School Association which holds an annual convention. At its session held May, 1893, there was reported within the State 5,079 Sunday Schools, having 42,321 officers and teachers, and 342,511 schollars, a total membership of 384,832; one person in each five of the population of the State, according to this report, being connected with Sunday school work. Many Sabbath schools are not reported to the Association.

Its report for 1892 embraced 4,782 schools, Worth county reporting the smallest number, 12; Winnebago and Palo Alto each reported 15, Woodbury county reported 100, Clinton 105, Jasper 135, Linn 140, and Polk 158. The average to the ninety-nine counties, according to the report for 1893, is 51.3 schools, a number that shows that our people are generously and earnestly engaged in this work.

The amount expended for the year ending May, 1893, for the support of Sunday schools, according to the report to the State Association was $129,414, not a meager sum to be voluntarily given for the support of this enterprise, Mrs. Mattie M. Bailey, Secretary of the Association, reports that 75 per cent. of the Sunday schools within the State are continued throughout the year, and that at least one million copies of Sabbath school papers are taken and that the libraries of these Sabbath schools contain at least 100,000 volumes.

PAROCHIAL SCHOOLS, DENOMINATIONAL AND NON-SECTARIAN COLLEGES AND UNIVERSITIES.

A census of church work in Iowa would not be complete nor would our educational work be fully shown, unless some report was made of the parochial schools and the denominational and secular universities and colleges maintained within the State.

Our laws make no provision for exempting persons of any denomination or sect from the payment of school taxes, it matters not how much they may have paid to support schools maintained by their own sect or church. Neither do our laws preclude any church or sect from maintaining schools for the education of its youth. The colleges and universities of the State are mostly built and maintained by religious denominations. No appropriation of any part of the school funds raised by taxation can be legally made for the support of denominational schools.

The three State schools, the Iowa State University, the Agricultural College, and the State Normal School are entirely non-sectarian. We have many other secular schools of high grade.

CHURCHES AND CHURCH WORK IN IOWA.

STATE SCHOOLS.

NAME OF SCHOOL	No. of Students Male	F'male	Total	No. of Instructors Male	F'male	Total	Volumes in Library	Endowment	Yearly Income	Value of Grounds and B'ld'gs
Iowa State Normal	191	515	706	9	9	18	5,000	$	$ 21,000	$ 75,000
Iowa State Agricultural College	454	93	547	43	6	49	9,390	$629,284	80,000	450,000
Iowa State University	752	152	904	69	2	71	28,000	281,964	100,000	300,000
TOTALS	1,397	760	2,157	100		122	42,390	$911,248	$ 221,000	$ 825,000

OTHER SECULAR SCHOOLS.

NAME OF SCHOOL	No. of Students Male	F'male	Total	No. of Instructors Male	F'male	Total	Volumes in Library	Endowment	Yearly Income	Value of Grounds and B'ld'gs
Audubon Normal College	190	173	363	8	5	13	2,500	$ 40,000	$ 4,000	$ 40,000
Amity College	261	211	472	10	2	12			8,000	4,250
Decorah Institute	220	110	310	4	2	6	300		1,000	5,000
Iowa City Academy	165	108	313	5	4	9			25,000	40,000
Dexter Normal College	137	23	160	7	5	12	2,756			25,000
Keokuk Medical College	98		98	15		15	652			10,000
Guthrie County High School	104	101	205	4	1	5	300			30,000
LeMars Normal School and Business College	111	171	272	3		10	1,000		4,000	40,000
Afton Normal School and Business College	98	92	190	5	2	7	300	10,000		40,000
National Normal School and Business College	100	90	190	5	3	9	900			30,000
Highland Park Normal College			1,262			26	5,500			450,000
TOTALS	1,358	1,185	3,830	75	38	113	13,108	$ 50,000	$ 45,000	$ 634,250

* Supported by tax on county, it being a county institution.

DENOMINATIONAL UNIVERSITIES.

NAME.	No. of Students. Male	F'male	Total	No. of Instructors. Male	F'male	Total	Volumes in Library.	Endowment.	Yearly Income.	Value of Grounds and B'ld'gs.	Denomination.
Iowa Wesleyan University	74	78	387	14	4	18	5,000	$62,600	$	20,000	Methodist
Central University of Iowa			162	5	3	8				706,067	Baptist
Drake University			862	33	6	40		128,755	21,688		Disciple
Upper Iowa University	329	155	484	11	11	22	5,322	15,000	7,000	75,000	Methodist

DENOMINATIONAL COLLEGES.

NAME.	No. of Students. Male	F'male	Total	No. of Instructors. Male	F'male	Total	Volumes in Library.	Endowment.	Yearly Income.	Value of Grounds and B'ld'gs.	Denomination.
Elkhorn College	100	80	180	5	2	7	500	$	$	10,000	Lutheran
The Norwegian College	213		213	8		8	6,500	7,500		80,000	Lutheran
Lenox College	57	58	115	4		4	1,400	11,000	4,000	20,000	Presbyterian
Parsons College			149					150,000	12,000	100,000	Presbyterian
Coe College	69	80	149	5	3	8	2,500	80,000	10,000	250,000	Presbyterian
Tabor College	95	127	222	7	6	13	5,500	140,000	10,000	50,000	Congregational
Cornell College	230	320	650	16	9	25	11,000	140,000	28,000	125,000	Methodist
Simpson College	224	188	416	10	4	14	2,500	60,000	75,000	100,000	Methodist
Iowa College	133	20	153	19	6	25	10,000	300,000	30,000	150,000	Congregational
Des Moines College	87	71	158	6	6	12	3,000	100,000	5,587	13,000	Baptist
Penn College			296	8	5	13	3,000	30,000		72,000	Friends
Western College	229	180	409	15	4	19	3,000	30,000	10,000	105,000	United Brethren
St. Ambrose College	80		80	6		6	3,500	25,000	10,000	30,000	Roman Catholic

SEMINARIES.

NAME.	No. of Students. Male	F'male	Total	No. of Instructors. Male	F'male	Total	Volumes in Library.	Endowment.	Yearly Income.	Value of Grounds and B'ld'gs.	Denomination.
Epworth Seminary	125	100	225	8	4	12	1,500	$30,000	$5,000	$30,000	Methodist
Cedar Valley Seminary	157	110	267	4	4	8	1,500		3,000	30,000	Baptist
Burlington Institute	90	124	214	5	2	7	2,500	30,000	1,500	40,000	Baptist
Albion Seminary	41	39	80	3		3	400		1,500	5,000	Methodist
St. Katherens Hall		110	110	1	11	12	1,000	10,000	25,000	60,000	Protestant-Episcopal

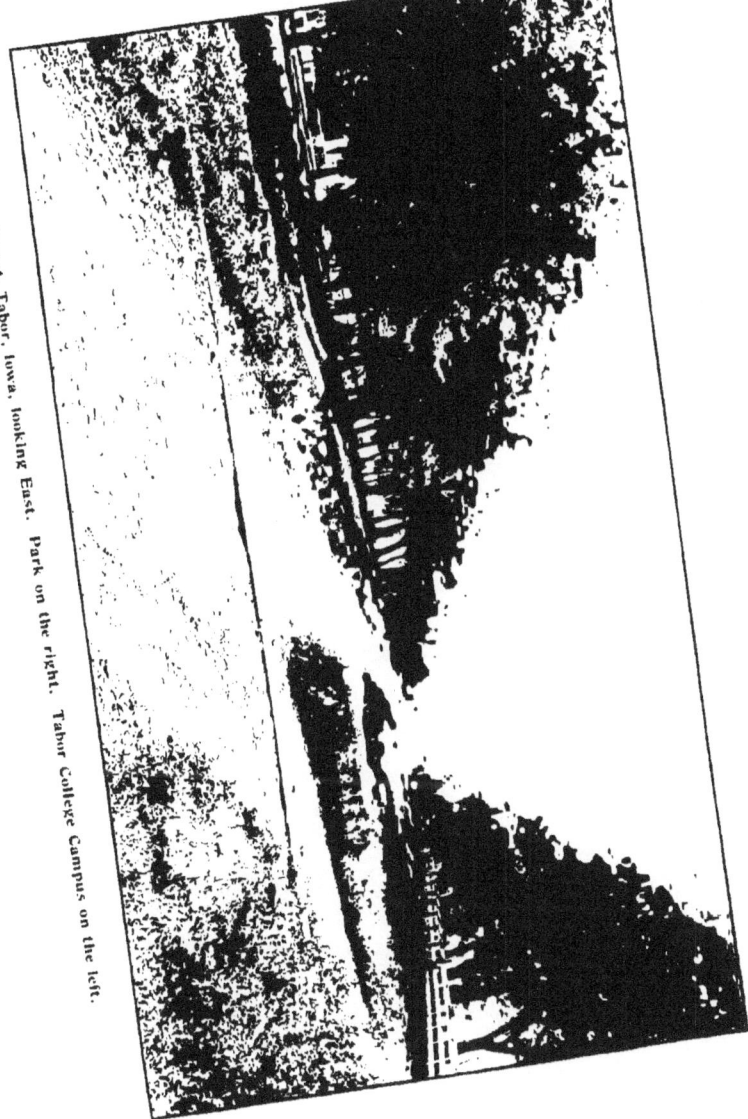

Elm Street, Tabor, Iowa, looking East. Park on the right. Tabor College Campus on the left.

PAROCHIAL SCHOOLS.

The Roman Catholic, several branches of the Lutheran body, and some other churches maintain denominational schools. Desiring as a part of their education, the instruction of their youth in their religious doctrines and usages, they spend large sums for the maintainance of their parochial or church schools. In the Diocese of Davenport there are 145 Catholic churches, six academies instructing 1,100 students, and 37 parochial schools with 4,510 pupils. The church also maintains hospitals and orphan asylums at large expense. In the Diocese of Dubuque there are 250 churches 1 seminary, 1 college, 8 academies and 100 parochial schools with 12,500 pupils. We addressed circular letters to upwards of 100 of these schools and received replies from twenty-two. They reported 2,755 pupils, namely, 1,305 males and 1,405 females, they having six male and sixty-five female instructors, with 2,415 volumes in their libraries. Ten of the twenty-two schools reported an aggregate yearly income of $4,750, and eighteen reported an endowment of $142,200.

We have been unable to obtain the statistics of the Luthern schools, as the several Lutheran Synods are not bounded by State lines and do not gather their statistics with reference to such lines, some Synods embracing several States. Rev. Geo. H. Schnurr of Nevada, Iowa, a gentleman who very kindly aided us in collecting facts regarding the Lutheran body, wrote us under date of July 7, 1893: "I am not able to give you the figures desired. The fact is that parochial school statistics have never been gathered or arranged by States. From incomplete statistics that I have seen, a safe estimate could be made at 15,000 pupils."

It is an encouraging fact that the several religious denominations within this State are earnestly interested in securing for their youth most liberal educational advantages. These parochial schools and denominational seminaries colleges and universities, furnishing educational advantages, many of them in the higher grades require large sums, which are generousiy given for their support.

We recognize fully the incompleteness of this report of church and school work within the State. Our attempt has revealed to us the difficulty of gathering complete statistics on these lines. We trust, however, that the facts we present will interest intelligent readers. They have cost us great labor—having involved extensive correspondence and research. A proper effort in the coming State census might present a complete enumeration of those interesting matters.

IOWA'S PALACES.

Some seven years ago the palace idea for exhibiting agricultural, horticultural, mechanical and mineral productions and other resources originated in this State, the citizens of Sioux City being the first to attempt its development, they adopting corn as the principal material for the decoration of their structure which was worthily named the "Corn Palace." It was made a thing of beauty and its unique decorations won large favor and drew to the city thousands of visitors.

A number of counties in Southeastern Dakota, Northeastern Nebraska,

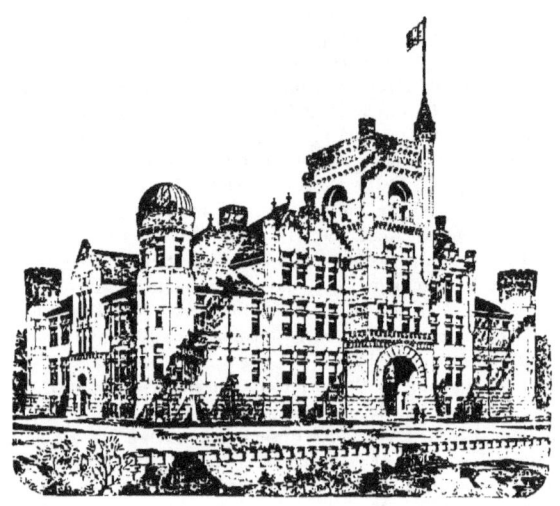

SIOUX CITY HIGH SCHOOL BUILDING.

MOUNT ST. JOSEPH'S ACADEMY, DUBUQUE, IOWA.

and Northwestern Iowa combined with the people of Sioux City to make exhibits of their resources and productions in the Palace Exposition, special booths or space being assigned to each county for its special exhibit. These exhibits at once demonstrated that Sioux City was central in a fine agricultural and fruit growing region, while the fine artistic and truly beautiful decorations of the spacious palace wrought out of corn and other grains and grasses at once won extended fame and favor.

The exterior as well as the interior of the Corn Palace was decorated with corn, all varieties of that cereal in size, color and tint being used in happy combination of form and shade which made the Corn Palace to the beholder, when the rich autumn sun light shone upon it, a thing of surprising grandeur. The decorations, while they were of Nature's perfect painting and so most pleasing to the eye, were not durable for external adornment and when the annual exposition closed the Corn Palace structure was removed and reconstructed the following year in entirely new architectural and decorative designs. This gave the artists drawing the designs for and superintending the decorations of the structure fine opportunity for studying the blending of the rich tints and many rich colors found in the numerous varieties of this kingly cereal so as to produce in its use the most marvelous, yet pleasing artistic effects. The use of corn as decorative material reaching a happy climax in the decoration of the Iowa Pavillion in the Agricultural Building and the Exhibition Hall in the Iowa Building at the Columbian Exposition, where the visiting thousands of intelligent people from foreign countries as well as from the eastern and southern states of our country were enraptured with the beauty of these Iowa structures. Their charming decorations accomplished by the intelligent artist's use of the simple products of Iowa's fertile farms and fields commanding their admiration. The Corn Palace was a grand advertisement of the energy, culture and enterprise of the people of the city giving it being.

THE FLAX PALACE.

Forest City, the county seat of Winnebago County, is central in the leading flax producing region west of the Mississippi river. Its stirring business men united their energies and capital for the erection of a Flax Palace. That important farm product being susceptible of use in beautiful ornamentation in the hands of persons of suitable taste. The city named and the people of the region surrounding it may not equal in wealth the larger and older palace cities of Iowa, but they energetically took hold of the project and the Flax Palace with an exhibit of the superior farm products of northern Iowa favorably advertised through the medium of visiting thousands the superior advantages of that beautiful region, abounding in natural advantages, and won thereto a large immigration and rapid development. The "Palaces" of Iowa by their unique structure, attractive adornment, novel and superbly fine exhibits of the resources of their surroundings attracting visitors from other states rendered valuable service in spreading knowledge of our excellencies and inviting desirable immigration with capital to assist in the further improvement and progress of the country surrounding them.

THE BLUE GRASS PALACE.

The enterprising citizens of Creston inspired by the success of Sioux City with its Corn Palace, conceived the idea of a "Blue Grass Palace," and a number of counties in the southwestern portion of the State were organized in what was named the Blue Grass League, to make an annual exhibit of their productions and resources in a structure in the erection and decoration of which the grasses, especially Blue Grass should predominate. A very commodious structure was erected and attractively decorated with the materials named. Space was assigned to the several counties forming the

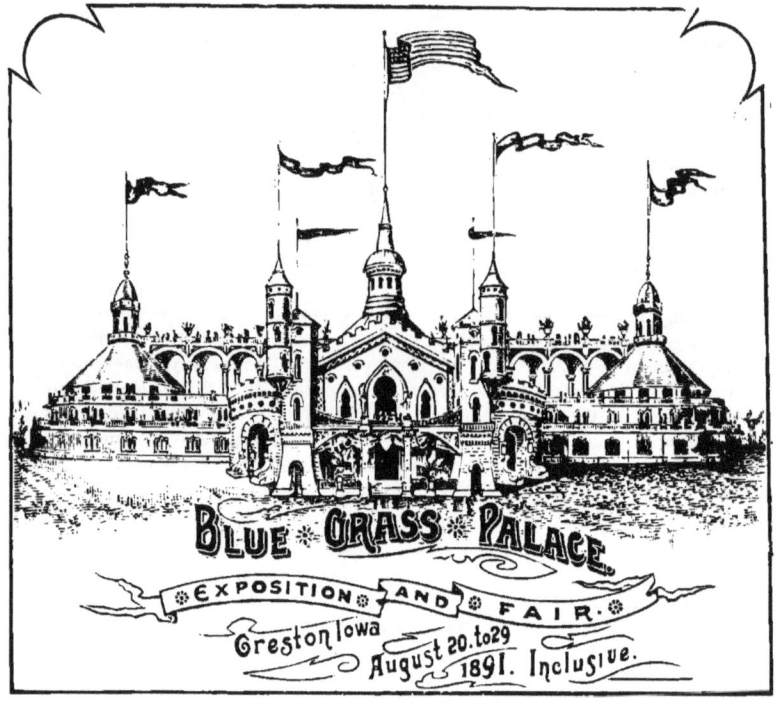

league. Each county decorating its booth and making exhibits therein. The varied productions of that wonderfully fertile portion of this queenly State were placed on exhibition and thousands were attracted from distant parts by the beauty of the unique structure and the rich and varied exhibit it contained. The Blue Grass Palace and its attractive ornamentation and industrial exhibits attracted scores of emigrants to the beautiful Blue Grass region.

THE COAL PALACE.

The citizens of the busy manufacturing city of Ottumwa, originated the idea of a Coal Palace. That city lies in a great coal producing region, has extensive water power and has developed important manufacturing industries. It planned for an annual exhibit of its productions in its Coal Palace. It may be thought by some that there could be no beauty developed from the dark, smutty black diamonds, but cultured architectural and decorative skill works out new forms of beauty often from very crude materials. The Coal Palace was made winsome in architectural design, and while it may not have been so richly or gorgeously beautiful as the Corn Palace it was made serviceable by its fine exhibits of the products of the fields, the orchards, gardens, mills, shops, and mines of the growing city and the region surrounding it, and Ottumwa is deservedly known as one of the Palace Cities of the State.

IOWA BOOKS AND AUTHORS.

By Mrs. Sara B. Maxwell.

It has been said that Iowa is too young and has no time nor opportunity to write "great" books. Iowa is young and has of necessity heretofore devoted her time and energy to developing her material resources. She therefore deserves the more credit for the literary progress she has made and for the many good books she has written ; books which compare favorably with those, in the same line, of any other place.

Theorists claim that we have not the environment necessary to the inspiration of the grandest themes. This may be so ; but the imagination of the Rev. Samuel McClurg Osmond needed not the aid of lofty mountain peak, or rapidly rolling river, when he penned the beautiful story of "Sulamith." A prairie flower called forth the sweet and tender "Golden Rod," from the heart of Rev. G. W. Crofts. No battle array, nor sound of clashing arms inspired the production of the "Siege of Calais," by Rev. A. L. Frisbie. We have no mountains ; no ruined castles ; no ancient history ; no ghostly inheritances to project themselves through our fancy ; but we have broad rolling prairies and an invigorating atmosphere which gives us broad views, humane hearts, and a common sense capable of grasping and analyzing the problems of life.

Book-making in Iowa began at an early day and we now have over seven hundred authors of books and pamphlets. The limits of this chapter allow the mention of only a few of the best known.

To Prof. James Pierson belongs the honor of having published the first poem of any length, viz: "The Judaid," a book of 267 pages, published in 1842.

Many Iowa books have attained national reputation and influence, and some are known beyond the seas, several having been translated into other languages ; notably, the ethical works of W. McIntosh Salter ; the scientific works of Prof. W. J. McGee, and of Charles Wachsmuth, who has been recognized by the Russian government as authority in his specialty.

Bishop W. Stevens Perry is known on both sides of the Atlantic as a scholarly writer on the annals of his church and other subjects of permanent interest. Two continents recognize Major S. H. M. Byers as a polished writer of both prose and poetry. "Sherman's March to the Sea" has immortalized him. The novels and stories of Miss Alice French (*Octave*

Thanet) and of Hamlin Garland are read and quoted everywhere. As a writer of field sports, W. Bruce Leffingwell has the reputation of being the best in the world. "The Medical and Moral Care of Female Patients in Hospital for the Insane," a paper read before the National Conference of Charities in Chicago, 1879, by Dr. Margaret A. Cleaves, moulded public opinion and had a far reaching influence. It was published by the government of New South Wales and has been quoted in English and American papers.

One of Iowa's most interesting and instructive books is Hon. D. N. Richardson's "Girdle Round the Earth," full of valuable information so charmingly given one wishes to read it again and again. "The History of the Amana Society," by Prof. W. R. Perkins, is said by competent critics to be the finest historical monologue ever written ; critical, analytical, scholarly, in every way a most valuable contribution to the literature of social science as well as history.

Our law writers stand with the best in the country.

May Rogers in her "Waverley Dictionary" has done for Scott's Waverley Novels, what G. A. Pierce did for the novels of Dickens in his "Dickens Dictionary."

Our good books embrace every class in the field of knowledge, but our greatest book is undoubtedly "The Evolution of Love," by Rev. Dr. Emory Miller. This has been called an "epoch making book." That it marks a distinct advance in the history of philosophy is acknowledged by many of the ablest philosophic minds and best informed scholars (in the history of philosophy) of the United States, who hail with profound delight the results of the Doctor's "hard years of thinking," recognizing that he has taken up the grand quest of philosophy—the finding "an ultimate unit of thought and thing" that will account for all variety, where Hegel, having like all his predecessors failed—left it, and that *he* has succeeded.

For convenience of reference, we will, according to the latest approved classification, group the books into nine classes without subdivision, except in 3 and 8, as follows: 1, Philosophy ; 2, Religion ; 3, Sociology ; 4, Philology ; 5, Natural Science ; 6, Useful Arts ; 7, Fine Arts ; 8, Literature ; 9, History, including Biography, Geography and Travels.

I. PHILOSOPHY, MENTAL AND MORAL.

In philosophy there are, as far as we know, twenty books. We mention the following :

Miller, Emory, D. D., LL. D., The Evolution of Love. 346 p. 12 Chic., 1892.
Patrick, *Prof.* G. T. W. Fragments of the Work of Heraclitus of Ephesus, on Nature. Translated from the Greek text of Bywater, with an introduction, historical and critical. 131 p., 8 Balto., 1889.
Salter, W. Macintosh. Ethical Religion. Phila., 1892.
First Steps in Philosophy. Phila. 1889.
Die Religion der Moral. Tr. into German by Prof. Dr George Von Gyzicki of the University of Berlin. 358 p., Leipzig, 1885.
Moralische Reder. Tr. same as above, 93 p , Leipz., 1889.
Zedelyke, Relige. Tr. into Dutch by Rev. P. H. Huganholtz, Trs. of Amsterdam. 277 p., Amsterdam, 1888.

NOTE. Many of Mr. Salter's lectures are translated into French.
Welch, *Dr.* A. S. Talks on Psychology. N. Y., 1889.
Wood, *Rev.* Stephen. Physics and Metaphysics, in the Light of the New Philosophy. 67 p., 8 , Chic. 1884.

II. RELIGION.

NOTE. In this class there are so many good books which have been widely circulated in the denominations to which the authors belong that it is difficult to select the few to fill the allotted space; therefore popular books may be omitted, from necessity. There are about two hundred religious books of Iowa authorship.

Adams, *Rev.* Ephraim The Iowa Band. A History of Early Congregationalism in Iowa. 184 p., 12 , Bost., 1870.
Archibald, *Rev.* Andrew The Bible Verified. New ed., 252 p., 16 Phila., 1892.
 Same in Spanish.
Blair, *Eld.* W. W. Joseph the Seer. 208 p., 16 , Lamoni, 1889.
Carpenter, *Rev.* G. T. The Bible vs. Spiritualism. 107 p., 16 , Oskaloosa, 1870.
Dunn, *Rev.* L. A. Foot-prints of the Redeemer in the Holy Land. 308 p., 12', D. M., 1880.
Ells, Eliza Truth Made Manifest. 391 p., 12 , Lamoni, 1891.
Fox, *Mrs.* Nettie Pease. Mysteries of the Border Land. 536 p., 12 , Ottumwa, 1883.
Hallock, *Mrs.* M. A. The Story of Moses il., 246 p., Phila., 1888.
Hattlestadt, *Rev.* O. S. Historiske Meddelelser om den Norske Augustana Synode i America. 264 p., 16 , Decorah, 1887.
Herron, *Rev.* G. D. A Plea for the Gospel. 108 p., 16 , N. Y., 1892.
 The Larger Christ. il., 122 p., 16 , Chic., 1891.
Hofer, Andrea. The Christ Child. 12 , Chic., 1892.
Johnson, *Rev.* B. A. Vision of the Age, or Lectures on the Apocalypse. 360 p., 12 , St. Louis.
Kempker, J. F. History of the Catholic Church in Iowa. 64 p., 16 , unb., I. C., 1886.
Lambert, *Eld.* J. R. What is Man? 249 p., 24 , Lamoni. 1891.
Magoun, H. W. The Asuri -Kalpa. A Witchcraft Practice of the Atharva-Veda. 33 p., 8 , Balto., 1889.
"Manuscript Found," or Manuscript Story of the Late Rev. Solomon Spaulding. 144 p., 16 , Lamoni, 1885.
Mikkelsen. *Rev.* A. Nogle af en Prests Erfaringer. 347 p., 12', Decorah, 1893.
Mitchell, *Rev.* S. H. Historical Sketches of Iowa Baptists. 504 p., 8 , Burl., 1886.
Perkins, *Prof.* W. R. Trappists of Melleray.
Perry, *Rt. Rev.* W: Stevens. Historical Collections of the American Colonial Church. (And some seventy other books.)
Taylor, *Rev.* Landon The Battlefield Reviewed. 375 p., 12 , Chic., 1881.
Wulfsberg, *Rev.* E. Praedikener over Kirke-Aarets Evangelier. 728 p., 9 , Decorah, 1888.

III. SOCIOLOGY.

NOTE. Under this head the sub-divisions Education and Law are given. There are about sixty-five books in this class and sixty in education. while the law claims about seventy titles, exclusive of supreme court reports, etc.

Ashby, N. B. Riddle of the Sphinx. 474 p., 8", D. M., 1890.
  Wealth and Civilization. 293 p., 12", Chic., 1891.
Baker, E. P. The Money Monopoly. 189 p., 16", D. M., 1892.
Baylies, Nicholas. Political Controversy Between the United States and Great Britain. 196 p., 12", D. M., 1885.
Brown, Leonard. Pending Conflict. 144 p., 8", D. M., 1890.
  Rights of Labor. 68 p, D. M., 1875.
Cloud, D. C. Monopolies and the People. 462 p., 8", Davenport, 1873.
Dean, H. Clay. Crimes of the Civil War, and Curse of the Funding System. 512 p., 8 , Balto., 1868.
Duryea, J. B. Business of Banking and Commercial Credits. Ed. 2, 423, p., 8 , D. M., 1892.
Gibbons, J. Tenure and Toil. 316 p., 16 , Phila., 1888.
Macy, *Prof.* Jesse Our Government; How It Grew, What It Does, and How It Does It. Rev. Ed. 296 p., 16 , Bost., 1890.
Miller, *Dr.* Ign. Communism. 24 p., *pam.*
Price, Hiram Speeches and Letters. 399 p., 8", Wash , 1889.
Van Valkenberg, J. Knights of Pythias Manual and Text Book. 502 p., 12 , Canton, O. 1889.

III. SOCIOLOGY. EDUCATION.

Bell, Hill M. Rhetoric Book for the Use of Students. sq. 8 , 1891.
Blakeslee, *Prof.* T. M. Academic Trigonometry, Plane and Spherical Chart. 35 p., 16 , Bost., 1888.
Ensign *Prof.* Laura Outlines, Tables and Sketches in United States History. 82 p., 16 , Chic., 1885.
Gates, *Pres.* G. A. Iowa College—Baccalaureate Sermons, 1887, '89 '91.
Kratz, *Prof.* H. Naturalism in Pedagogy, *pam.*
King, *Rev.* W. F. Cornell College—Baccalaureate Sermons, 1883, '88.
Macy, *Prof.* Sherman R. Outline Course of Theoretical Pharmacy. 127 p., 24 , D. M., 1891.
Morris, R. Anna Physical Education, 192 p., 11 , Chic., 1892.
Parish, *Prof.* L. W. Analysis of Compayres Pedagogy. 105 p., 16", C. F. 1892.
Scott, *Dr.* C. Etymological Outlines of the Elements of Physiology and Anatomy. 92 p., 24", 1890.
Shoup, *Prof.* W. J. Graded Didactics, 2v. 12 , Chic., 1889.
  History and Science of Education. 303 p., 12 , Chic., 1891.
Thompson, Albert H. Examiner's Companion. 380 p., 12 , Chic., 1890.
Throndsen, K. Norske Laesebog. 2v. Decorah, 1892.
Warman, *Prof.* E. B. How to Read, Recite and Impersonate.
  Gestures and Attitudes; An Exposition of the Delsarte Philosophy. 416 p., 8", Chic., 1892.
  Physical Training ; or the Care of the Body. 190 p., 12 , 1890.

Welch, W. N. How to Organize, Classify and Teach a Country School. 107 p., 12°, Chic., 1886.
Ylvisaker, *Rev.* Joh. Norwegian Luther College, Decorah, Iowa. History from 1861 to 1890. 68 p., ob. 12°, Decorah, 1890.
Same in Norwegian.

III. SOCIOLOGY. LAW.

Baker, Andrew J. Annotated Constitution of the United States. Chic., 1892.
Brown, Timothy Commentaries on the Jurisdiction of Courts. 8°, Chic., 1891.
Dillon, *Judge* J: F. Law of Municipal Bonds. 8°, St. L., 1876.
    Removal of Causes from State to Federal Courts. Ed. 1, 2, 3, 4 and 5, St. L., 1876, '79.
    Treatise on the Law of Municipal Corporations. Ed. 1, 2, 3 and 4, 1872-'90.
Field, G. W. Doctrine of Ultra Vires. 8°, D. M. 1881.
    Lawyers' Briefs. 6v., 8°, Phila., 1884, '86.
    Treatise on the Law of Damages. 8°, D. M. 1876.
Kinne, *Judge*, G. L. Pleading, Practice and Forms. 8°° Chic., 1888.
Lacey, J. F. Digest of Railway decisions. 2v., 8°, Chic., 1875.
McClain, *Prof.* Emlin Annotated Code and Statutes of Iowa. 2v., 8°, Chic., 1888.
McCrary, G. W. American Law of Elections. Ed. 2 and 3, 1880-1887.
Miller, *Justice* Samuel F. Constitution of the United States ; Three Lectures before the University Law School of Washington. 8°, Wash., 1880.
    Biographies of the Judges of the United States Supreme Court. *Rev.* ed. D. M., 1875.
Miller, *Judge* W. E. Probate, Law and Practice in Iowa. 8°, D. M., 1890.
    Revised Annotated Code of Iowa. 2 v, 8°, D. M., 1890.
    Treatise on Pleading and Practice in the Courts of Iowa Under the Code. Rev. ed. 8°, D. M., 1875.
Rorer, *Judge* David American Inter-State Law. Ed. 2, 8°, Chic., 1878.
    Law of Railways. 2v. 8°, Chic., 1884.
Shiras, *Judge* O. P. Equity Practice in the United States Courts. 12°, Chic., 1889.
Withrow, T. F. *Ed.* American Corporation Cases. 4v. N. Y.

IV. PHILOLOGY.

NOTE. So far as ascertained, thirty titles comprise the books in Philology.

Bell, *Prof.* Hill M. Orthoepy and Orthography. D. M., 1892.
Currier, *Prof.* Amos N. Table of Latin Suffixes and a Table of Prefixes. 1889.
Ely, *Prof.* E. H. Latin in the Public Schools. pam.
Pollard, *Mrs.* Rebecca S. Manual of Synthetic Reading. 217 p., 8°, Chic., 1892.
Shoup, *Prof.* W. J. Graded Speller. St. Paul, 1888.

Warman, *Prof.* E. B. Practical Orthoepy. Chic., 1889.
Wright, *Prof.* D. Sands Drill Book in English Grammar. 16°, Chic., 1887.

V. NATURAL SCIENCE.

NOTE. Our catalogue contains seventy-five titles; there are probably one hundred.

Bennett, *Prof.* A. A. Inorganic Chemistry. Pt. 1, 357 p., 16°, B., N. Y. and Chic., 1892.
Bessey, *Prof.* C. E. The Essentials of Botany. N. Y., 1889.
Call, *Prof.* R. Ellsworth Annual Report of the Geological Survey of Arkansas. 1889. v2, 283 p., 8°, L. R. 1891.
    Artesian Wells in Iowa, Sketch of the Physical Geography of Iowa (and many other valuable papers).
McGee, *Prof.* W. J. Pleistocene History of Northeastern Iowa. From the 11th Report of the United States Geo. Survey, 1889-90. 568 p., f°, Wash., 1791. (And a great many valuable monographs).
McLennan, Evan. Cosmical Evolution. 12°. Chic., 1891.
Macomber, J. K. Matter and Force. 93 p., 16°, Ames, 1876.
Matthews, *Dr.* Washington On Composite Photography as Applied to Craniology. pls. 4°, Wash.
    Ethnography and Philology of the Hidatsa Indians. 239 p., 8°, Wash., 1877.
Wacksmuth, C: and Frank Springer. Revision of the Palaeocrinoidea. pts. 1 and 2, and pt. 3 of Sections 1 and 2. 8°, Phila., 1879-1886.
White, C. A. Report of the Geological Survey of Iowa. 1870. 2v., 8°, D. M., 1870.

VI. USEFUL ARTS.

Sixty books and pamphlets.

Anderson, Nellie Van The Right Knock. 316 p., 16°, Chic., 1889.
Carpenter, C. C. Instructions to Surveyors. 129 p., 12°, D. M., 1870.
Cleaves, *Dr.* Margaret A. Colony of the Insane at Gheel, Belgium, 1891.
    Medical and Moral Care of Female Patients in Hospitals for the Insane. 1879.
Clute, Oscar (*John Allen*) The Blessed Bees. 172 p., 16°, N. Y., 1878.
Davis, *Prof.* Floyd Potable Water. 118 p., 12°, B., N. Y. and Chic., 1891.
Dodge, *Gen.* G. M. Union Pacific Railroad; Reports of the Chief Engineer for 1867, '68, '80.
Eaton, *Dr.* C. W. Things Young Men Should Know. 584, 187 p., D. M., 1884.
Goodyear, S. H. Theory of Accounts. 228 p., 8°, C, R. 1890.
Hutchinson, *Dr.* Wools *Ed.* Vis Medicatrix. D. M., 1891.
Scott, *Mrs.* Mary Indian Corn as Human Food. 16°, Nevada, 1891.

VII. FINE ARTS.

Twenty titles, not including sheet music.

Bartlett, *Prof.* M. L. Class and Chorus. 176 p., 8°, Chic., 1890.
Dinsmore, G. A. Old Violins.
Dunham, *Prof.* J. R. The Banner. 160 p., ob. 16°, Chic., 1886.
Forscutt, Mark *Ed.* Saints Harmony. 565 p., 4°, Lamoni, 1889.

Leffingwell, W. Bruce Shooting on Upland, Marsh and Stream. 437 p., 8 ,
    Chic. and N. Y., 1890.
    Wild Fowl Shooting. 373 p., 8 , Chic., 1890.
Parker, *Rev.* H. W. The Spirit of Beauty. Essays, Scientific and Esthetic
    Ed 2, 252 p., 12°, N. Y., 1891.
Psalmabog for den Norske Evangelisk Luteriske Kirke i Amerike. 192 p.,
    16 , Decorah, 1877.
Randall, R. H. Bethel Chimes. 144 p., 12 , Marion, Iowa, 1891.
Taylor, Virgil C. The Enchanter. 176 p., N. Y., 1864.
Woolett, J. Songs. The Autumn Time ; Bring Sweet Flowers ; Home of
    Our Fathers ; and My Maude.

VIII. LITERATURE.

Thirty books.

NOTE. This class is divided into general and miscellaneous, poetry and
fiction.

Anderson, L. J. and Nellie V. Every Day Helps. 24 , Chic., 1890.
Burdett, Robert J. Rise and Fall of the Mustache. (*humorous*).
Davidson, C. Studies in the English Mystery Plays. 173 p., 8 , *unb*., 1892.
Folsom, Moses Treasures of Science, History and Literature. 8 , 1876.
Jones, *Prof.* R. Literature as a Means of Culture. 65 p., 16 , *unb*.
Rogers, May. The Waverley Dictionary. 12°, Chic., 1885.
Springer, J: The Caxton Reproductions, with the Early Press of Iowa. l.
    C. 1880.
Throndsen, R. Skolelaereren og hans Son. 112 p., 12 , Decorah, 1886.
Wilkie, Frank B. Davenport, Past and Present.
Wynn, *Rev.* W. H. Addresses and Reviews. 12 , n. t. p., n. d.

VIII. LITERATURE. POETRY.

Sixty-five books.

Boylan, Will M. Life's Purest Gold. 8 , Eldora, 1889.
Butz, Caspar. Gedichte eines Deutch-Amerikaners. 8 , 312 p., Chic., 1879
Byers, S. H. M. Happy Isles and other poems. 162 p., Ed. 2, N. Y. 1891
Collier, *Mrs.* Ada L. Lilith, The legend of the First Woman. 104 p., 16 .
    Bost., 1885.
Crofts, *Rev.* G. W. Golden Rod. 207 p., 12 , Omaha, 1889.
Fearing, Lilian Blanch. City by the Lake. 192 p., Chic., 1892.
Frisbie, *Rev.* A. L. The Siege of Calais and other poems. 166 p., 16 , D·
    M., 1880.
Gonner, NS. Prairieblummen. 166 p., 8 , Dubuque, 1883.
Judd, *Rev.* T. E. The Owls. 143 p., 8 , Marshalltown, 1888.
McCreery, J. L. Songs of Toil and Triumph. 143 p., 16 , N. Y., 1883.
Manning, Jessie Wilson. Passion of Life. 75 p., 16 , Cin., 1837.
Osmund, *Rev.* S. McClurg. Sulamith. 211 p., 12 , Phila., 1892.
Parkhurst, Clint. Poems. 153 p., 16 , Chic., 1874.
Percival, *Rev.* C. S. Poetic Parallels and Simile in Song. 162 p., 13°,
    Cleve., 1892.
Pierson, Johnson. The Judaid. 267 p., 12 , 1842.
Richman, DeWitt C. The Talisman and other poems. 152 p., 12 , Muscatine, 1867.

Smith, *Mrs.* D. (*Maude Meredith.*) The Rivulet and Clover Blooms. 75 p., 24 , N. Y. and Chic., 1881.
Throndsen, K. Orkenblomster. 240 p., 24 , Decorah, 1890.

VIII. LITERATURE. FICTION.

One hundred books.
Anderson, Nellie Van. It is possible. Chic., 1891.
Baldwin, *Mrs.* Mary R. Along the Anataw. N. Y., 1891.
    Around Brenton. N. Y., 1891.
Claggett, Sue Harry. Her Lovers. Phila., 1877.
French, *Miss* Alice, (*Octave Thanet.*) Expiation. N. Y., 1892.
    Knitters in the Sun. B. and N. Y., 1892.
    Otto the Knight, and other trans-Mississippi Stories. B. and N. Y., 1891
    We All. N. Y. 1891.
Garland, Hamlin. Jason Edwards. B., 1892.
    Main Travelled Roads. B., 1892.
Harbet, Lizzie Boynton. Amore. Chic., 1892.
    Out of Her Sphere. D. M., 1871.
Leffingwell, W. Bruce. Manulito; or a Strange Friendship. Phila., 1892.
Smith, *Mrs.* D. (*Maude Meredith.*) The Parson's Sin. Chic., 1892.
Vittum, *Rev.* Edw. M. Head of the Firm. Bost., 1891.
Wetmore, *Mrs.* Mai M. (*Oaks.*) Wee Folks in No-Man's Land. Chic., 1893.

IX. HISTORY.

Including Biography, Geography and Travels. One hundred books exclusive of County histories.
Aldrich, C., *Ed.* Life and Times of A. B. F. Hildreth. 556 p., 12 , D. M.. 1891.
Baylies, Nicholas. Life of General Eleazer Wheelock Ripley of the War of 1812. 12°, D. M., 1890.
Burrows, J. M. D. Fifty Years in Iowa. 16 , Dav., 1888.
Byers, S. H. M. Iowa in War Times. 615 p., 8 , D. M., 1888.
Chapin, *Mrs.* Nettie S. American Court Gossip; or Life at the National Capitol. 269 p., 13 , Marshalltown, 1877.
Clark, *Capt.* J. S. Thirty-Fourth Iowa Regiment. Brief history.
Crooke, *Adj.* G. Twenty-First Regiment of Iowa Volunteer Infantry. 232 p., 8°. Milwaukee, 1892.
Fuller, C. E. Reminisences of James A. Garfield. 441 p., 8 , Cin., 1886.
Fulton, A. R. Notes of the Northwest. 255 p., 8 , D. M., 1878.
    Red Men of Iowa. ll. 559 p., 8 D. M., 1882.
Grinnell, Josiah B. Men and Events of Forty Years. 426 p., 8 , Chic., 1891
Ingersoll, L. D. History of the War Department. 613 p., 8 , Wash., 1880.
Landers, Frank E. Historical Geographical Atlas of the U. S. A., from the Earliest Colonial Days to the present time. F°, 1889.
Lathrop, *Dr.* C. H. History of the First Iowa Volunteer Cavalry. 231 p., Milwaukee, 1891.
Nourse, C. C. Iowa and the Centennial. 42 p., 12 , D. M., 1876.
Perkins, *Prof.* W. R. History of the Amana Society. 94 p., 8 , 1891. *Pam.*
Reid, Harvey. Biographical Sketch of Enoch Long. 184 p., 8 , Chic., 1884.
Richardson, D. N. Girdle Round the Earth. 451 p., 8 , Chic., 1890.

Rouse, *Mrs.* Clara B. Iowa Leaves. Six chapters. 451 p., 12 , Chic., 1891.
Salter, *Rev.* W. Life of James W. Grimes, Governor of Iowa, 1854-58. A Senator of the U. S. 398 p., 8 , N. Y., 1876.
Augustus C. Dodge, Senator of the U. S. from Iowa. 38 p., 8 , I. C., 1887.
Columbian Calendar, the Voyage of Christopher Columbus from the third day of August to the Discovery of America, A. D. 1492, Burl., 1892.
Sharp, Abbie Gardner. History of the Spirit Lake Massacre. 316 p., 12 , D. M., 1885.

IOWA AND PATRIOTISM.

When the permanent settlement of Iowa opened, after the Indian war of 1832, the contentions regarding negro slavery, that finally culminated in the civil war which overthrew that institution, had begun to agitate the country. The Missouri Compromise, adopted as a settlement of the slavery question in 1821, was, when the pioneers crossed the river in 1833 to found a permanent settlement at Dubuque, in its most vital force. By its provisions the area forming this State was consecrated to freedom. Yet under its territorial government a few slaves were held in Iowa, sixteen according to the National Census of 1840, being held within its borders. Ultimate freedom from slavery was however fully assured to this region. Immigrants from the New England states flocked to this new field bringing with them as one of their chief possessions, an intelligent patriotism, a legacy of patriotic sires, who stood bravely for freedom at Lexington, Bennington, and Bunker Hill. Other settlers coming from the central and eastern states to this free western country to establish a new commonwealth, brought with them a hearty affinity with that spirit. Others coming from the then slave-cursed south, came to enjoy a deliverance from the scenes and associations of that oppression. They believed that all men were endowed equally by the Creator, with the right to their own muscle, bone and mental powers, and with equal rights to free volition and action in the pursuit of happiness. When a National Administration, to maintain its party dominancy, consented to aid in the extension of the institution of slavery by the repeal of the Compromise that had, from its enactment, been regarded as a perpetual guaranty of freedom, to the great Northwestern portion of the country, the people of Iowa cast a decisive majority vote on the platform declaring, "We most unqualifiedly and emphatically disapprove of the efforts now being made in Congress to legislate slavery into the territory of Nebraska." The next year they declared by the largest majority the State had ever cast, down to that time, "That under the constitution and by right, freedom alone is national." They then believed that the broadest possible individual freedom was essential to the true happiness of the people, and the real prosperity of the State. They claimed civic freedom for themselves and their posterity, and patriotically gave voice and vote, that others, settling new territories throughout this broad west, should enjoy these same heaven-bequeathed advantages. Inspirations of the noblest patriotism determined the lines of development that have made Iowa, in its brief history, not only one of the freest and progressive but also one of the most orderly States of the Union.

When in April, 1861, the stirring message that rebel hosts assailing Fort Sumpter, had compelled the striking of the National banner to the Palmetto flag, and the proclamation of Mr. Lincoln summoned the states to send armed men to maintain the national authority and repossess the national government of its property, the citizens of no one of the twenty-four loyal states were more earnest in patriotic determination and deed than were the people of this State. The sturdy, patriotic, Kirkwood, Marylander by birth was then governor. With the hearty approval of the people he at once proceeded to fill the quota of troops then called for from the young State. No one of the loyal states responded more earnestly. The uprisings on the Patapsco and Potomac, cut him off for some days from communication with the national authorities, but the patriotism of the people precluded any dallying with doubtful questions. Governor Kirkwood, with their hearty approval, proceeded at once to raise the quota of troops, which telegrams, flashing through the country, announced that the general government was calling into the field, without waiting to receive the official notice sent out by the Secretary of War.

Governor Kirkwood took early steps to call the General Assembly to meet in Extraordinary Session. Responding to his call that body convened May 16, 1861,—but one month after the surrender of Ft. Sumpter. In his message to that body he said:

"In this emergency Iowa must not and does not occupy a doubtful position. For the Union as our fathers formed it, and for the Government founded so wisely and so well, the people of Iowa are ready to pledge every fighting man in the State, and every dollar of her money and credit, and I have called you together in Extraordinary Session for the purpose of enabling them to make that pledge formal and effective."

In that message Governor Kirkwood further informed the people that he was met at the outset by two difficulties. First. The State treasury was empty, there were no funds under his control to meet the necessary expenses of transportation and providing uniforms and other requisites for the troops volunteering to meet the call." Second. "There was no efficient military law under which to operate."

The first difficulty was obviated by the patriotic action of chartered banks and wealthy citizens of the State, who placed at his disposal, all the money the State authorities might need. Governor Kirkwood informed the General Assembly that he "determined although without authority of law, to accept their offer," trusting that that body would legalize his acts. He did not trust its patriotism in vain.

The Secretary of War asked that the troops be in readiness to proceed to the field by the 20th of May. The wise and patriotic action of the people, Governor Kirkwood informed the General Assembly enabled him "to place them in uniform on the eighth instant, twelve days in advance of the time named by the national authorities." He also stated "that they would have been there a week sooner had not the mob at Baltimore cut off all communications with the government and left him without instructions for two weeks."

The patriotism of the people brought out more people than the call required and a second regiment was placed in camp in anticipation of a second call. Gov. Kirkwood stated in his message that he had received a "tender of troops to form five full regiments when only one had been called for by the national authorities."

The people of no State were more patriotic or truly loyal or devoted to the maintenance of the Union of the States than were the people of Iowa in that terrible conflict. Her citizen soldiery toiled in almost every march, fought in almost every battle, and bravely fell everywhere at the front. Her generals from her shops and corn fields made honorable history and won renown on many fields. No spot nor stain tarnished the honor of Iowa in that terrible trial. With Lyon at Wilson Creek; Curtis in the Ozarks; with Banks on the Red River; with Steele in Arkansas; Thomas at Chickamauga, on the Chattanooga; in Sherman's march to the sea; the struggle through the swamps of the Carolinas; with Sheridan at Cedar Creek; Sherman and Grant at Vicksburg; Rosecrans at Murfreesboro, and Sherman at Bentonville, the courage and patriotism of the soldiers of Iowa were nobly attested, and none had better right to share in the pageant of the grand review. Forty-nine regiments of infantry (forty-eight of white troops and one colored), nine regiments and two extra companies of cavalry and four batteries of artillery were enrolled in the patriotic force,—a total of 56,364 men in duly organized and reported Iowa troops, while there were 19,155 enlistments of Iowa men in regiments in other states, making a grand army of 75,519 men enrolled, being one for each ten persons of her population at the close of the grim struggle. Of the troops reported in Iowa organizations 3,360 were killed or died of wounds received in battle, while 8,810 died of disease or fell by accident. Iowa's part in the conflict for perpetual, national unity in a redeemed country was costly in precious lives. Her homes were made sad by the sorrows of war, but her people faltered not when called to its stern duty; her sons freely going at their country's summons. The draft wheel made but few turns to secure her quotas.

When the rebellion terminated by the surrenders at Appomattox and Durham Station, Iowa citizen soldiery were too patriotic to be resentful and too intelligent to refrain from peaceful industry. Recognizing those who, but the preceding day they fought in war as rebels, in that day of proclaimed peace as friends, they recognized them then as citizens of one country, having mutual interests to be promoted by perpetual unity in its perfected freedom, the highest development of which was to be achieved by the united intelligence of a citizenship having mutual and equal rights to freedom and happiness. Under such patriotic inspirations Iowa has made her unexampled progress.

Situated in the central region of the grand constellation of States, Iowa favors their perpetual union. Her intelligent citizens regard each star with equal respect. In the national parliamentary halls her citizens have won honor: in the highest judicial chambers her citizens have gained honored name: in the high duties of cabinet councils and diplomatic offices her sons have rendered distinguished service. Exalting the fatherhood of God and the brotherhood of man, she recognizes each of her citizens as having equal rights to life, liberty, the advantages of her schools and the protection of her government.

IOWA AND ART.

In the difficulties and privations inevitable in the formation of a new state, the improvement of a new country and the accomplishment of the work necessary to be done in the construction of homes, roads, churches, schools and all the other public and private institutions necessary in the construction of a new commonwealth, so large in area as Iowa, and in the brief period of only sixty-three years in which this vast work has been done, it should not be a source of serious alarm if the attention of its people should be directed more to matters merely material than to such things as have only relation to taste, or the study of the beautiful.

The people of Iowa, however, in the pressure of the material matters which have directly and necessarily concerned them, have not been unconcerned about the arts. Nature filled the surroundings of their homes with bloom and beauty, and esthetical tastes were incited by the loveliness and grandeur of these broad landscapes that Nature's artists painted in gold and pearl.

Our people have been liberal patrons of the liberal and fine arts. We may not in our brief history have produced great masters, but that our accomplishments and creations have been respectable is well known. In music our bands have won respectful recognition in distant states and cities. In sculpture, architecture, and painting we have furnished names that are well known. The name of Mrs. Ketchum will by her work in sculpture and architecture be long perpetuated. The country that gave to the world the "Swedish Nightingale" had gained world-wide fame by its deeds of military heroism before Iowa was discovered, but in its longer history it has produced but one Jennie Lind. The names of England's great military heroes, statesmen, navigators and scientists are multitudinous, the list of her names great in architecture, sculpture and painting is brief.

The history of the pioneer days in Iowa is made. Her public schools, her colleges and her universities are now planted on enduring foundations. Her schools of art are passing from infantile condition, their patronage is respectable, and the "science of the beautiful" receives respectful attention. The work of Iowa artists has place in the Columbian Exposition. In the Woman's building their beautiful creations have place. In the Iowa building there is a very inviting exhibition.

During the past year a State Art Association was formed with a membership respectable in numbers and accomplishments. Its annual meetings will inspire an honorable enthusiasm in esthetical study.

IOWA AND WORLD'S FAIRS.

THE CENTENNIAL.

The first effort made by this State to present its resources in a world's Exposition was made in the Philadelphia Exposition, the Centennial of 1876. The Fifteenth General Assembly met in January, 1874, and adjourned in March following, but took no action looking toward an exhibit of the resources of the state in the then pending Exposition. In the summer of 1875 fuller information regarding that Exposition having been disseminated, the people became interested in the improvement of that opportunity to present their resources, accomplishments and possibilities to the knowledge of the nations. To effect this purpose a voluntary organization of citizens was effected, which gave time and means to raise the necessary material and money to secure a creditable presentation of the industries, agricultural, and mineral resources and educational advantages and facilities of Iowa therein. The Sixteenth General Assembly, convening in January preceding the opening of the Exposition in May, appropriated $20,000 for an exhibit, and provided for a commission to take the matter in charge. The citizens' organization then turned the means it had raised and the material it had gathered over to the State commission, and an exhibit of the resources, soils, products and educational work of the State was made that won it great favor. The display of the soils of Iowa made in glass tubes six inches in diameter and showing the soil as it was taken from the ground to the depth of six feet, was unique and being true to the natural condition attracted great attention. The exhibits of Iowa fruits, which won high awards, and the exhibit of dairy products taking the highest prizes won, honors that proved of great financial advantage to Iowa, opening a wide and ready market for her fruit and dairy products that had previously been unknown in distant markets. The efforts in that exposition resulted in great advantage to the State.

THE WORLD'S INDUSTRIAL AND COTTON CENTENNIAL.

In February, 1893, the Congress of the United States took action to constitute an International Exposition of the resources, industries, productions, arts and accomplishments, especially of the North, Central and South American States; they each being especially invited to unite therein. This Exposition was opened in the City of New Orleans, in December, 1884. The exhibit that Iowa there made was gathered, installed and managed solely by private enterprise, the State authorities making no appropriation to assist in the work. On the recommendation of Governor Sherman, the President appointed Mr. H. S. Fairall, of Iowa City, Commissioner for the State. An Iowa Commission was also formed by voluntary organization, Governor Sherman being President.

In the Horticultural department of this Exposition Iowa made a most commendable display. Her fine show of pomaceous fruits won a gold medal and the first prize of $200 for the largest and best display of apples, not exceeding two hundred varieties, and gaining twelve other valuable premiums. This State also won twenty-two first premiums in its agricultural display. In the Dairy department Iowa carried off the honors, making the largest display of butter ever exhibited up to that time by any state at any dairy fair or exposition, and winning the highest premiums.

In the department of Education an exhibit was made under the supervision of Hon. J. W. Akers, State Superintendent of Public Instruction, presenting the work of our public school system. It was representative, comprehensive and complete, and placed Iowa in the foremost rank; thirty-nine honorable awards being won by her educational exhibit in that exposition.

The plans of the Commission were greatly frustrated by a railroad wreck which occurred on the Burlington, Cedar Rapids and Northern railway, in which a large portion of the material intended for the exhibit was totally destroyed, many articles being utterly ruined, the principal portion being damaged beyond use. The accident was costly to the State in the results of the Exposition, as the lateness of the season at which it occurred, to a large degree, precluded replacing the articles damaged or destroyed; the wreck occurred December 1st, 1884.

At the Exposition of 1889, at Paris, Iowa was represented by a few exhibits, a full report of which was made to Governor Larrabee by Commissioner James O. Crosby. Two gold medals were awarded. One to the State of Iowa for an exhibit of its school system made by Hon. Henry Sabin, State Superintendent of Public Instruction. The other was for Hall's Report of the Geological Survey of Iowa, exhibited by a son of the author.

IOWA IN THE COLUMBIAN EXPOSITION.

In April, 1890, the Twenty-third General Assembly of this State took action to provide for an exhibit of its agricultural, mineral, mechanical, industrial, educational, and other resources in the World's Columbian Exposition. Iowa was the first of the states of the Union to take action providing for an exhibition therein.

Its Legislative Assembly, meeting only biennially, was in session when the National Congress was considering the matter of providing for the Exposition. When the lower house in that body passed its measure for making provision for the great Fair, our General Assembly was on the eve of closing its session. It was evident that the National Senate would enact the House bill into law. If Iowa should make an exhibit of her resources in the contemplated Exposition, under the auspices of State authority, it was necessary that immediate action should be taken, as that body would not again convene until January, 1892, a short time before the opening of the Fair if it should be held, as was then proposed, in 1892. Under these circumstances the Legislature, taking hasty action in the premises, enacted the following measure which was approved by the Governor ten days before the National enactment was approved by the President:

AN ACT to Provide for a Creditable Exhibit of the Resources of the State of Iowa in the "Columbian Exposition" or the World's Fair, to be held in Chicago.

WHEREAS, Congress is now considering, and the House of Representatives has already passed a bill, providing for a World's Fair, to be known as the "Columbian Exposition," and held at Chicago during the year 1892 or 1893 ; and

WHEREAS, It is highly desirable that the agricultural, mineral, mechanical, industrial, educational and other resources and advantages of the State of Iowa shall be creditably represented in such exposition, therefore,

Be it Enacted by the General Assembly of the State of Iowa:

SECTION 1. That the Executive Council be and is hereby authorized and directed to appoint an exhibition committee to be known as the "Iowa Columbian Commission." Such commission shall consist of eleven members, to be selected one from each congressional district in the State, not more than six of whom shall be from the same political party, and shall have full power to devise and execute plans for the State Exhibit herein contemplated, take charge of the same and disburse the appropriations. It may appoint such officers as in its judgment may be necessary for carrying out this act, including the right to delegate to an Executive Committee the duty and power to execute all or any plans that may be devised or ordered by such Commission. One member thereof shall be chosen to act as Treasurer, and he shall be (*ex-officio*) custodian of the moneys herein appropriated; but before entering upon the duties of such position he shall furnish a bond, subject to the approval of the Executive Council, and running to State of Iowa in the penal sum equaling amount herein appropriated. If the said "Columbian Exposition" is held during the year 1892, the Commission created by this section shall be appointed at some time prior to January 1st, 1892. Any vacancy occurring in said Commission shall be filled by the Executive Council by the choice of some citizen residing in the congressional district wherein such vacancy occurs. The Commission herein created shall receive as compensation for the service of its members not to exceed five dollars for each day actually and necessarily engaged in the work of the Commission, and actual railroad fare paid.

SECTION 2. The sum of Fifty Thousand Dollars is hereby appropriated out of any money in the State Treasury not otherwise appropriated, for the purpose of carrying into execution the intent of this act; Provided that, if said Fair or Exposition be not held before 1893, not more than ten per cent. of the sum hereinbefore named shall be drawn from the State Treasury before the convening of the Twenty-fourth General Assembly and the remainder shall be covered back into the Treasury, and the subject of further appropriation shall be referred to the said Twenty-fourth General Assembly; but no part of any such appropriation shall be drawn from the State Treasury until the commission through its duly chosen officers, shall certify to the Auditor of State that the same is actually necessary for disbursement, and shall then be drawn only in portions, not exceeding one-fourth the amount appropriated, as may from time to time become requisite. All payments of money by the Treasurer must be under complete vouchers and under conditions to be fixed by said commission. At the close of its services the commission shall make to the Governor a statement of its proceedings, which shall include a list of all disbursements, with complete vouchers therefor attached. Provided further, no appointments under this act shall be made, nor shall any money herein appropriated be drawn or any charge or expense made until it is definitely known when the exposition is to be held. Provided further, that said commission shall be restricted in expenditures to the amount herein appropriated.

Approved, April 15th, 1890.

In pursuance of this enactment, the Executive Council appointed the following persons to constitute the commission provided by the law:

       First District, Edward Johnstone, of Keokuk.
       Second   "   H. W. Seaman, of Clinton.

Third	"	F. N. Chase, of Cedar Falls.
Fourth	"	James O. Crosby, of Garnavillo.
Fifth	"	James Wilson, of Traer.
Sixth	"	J. W. Jarnagin, of Montezuma.
Seventh	"	Henry Stivers, of Des Moines.
Eighth	"	S. H. Mallory, of Chariton.
Ninth	"	Charles Ashton, of Guthrie Center.
Tenth	"	John F. Duncombe, of Fort Dodge.
Eleventh	"	Wm. H. Dent, of Le Mars.

On the call of the Governor the several appointees met in the capitol, at Des Moines, and having duly qualified, on the second day of September, 1890, organized the Commission, elected the following officers, appointed the following committees, and entered upon its work.

President.
Edward Johnstone, Keokuk.

Vice President.
James Wilson, Traer.

Secretary.
F. N. Chase, Cedar Falls.

Treasurer.
Wm. H. Dent, Le Mars.

Executive Committee.
S. H. Mallory, Chariton.
J. W. Jarnagin, Montezuma.
J. F. Duncombe, Fort Dodge.

Auditing Committee.
James Wilson, Traer.
Henry Stivers, Des Moines.
James O. Crosby, Garnavillo.

Committee on Rules.
H. W. Seaman.
Chas. Ashton.
Jas. O. Crosby.

This was one of the first State Commissions organized. It took early action to secure a site for an Iowa State building in the park selected for the Exposition. The act of Congress deciding that the Fair should be held in 1893, left the Commission with only $5,000 at its command prior to an appropriation by the ensuing General Assembly. It proceeded however to form plans and take the necessary preliminary steps to secure such an exhibition of the resources of the State as was contemplated by the act constituting it.

The Twenty-fourth General Assembly enacted the following law, making a final appropriation for the work of the Commission, which was approved by the Governor April 8th, 1892.

AN ACT making appropriation for an exhibit of the resources of the State of Iowa at the World's Columbian Exposition of 1893, to be held in the city of Chicago.

Be it Enacted by the General Assembly of the State of Iowa:

SECTION 1. That the sum of One Hundred and Twenty-five Thousand Dollars ($125,000) is hereby appropriated out of any money in the State Treasury, not otherwise appropriated, for the purpose of carrying out the intent of chapter 126 of the acts of the Twenty-third General Assembly, an act entitled, "An act to provide for a creditable exhibit of the resources of the State of Iowa in the Columbian Exposition or World's Fair to be held in Chicago." Said sum hereinbefore named is the whole amount to be used and expended by said Columbian Commission; the unexpended appropriation by the Twenty-third General Assembly being considered as covered into the State Treasury and no longer available for the uses of said Commission.

SECTION 2. No part of the moneys appropriated by this act shall be drawn from the State Treasury until the Commission, through its duly chosen officers, shall certify to the Auditor of State that the same is actually necessary for disbursement at the time requisition is made, *provided*, that not more than sixty (60) per cent of the amount herein appropriated shall be drawn from the State Treasury in the year 1892. *Provided further* that not more than twelve and one-half per cent. of the moneys hereby appropriated shall be expended for salaries and other expenses of employes.

SECTION 3. This act being of immediate importance shall take effect and be in force from and after its publication in the *Iowa State Register* and *Des Moines Leader*, newspapers published in Des Moines, Iowa.

In February, 1891, a vacancy occurred in the Commission by the resignation of Hon. James Wilson, who having been elected to a professorship in the Iowa Agricultural College, found it necessary to resign his place in the body. Hon. S. B. Packard, of Marshalltown, was appointed to fill the vacancy.

In May, 1891, a second vacancy occurred in the body by the death of the Hon. Edward Johnstone, its able and honored President, who departed this life in his seventy-sixth year. He came to Iowa in 1837, and for upward of half a century had occupied high position in social, business and political relations. Hon. Theodore Guelich, of Burlington, was appointed to succeed him.

A third vacancy occurred through the death of Mr. Guelich, January 27th, 1893. This gentleman had proved himself a most useful and respected member of the body. He was succeeded by Dr. A. C. Roberts, of Fort Madison.

The two enactments appropriated a total of $130,000 for the work of the Commission. This body knew the sum to be meager, considering the magnitude of the work in its hands. To secure the best exhibit possible of the resources and accomplishments of the State by the most economical use of the funds appropriated, it reorganized the Commission, elected the following officers, constituted the following committees, and arranged its work in the following departments, which were placed in charge of members of the Commission as follows:

President—James O. Crosby.
Vice-President—John F. Duncombe.

Treasurer—Wm. Hamilton Dent.
Secretary—Frank N. Chase.
Executive Committee—S. H. Mallory, S. B. Packard, H. W. Seaman.
Auditing Committee—Theodore Guelich, S. B. Packard, Henry Stivers.
Archaeological, Historical and Statistical Committee—Charles Ashton, James O. Crosby, J. W. Jarnagin.

DEPARTMENTS.

A	Live Stock	S. B. Packard
B	Agricultural and Dairy	F. N. Chase
C	Horticulture	W. H. Dent
D	Mineral and Geological	John F. Duncombe
E	Press	Henry Stivers
F	Woman's Work	James O. Crosby
G	Manufacturing and Machinery	H. W. Seaman
H	Education and Fine Arts	J. W. Jarnagin
I	Forestry	Theo. Guelich

After the death of Commissioner Guelich, his successor, Dr. A. C. Roberts, was appointed to fill his place in the department of Forestry.

The Commission decided to make a collective exhibit in the Iowa State building, competitive exhibits in the several general buildings providing for such exhibits in the Agricultural, Mineral, Horticultural, Manufacturing and Liberal Arts and Forestry buildings and in the Live Stock Department. Ample space was secured for such exhibits in the several buildings named.

In the Agricultural building the space was in a most desirable location, in section D, at the northeast corner of the section, and at the crossing of the main intersection aisles of the building. At their intersection there is a large circular open space, which makes the location a prominent and inviting one. The northeast corner is occupied by Great Britain; the northwest by Germany; the southwest by Iowa; and the southeast by Pennsylvania. This fine position was improved by the erection of a beautiful pavillion of unique architecture designed by Messrs. Milward and Clark, decorators, of Sioux City, and was appropriately decorated with products from the fields and farms of the State under their supervision. A fine exhibit of the grains, seeds and other agricultural products of the State is installed therein. The space embraces two thousand seven hundred square feet.

MINERAL AND GEOLOGICAL.

In this department Iowa has installed a very full and interesting display, prominently located in the south portion of the mining building, and along the south wall. The installation of the exhibit is unique and attractive. The display of valuable minerals, building stone, marble and other qualities of stone suitable for ornamental and monumental work, clays for brick and pottery manufacture, molding and glass sands, are a surprise to all who have not given careful investigation to this class of Iowa's resources. Upwards of one hundred different exhibits are shown in this department, some of which are of great value. The ornamental mantelpiece worked in the several varieties of Floyd county marble exhibited by Messrs. Bishop and Treat, of Charles City, is especially attractive. There are also interesting exhibits of gypsum, sewer tile, building and paving brick and pottery work. The ladies of Dubuque have added to this exhibit a grotto which contains a fine display of lead and zinc ores, obtained in that vicinity, and also many beautiful specimens of stalactites, stalagmites, and other interesting formations found in caves in the vicinity of their city. There is also a fine display of the iron ores found in abundance in Allamakee county, which is a surprise even to Iowa people. The mineral exhibit occupies six hundred feet of floor and one thousand feet of wall space.

THE EDUCATIONAL EXHIBIT.

This important exhibit is centrally located in the space assigned for educational exhibits in the Gallery of the Manufacturers' and Liberal Arts building. The educational displays of the states of New York, Pennsylvania, Nebraska and Colorado immediately surround the space occupied by Iowa. Our exhibit is very complete, showing the work of our common and higher schools. We regret that only one of the three great State schools have part therein. This we do the more because similar great schools of the other states named have added very large interest to their state exhibits by their cabinets and the work of their students. There are numerous photographs of country and city school houses, of the interior of school rooms, showing the pupils at actual work. Our school statistics are presented in a new and original manner. A map drawn by a pupil of the Montezuma schools presents at a glance the location of each one of the 13,275 public schools of the State. Iowa has made honorable presentation in this great and comprehensive display of the educational modes and work of states and nations, the most complete ever presented, inviting the thorough and studious examination of all educators of all countries.

The important Iowa schools for the unfortunate classes have full exhibits of their work in their proper departments. Of these we mention the institution for the feeble minded, the blind and the mute. These have also very interesting displays of their work in the State building.

MACHINERY AND MANUFACTURES.

In these departments there are numerous exhibits in the appropriate buildings and groups, the displays embracing farm machinery and tools, dairy appliances, quarrying and mining tools and machines, mechanics' tools and railroad inventions.

HORTICULTURE.

Early in the summer of 1892 the Iowa Columbian Commission contracted with the Iowa State Horticultural Society to make the Horticultural exhibit. The failure of the fruit crop throughout the State in 1892 added some unexpected difficulties to this work. Iowa won great honor by her displays in this department in the Philadelphia and New Orleans Expositions, and her honor will be duly maintained on this more important occasion. The Iowa exhibits of fruits thus far in the Columbian Exposition has been formed chiefly of apples, the product of the crop of 1891. It speaks volumes in praise of the fruit interests of the State that the apples produced in her soil and climate possess such keeping qualities.

WOMANS' WORK.

In the Woman's building the work of our womanhood has respected place. In other parts of the Fair her work is also seen. In the building named the women of Sioux City have erected a pavillion and decorated it beautifully with the products of the field, after the manner of the corn palaces that have so well advertised the enterprise and energy of their city. This is the first instance of the womanhood in the history of the world's expositions undertaking an exhibit of the products of the farm. By the attention it attracts their exhibit redounds to the honor of their city and the State. In this fine building there are many displays of the handiwork of Iowa women and of their culture and taste.

The work of the women of Iowa is largely seen in our educational exhibit. The work of education being largely in their hands, not only are women in the majority as teachers in our district, but they have place also in our high schools and colleges, and largely direct our educational interests thirteeen counties having elected women to fill the county superintendent's office. In law and medicine, in authorship, in the work of the press, in sculpture and painting, and in important invention women in Iowa have rendered useful service. Their work is shown in every department in which Iowa makes an exhibit.

THE DAIRY.

In this important department Iowa presents a display that will sustain the high reputation and honor her dairymen have heretofore gained. In the dairy tests her famed cows are present to compete for first prizes. Her dairies and creameries are placing their products in the competition and are highest honors.

LIVE STOCK.

In the numerous divisions and classes of the live stock department Iowa stockmen will be found in honorable competition for first honors. We cannot now give the names or number of exhibitors, but numerous valuable animals of the best improved breeds will be shown.

THE GENERAL EXHIBIT.

This is made in the Iowa State building, a fine structure in a fine location. No State building is more generally visited by the masses who visit the Exposition, nor is any state Structure the subject of more general praise.

The architecture and the decorations of the building are an exhibit of Iowa art, the Josleyn & Taylor Company, of Cedar Rapids, architects, designing and superintending its construction. Messrs. Milward & Clark, decorators, of Sioux City, having charge of the decorations of the exhibition hall. Their artistic skill is evident to the thousands who look with delight upon the beautiful creations wrought out by those gentlemen with the simple grains and grasses gathered from our fields. In the reception hall and ladies' parlors there are several decorative pieces in Goeblin Toile, wrought out by Messrs. Andrews & Noel, of Clinton, that attract attention by their excellence of design and the skill and delicacy of their execution. In this building the work of the press, the schools and authorship, the art, the quarry, the mine, and the farms and shops of Iowa are shown. The Iowa building and the exhibits displayed therein will carry the name of Iowa in favorable mention through every civilized country. "The Peri," a piece

IOWA'S HOME, COLUMBIAN EXPOSITION.

carved in the finest Italian marble by the late Mrs. Harriet Ketcham, of Mt. Pleasant, a beautiful piece of art exhibited in the art department of the Iowa building, wins high praise.

THE DEDICATION.

In the dedicatory exercises of Jackson Park and its great buildings to the purposes of the Fair in October last, proper services were held on the following day dedicating the Iowa building to its important purpose. A full account of these exercises are given in the beautiful Souvenir published by order of the Commission and under the supervision of the Hon. James O. Crosby, its President.

THE OPENING OF THE FAIR.

On the opening day of the great Fair, May 1st, 1893, appropriate exercises were held in the Iowa building, which was one of the few State buildings at that time so near completion and having its exhibits in such state of forwardness as to be ready for the reception of visitors. President Crosby, of the Commission, presided. The Iowa State Band furnished excellent and appropriate music. The audience was led in invoking the divine blessing by Rev. Charles Ashton, of the Commission, and an able oration in response to a brief but pertinent address by President Crosby was delivered by Hon. W. M. McFarland, Secretary of State, who spoke to the great edification of the large audience filling the large assembly hall of the beautiful Iowa building. Iowa won praise by the completeness of her building and her exhibits at that time, as she has continued to receive praise for the artistic beauty of the decorations of the structure and the harmony of design and the excellence of the exhibit made of her wonderful productiveness.

POPULATION.

We give the population by counties for each national census taken since the settlement of Iowa:

COUNTIES	1840	1850	1860	1870	1880	1890
Adair			984	3,982	11,667	14,534
Adams			1,533	4,614	11,888	12,292
Allamakee		777	12,237	17,808	19,791	17,907
Appanoose		3,131	11,931	16,456	16,636	18,961
Audubon			454	1,212	7,448	12,412
Benton		672	8,496	22,454	24,888	24,178
Black Hawk		135	8,244	21,706	23,913	24,219
Boone		735	4,232	14,581	20,838	23,772
Bremer			4,915	12,528	14,081	14,630
Buchanan		517	7,906	17,034	18,546	18,997
Buena Vista			57	1,585	7,537	13,548
Butler			3,724	9,951	14,293	15,463
Calhoun			147	1,602	5,595	13,107
Carroll			281	2,451	12,351	18,828
Cass			1,612	5,464	16,943	19,645
Cedar		1,253	3,941	12,949	19,731	18,936	18,253
Cerro Gordo			940	4,722	11,461	14,864
Cherokee			58	1,967	8,240	15,659
Chickasaw			4,336	10,180	14,534	15,019
Clark		79	5,427	8,735	11,513	11,332
Clay			52	1,523	4,248	9,309
Clayton		1,101	3,873	20,728	27,771	28,829	26,783
Clinton		824	2,822	18,938	35,357	36,763	41,199
Crawford			383	2,530	12,413	18,894
Dallas			854	5,244	12,019	18,764	20,479
Davis			7,264	13,764	15,565	16,408	15,258
Decatur			965	8,677	12,018	15,336	15,643
Delaware		168	1,759	11,024	17,132	17,950	17,349
Des Moines		5,577	12,988	19,611	27,256	33,099	35,324
Dickinson			180	1,389	1,901	4,328
Dubuque		3,059	10,841	31,164	38,969	42,996	49,848
Emmet			105	1,392	1,550	4,274
Fayette			825	12,073	16,973	22,258	23,141
Floyd			3,744	10,768	14,677	15,424
Franklin			1,309	4,738	10,249	12,871
Freemont		1,244	5,074	11,174	17,652	16,382
Greene			1,374	4,627	12,727	15,797
Grundy			793	6,399	12,639	13,215
Guthrie			3,058	7,061	14,334	17,380
Hamilton			1,699	6,055	11,252	15,319
Hancock			179	999	3,453	7,621
Hardin			5,440	13,684	17,807	19,003
Harrison			3,621	8,931	16,649	21,356
Henry		3,772	8,707	18,701	21,463	20,986	18,895
Howard			3,168	6,282	10,837	11,182
Humboldt			332	2,596	5,341	9,836
Ida			43	226	4,382	10,705
Iowa			822	8,029	16,644	19,221	18,270
Jackson		1,411	7,210	18,493	22,619	23,771	22,771
Jasper			1,280	9,883	22,116	25,963	24,943
Jefferson		2,773	9,901	15,038	17,839	17,463	15,184
Johnson		1,491	4,472	17,573	24,898	25,429	23,082
Jones		474	3,007	13,306	19,731	21,052	20,233
Keokuk			4,822	13,271	19,434	21,258	23,862
Kossuth			416	3,351	6,178	13,120
Lee		6,093	18,861	29,232	37,210	34,859	37,715
Linn		1,373	5,441	18,947	31,080	37,237	45,303
Louisa		1,927	4,939	10,370	12,877	13,142	11,873
Lucas			471	5,776	10,388	14,530	14,563
Lyon				221	1,968	8,680
Madison			1,179	7,339	13,884	17,224	15,977
Mahaska			5,989	14,816	22,508	25,382	28,805
Marion			5,482	16,813	24,436	25,111	23,058
Marshall			338	6,015	17,576	23,752	25,842
Mills				4,481	8,718	14,137	14,584
Mitchell				3,409	9,582	14,363	13,299
Monona				832	3,654	9,055	14,515
Monroe			2,884	8,612	12,724	13,719	13,666
Montgomery				1,256	5,934	15,869	15,848
Muscatine		1,942	5,731	16,444	21,688	23,170	24,504
O'Brien				8	715	4,155	13,060
Osceola						2,219	5,574

POPULATION—CONTINUED.

COUNTIES.	1840.	1850.	1860.	1870.	1880.	1890.
Page		551	4,419	9,975	19,667	21,341
Palo Alto			132	1,336	4,131	9,318
Plymouth			148	2,199	8,566	19,568
Pocahontas			103	1,446	3,713	9,553
Polk		1,513	11,625	27,857	42,395	65,410
Pottawattamie		7,828	4,968	16,893	39,850	47,430
Poweshiek		615	5,668	15,581	18,936	18,394
Ringgold			2,923	5,691	12,085	13,556
Sac			246	1,411	8,774	14,521
Scott	2,140	5,968	24,959	38,599	41,266	43,164
Shelby			818	2,540	12,696	17,611
Sioux			10	576	5,426	18,370
Story			4,051	11,651	16,906	18,127
Tama		8	5,285	16,131	21,585	21,651
Taylor		204	3,590	6,989	15,635	16,384
Union			2,012	5,986	14,980	16,900
Van Buren	6,146	12,270	17,081	17,672	17,043	16,253
Wapello		8,471	14,518	22,346	25,285	30,426
Warren		961	10,281	17,980	19,578	18,269
Washington	1,594	4,957	14,235	18,952	20,374	18,468
Wayne		340	6,409	11,287	16,127	15,670
Webster			2,504	10,484	15,951	21,582
Winnebago			168	1,562	4,917	7,325
Winneshiek		546	13,912	23,579	23,938	22,528
Woodbury			1,119	6,172	14,996	55,632
Worth			756	2,892	7,593	9,247
Wright			653	2,392	5,062	12,057
TOTALS	43,112	192,214	674,913	1,194,020	1,624,615	1,911,896

POPULATION OF IOWA—NATIVITY AND SEX.

As shown by the above table the population of the State in 1890 was 1,911,896. Of this population 324,069, but 17 per cent were persons of foreign birth, while 1,587,827 were born in this country. 994,453 persons in the State were males and 917,343 were females.

STATE GOVERNMENT AND INSTITUTIONS.

The Iowa territory was separated from the territory of Wisconsin and given a separate territorial organization by act of congress, approved by Martin Van Buren, President, June 12, 1839, who appointed Robert Lucas, a well known democratic statesman of his day, who had served through two terms as Governor of Ohio, Governor of the new territory. The first legislative assembly of the territory convened at Burlington, November 12th, of that year. Two sessions of the territorial legislature of Wisconsin had previously met at Burlington and provided for the organization of sixteen counties west of the Mississippi.

In the political changes resulting from the famous campaign of 1840, John Chambers, whig, of Kentucky, was appointed by President William Henry Harrison, to succeed Governor Lucas. After the presidential election of 1844, President Polk appointed Hon. James Clark to succeed Governor Chambers. Mr. Clark was a Pennsylvanian by birth, learned the printing trade in boyhood, came to Iowa in 1836, and established the second newspaper published in the territory. He was appointed Secretary of the Territory by Martin Van Buren in 1839. By act of congress, approved December 28th, 1846, Iowa was admitted as a State. It had at that time twenty-seven organized counties with a population of nearly 160,000, and the frontier settlements were well advanced toward the Missouri River. Hon. Ansel Briggs was elected Governor of the new State.

The Missouri River being fixed as its western boundary, Iowa City was far east of its center and it was deemed wise to establish the State capital at a point more nearly central in its territory, and the first session of its General Assembly enacted a law providing for the re-location of the seat of government, the capitol building and its site, ten acres of land at Iowa City, being appropriated for the State University. This action ultimately led to the location of the State Capital at Des Moines. The beautiful site of the present fine capitol structure was selected in 1856. The three constitutional conventions in the State were held in Iowa City. The city of Des Moines was declared to be the capital of the State by the proclamation of Governor Grimes, issued October 19, 1857. The old capitol at Iowa City then became the property of the State University. In 1870 the General Assembly made an appropriation and provided for the appointment of a board of commissioners to commence the construction of the present capitol edifice. This board embraced honored names. Governor Samuel Merrill being *ex-officio* its President, Granville M. Dodge of Councill Bluffs, James F. Wilson of Fairfield, James Dawson of Washington, Simon G. Stein of Muscatine, James O. Crosby of Garnavillo, Charles Dudley of Agency City, John N. Dewey of Polk county, and William M. Joy of Woodbury county were its members, with Alexander R. Fulton of Des Moines Secretary. The first Board of Capitol Commissioners was appointed for a term of two years. In making its report to the General Assembly it recommended the reorganization of the board and a reduction of its number to five. The General Assembly enacted a law April 10th, 1872, embodying its suggestions, and Messrs John G. Foote of Burlington, Martin L. Fisher of Farmersburg, Peter A. Dey and R. S. Finkbine of Iowa City, were appointed thereon, the Governor being *ex-officio* its President. The new board elected A. H. Piquenard, of Springfield, Illinois, Architect, General Ed. Wright its Secretary, Robert Finkbine Superintendent of Construction, and John G. Foote, Superintendent of Finance. This organization continued until the completion of the structure, except as changes resulted from deaths. In November, 1876, Mr. Piquenard died, and Messrs. Bell and Hackney, both young men who had assisted him, were elected to succeed him as architect. In February, 1879, Mr. Fisher died, and Mr. Cyrus Foreman of Osage was appointed his successor. The gentlemen composing these boards discharged their important trust with eminent fidelity and ability, giving to the State one of the finest State capitols of the country.

The following gentlemen have filled the executive chair of the State in the line of succession from Governor Briggs:

Hon. Stephen Hempstead, of Dubuque county.
Hon. James W. Grimes, of Des Moines county.
Hon. Ralph P. Lowe, of Lee county.
Hon. Samuel J. Kirkwood, of Johnson county.
Hon. Wm. M. Stone, of Marion county.
Hon. Samuel Merrill, of Clayton county.
Hon. Cyrus C. Carpenter, of Webster county.
Hon. Joshua G. Newbold, of Henry county.
Hon. John H. Gear, of Des Moines county.
Hon. Buren R. Sherman, of Benton county.
Hon. Wm. Larrabee, of Fayette county.
Hon. Horace Boies, of Black Hawk county.

Hon. Joshua G. Newbold was elected Lieutenant-Governor, but became Governor on the resignation of Hon. Samuel J. Kirkwood upon his election as United States Senator.

THE JUDICIAL SYSTEM.

In our country townships we have magistrates called Justices of the Peace, who are elected by the people and hold their office for two years. In our incorporated towns and cities we have Mayor's and Police Courts.

For the higher courts the State is divided into eighteen districts. Of these, two districts, the eighth and seventeenth, elect one Judge each; the first, third, twelfth, thirteenth, fourteenth, sixteenth, and eighteenth each elect two Judges; the fifth, sixth, ninth, tenth and eleventh each elect three; and the second, fourth, seventh and fifteenth each elect four. The several Judges are elected for terms of four years. There are courts in four cities of the State called Superior Courts, namely: in Cedar Rapids, Creston, Council Bluffs and Keokuk. These have each one Judge. From these District and Superior Courts appeals may be taken to the Supreme Court.

THE SUPREME COURT.

The supreme judicial body of the State is composed of five Judges, elected by the people for a term of six years, one Judge being elected yearly, the sixth year there being no election. As prosecutor an Attorney General, elected by the people, appears in behalf of the people. The court is now constituted as follows, the position of Chief Justice comes to the several Judges by rotation in the last year of their term.

Chief Justice: Gifford S. Robinson, Storm Lake.

Justices: Charles T. Granger, Waukon; Josiah Given, Des Moines; Jas. H. Rothrock, Cedar Rapids; L. G. Kinne, Toledo.

Attorney General: John Y. Stone, Glenwood.

The Supreme Judges are elected by the voters of the whole State. The District Judges by the voters of their several districts. The Judges of the Superior Courts by the voters of the city in which the court is located.

CONGRESSIONAL.

The State has eleven representatives in the National Congress. For their election the State is divided into eleven Districts.

The First District, composed of Lee, Van Buren, Jefferson, Henry, Des Moines, Louisa and Washington counties, is represented by Hon. John H. Gear, of Burlington.

The Second District, composed of the counties of Iowa, Johnson, Muscatine, Scott, Clinton and Jackson, is represented by Hon. Walter I. Hayes of Clinton.

The Third District, composed of the counties of Wright, Franklin, Hardin, Butler, Bremer, Black Hawk, Buchanan, Delaware and Dubuque, is represented by Hon. D. B. Henderson, of Dubuque.

The Fourth District, composed of the counties of Worth, Cerro Gordo, Floyd, Mitchell, Howard, Chickasaw, Fayette, Winneshiek, Allamakee and Clayton, is represented by Hon. Thomas Updegraff, of McGregor.

The Fifth District, composed of the counties of Grundy, Marshall, Tama, Benton, Linn, Jones and Cedar, Hon. Robert G. Cousins, is its Representative.

The Sixth District, composed of the counties of Jasper, Poweshiek, Keokuk, Mahaska, Monroe, Wapello and Davis, Hon. John F. Lacey, Representative.

The Seventh District, composed of the counties of Story, Polk, Dallas, Madison, Warren and Marion, Hon. J. A. T. Hull, Representative.

The Eighth District, composed of the counties of Appanoose, Wayne, Lucas, Clark, Decatur, Ringgold, Union Adams, Taylor, Page and Fremont, Hon. W. P. Hepburn, Representative.

The Ninth District, composed of the counties of Adair, Guthrie, Audubon, Cass, Montgomery, Mills, Pottawattamie, Shelby and Harrison, Hon. A. L. Hagar, Representative.

The Tenth District, composed of the counties of Boone, Greene, Carroll, Crawford, Calhoun, Webster, Hamilton, Humboldt, Pocahontas, Palo Alto, Emmet, Kossuth, Hancock and Winnebago, Hon. J. P. Dolliver, Representative.

The Eleventh District, composed of the counties of Monona, Woodbury, Ida, Sac, Buena Vista, Cherokee, Plymouth, Sioux, O'Brien, Clay, Dickinson, Osceola and Lyon, Hon. George D. Perkins, Representative.

CABINET OFFICERS.

Three citizens of Iowa have held Cabinet positions, Hon. James Harlan was Secretary of the Interior in the second administration of Abraham Lincoln. Hon. W. W. Belknap was secretary of War in Gen. Grant's administration, and Hon. S. J. Kirkwood was Secretary of the Department of the Interior in the administration of Presidents Garfield and Arthur.

In the United States Judiciary several of her citizens have won honorable reputation.

The following gentlemen have represented Iowa in the United States Senate:

Geo. W. Jones, Dubuque, 1848 to 1859.
Augustus C. Dodge, Burlington, 1848 to 1855.
James Harlan, Mt. Pleasant, 1855 to 1865.
James W. Grimes, Burlington, 1858 to 1870.
Samuel J. Kirkwood, Iowa City, 1866 to 1867.
James Harlan, Mount Pleasant, 1867 to 1873.
James B. Howell, Keokuk, Jan. 20, 1871, to March 4, 1871. (To fill vacancy caused by the death of James W. Grimes.)
George G. Wright, Des Moines, 1871 to 1877.
William B. Allison, Dubuque, 1873 to the present time.
Samuel J. Kirkwood, 1877 to 1881.
James W. McDill, 1881 to 1883.
James F. Wilson, Fairfield, 1883 to the present time.

The following gentlemen now constitute the Executive Council of the State:

Hon. Horace Boies, Black Hawk county, Governor.
Hon. Wm. McFarland, Emmet county, Secretary of State.
Hon. C. G. McCarthy, Story county, Auditor of State.
Hon. Byron A. Beason, Marshall County, Treasurer of State.

The other elective Executive State officials are:

Hon. J. B. Knoepfler, Allamakee county, Superintendent of Public Instruction.

Railroad Commissioners:

Hon. John W. Luke, Franklin county.
Hon. Peter A. Dey, Johnson county.
Hon. Geo. W. Perkins, Fremont county.

THE GENERAL ASSEMBLY.

The Legislative Department of the State government is composed of two houses. The Senate or Upper House consists of fifty members so divided that about one-half of its members are elected bi-ennially, the official term being four years. The Lower House or House of Representatives has one hundred members, elected bi-ennially. The Constitution provides that the sessions of the General Assembly shall be bi-enual. In cases of emergency extra sessions may be called.

The first extra session convened at Iowa City on the second day of July 1856, for the purpose of accepting the grant of lands by Congress in aid of railway construction, and to carry into execution the trust conferred upon the State. Grants were made to the Burlington & Missouri, the Mississippi & Missouri, the Air Line and the Dubuque & Pacific railroad companies.

An extra session was held in May, 1861, for the purpose of placing the State on a war footing to maintain the Union of the States.

A third extra session convened on the third day of September, 1862, and was occupied principally with military matters.

An adjourned session of the Fourteenth General Assembly was begun on the third Wednesday of January, 1873, for the purpose of considering and passing upon the report of the Codifying Commission. The revision of the laws at that adjourned session was designated as the "Code," though by way of distinction it is called the "Code of 1873."

STATE INSTITUTIONS—STATE UNIVERSITY.

This great school was established early in the history of the State. In July, 1840, Congress passed an act providing for the setting apart of 45,928 acres of land within the territory of Iowa for the use and support of a state university, whenever the territory should become a state. By the adoption of the constitution of 1846, the people of the State accepted the grant. At the first session of the General Assembly, February 25, 1847, an act was passed locating and establishing the State University at Iowa City. That act set apart the public buildings with the ten acres of land on which

STATE UNIVERSITY, IOWA CITY.

the same were situated for the use of the university, provided the capitol should be used for state purposes until otherwise provided by law. The first session of the university opened in March, 1855.

The Collegiate Department embraces four courses of study: Classical, Philosophical, Scientific and Engineering. Four years are required to graduate in any of the courses. In the Law Department the course of study covers two years. The Medical Department requires three terms of six months each. The Dental and Pharmacy Departments cover two years each.

The General Assembly at each session makes liberal appropriations for its support. The Twenty-third General Assembly appropriated $125,000, the twenty-fourth $78,000.

During the past school year a total of 904 students were enrolled in its classes, namely: females 152, males 752. Seventy five persons were employed as instructors. There are 28,000 volumes in its library. Its yearly income is reported at $120,000. Value of grounds and buildings, $300,000.

THE STATE AGRICULTURAL COLLEGE.

This state school was established in 1858. The legislature of that year appropriated $10,000 to purchase a farm for the location of the college buildings and for experiments in agriculture.

In 1859 a farm of 640 acres, near Ames, Story county, was purchased. In 1862 Congress passed a bill granting to each state public lands to the amount of 30,000 for each Senator and Representative to which the states were then entitled. The conditions of that act and the grant thereunder was accepted by the General Assembly of the State in September, 1862.

In 1887 Congress passed a bill establishing Agricultural Experiment stations in connection with the Agricultural College and appropriated $15,000 annually for the support of each.

In August, 1890, a bill for the more complete endowment and support of Agricultural Colleges was approved by President Harrison. This bill provided for increased appropriations for their support. The annual income of the Iowa college from the several appropriations of the General Government is now $78,000. The State erects and keeps in repair all buildings, and for this purpose it has appropriated about $855,000 for the exclusive use of the several departments of the college. The main college building is five stories high. The college domain now embraces 900 acres. The school has courses in agriculture and dairying, veterinary science, mechanical engineering, civil engineering, electrical engineering, science, and a special course for lady students.

The Twenty-fourth General Assembly appropriated $56,500 for this school. It reported last year an enrollment of 547 students, namely: 454 males and 93 females. Instructors, 29. Its library contains 9,300 volumes. The value of its endowments are reported at $679,784, its yearly income $80,000, and value of grounds and building at $450,000.

STATE NORMAL SCHOOL.

This important school was established by the Sixteenth General Assembly for the special training of teachers for the common schools of the State. It was organized by the board of directors June 7th, 1876, and was opened for the reception of students September 6th, 1876. The first year 155 students were enrolled in its classes. The last year it had an enrollment of 746, namely: 191 male and 515 female students.

The province of this school is in no respect a duplicate of other educational institutions of the State. It adheres strictly to the object assigned at its founding—that of preparing professional teachers for public schools. For its support and improvement the General Assembly makes liberal appropriations.

This important school has 5,000 volumes in its library. The value of its grounds and buildings is reported at $75,000.

These three important State schools are doing good work in securing to the State in professional life men and women of cultured intellect and special qualifications.

OTHER STATE SCHOOLS.

The Iowa College for the Blind was first opened in Iowa City in 1853 d removed to its present location at Vinton in 1862. During the forty years of its existence it has received from the State for improvements, repairs, clothing for pupils, support and current expenses upward of $870,-000.

The design of this institution is to furnish to the blind children of the State equal educational advantages with children who enjoy the boon of sight. The branches taught are raised print, point system, arithmetic, spelling, geography, history, grammar, natural philosophy, algebra, rhetoric, physiology, zoology, chemistry, moral philosophy, civil government, political economy, geometry, and English and American literature. The department of music is supplied with twenty-three pianos, one pipe organ, three cabinet organs and a sufficient number of violins, guitars, bass viols and brass instruments. Every student capable of receiving it, is given a complete course in this branch.

In the industrial department the girls are required to learn knitting, crocheting, fancy work, hand and machine sewing. The boys, netting, mattress-making and cane seating. Those of either sex who so desire may learn carpet weaving and broom making. The advantages of the school are free to every person either blind or of defective vision, and of suitable age and capacity in the State. The pupils are treated free of charge by skilled oculists.

INSTITUTION FOR THE DEAF AND DUMB.

This institution is located in Pottawattamie county near the city of Council Bluffs. The education it offers is free. Pupils are received from the age of nine to twenty-five who are sound of mind and free from offensive or contagious diseases. A competent corps of instructors of long and successful experience is employed in every department. The trades taught in the institution are printing, shoe-making, carpentering, dressmaking, farming and gardening, drawing and painting, light house work, plain sewing and knitting are also taught.

The last General Assembly appropriated $26,050 for this school.

INSTITUTION FOR THE FEEBLE MINDED.

This worthy institution is located at Glenwood, Mills county. The first child was admitted September 1876. For a time there was an unwillingness on the part of parents of this class of children to turn them over to its care. That diffidence is now largely outgrown. The object of the institution is to provide special means for this unfortunate class. The course embraces not only the course of the common schools where that is practicable, but a course of training in the practical matters of every day life, the cultivation of proper personal habits, and the fitting of the pupil for useful occupation.

The value of the lands and buildings pertaining to this worthy institution is now about $100,000.

INDUSTRIAL HOME FOR ADULT BLIND.

The object of this worthy institution is to provide a working home and means for the blind to earn their own subsistence. The institution was established by an act of the twenty-third General Assembly which appropriated $40,000 for the purchase of grounds and erection of buildings. It was located by the Commission at Knoxville, Marion county. Accommodations were designed for two hundred inmates. The institution was opened for the reception of eligible persons in 1862.

THE SOLDIERS' ORPHANS' HOME.

This institution was opened for the reception of children July 13th, 1864. The eleventh General Assembly assuming control, providing a special fund for its maintenance, and providing for its management and its permanent location at Davenport.

There is in connection with this worthy charity a well lighted, pleasant and commodious school building. It is the purpose of the Board of Management to have the course of instruction reach a high standard of practical usefulness.

In 1880 the General Assembly widened the sphere of usefulness of this institution by opening its doors to other dependent children. There were on the thirtieth of June, 1893, —— soldiers' orphans and other dependent children enjoying its advantages. Great attention is given to the moral instruction of children placed in its care.

The library of the institution contains about 800 volumes of carefully selected juvenile literature.

THE SOLDIERS' HOME.

This institution was created by the twenty-first General Assembly. The main building being completed was opened with proper ceremonies November 30th, 1887. Since that time enlargements and improvements have been made by authority of the succeeding sessions of the body creating it.

The hospital is 131 feet in length, 60 feet in width, two stories in height above basement, with spacious verandas and balconies. Great care was taken to secure good ventilation. The home is a worthy monument of the grateful patriotism of the people of the State towards its defenders who, broken in health, or suffering from wounds received in their country's dangerous service, now need its care. Down to June 30, 1891, 743 persons had been admitted to its care and comforts.

Since the adjournment of the twenty-fourth General Assembly, a number of cottages have been erected for the accommodation of married veterans needing the advantages of this home.

INSANE ASYLUMS.

Liberal provision has been made by the people of the State for the care of this unfortunate class.

The hospital at Mt. Pleasant is the oldest of the three institutions established by the State for the care and treatment of insane persons. It was established by the act of the Fifth General Assembly, approved January 24, 1855. It was formally opened March 6, 1861.

The hospital at Independence, Buchanan county, was opened on the first day of May, 1873.

The hospital at Clarinda, Page county, was opened for the reception of patients December, 15, 1888. The original plans for this institution, not yet fully carried out, contemplated accommodations for one thousand patients. The appropriation by the twenty-third General Assembly for the three

IOWA HOSPITAL FOR THE INSANE, INDEPENDENCE, IOWA.

institutions reached in the aggregate $237,500. The special appropriations made by the twenty-fourth General Assembly for repairs and improvements were $91,300.

These institutions are each controlled by a board of trustees elected by the General Assembly, composed of men of different political parties. Full staffs of eminent medical service is secured. The treatment of the unfortunate inmates is humane and wise, and care is given to promote their restoration to reason.

INDUSTRIAL OR REFORMATORY SCHOOLS.

Of these the State supports two; one for boys at Eldora, Hardin county. The persons eligible for commitment to its instructions and care are boys from eight to sixteen years of age, whose natures are yet susceptible to good impressions and who may be influenced to a better life by kindness, moral training and a proper discipline. This school was opened September 1st, 1868. In the almost twenty-three years elapsing from its opening to June 30, 1891, there were admitted 1,655 boys; of these 1,254 had been discharged and otherwise released, 401 still remaining under its care.

Care is taken to give its inmates useful instruction and correct moral training. The work of the institution has been most valuable to its inmates and honorable and serviceable to the State.

THE GIRL'S INDUSTRIAL SCHOOL.

Is located at Mitchellville, Polk county. This is virtually a branch of the Eldora school, designed for the moral training of wayward girls. The buildings and grounds of the Universalist Seminary at Mitchellville were purchased in 1879 and this school was established at that time. "The discipline is gentle and home like," and it has been estimated that seventy per cent. of those committed to the institution leave it reformed in character and conduct.

THE PENITENTIARIES.

Iowa has two such institutions, and may boast of the small percentage of its population classed as criminals.

The oldest of its penal institutions was located at Ft. Madison, Lee county, and was established by act of the Legislature of Iowa territory, January 25, 1839.

By an act of the fourteenth General Assembly of the State, commissioners were appointed to "locate and provide for the erection of an additional penitentiary." That commission located the additional institution at Anamosa, Jones county.

The number of convicts in the Anamosa penitentiary, March 23 last were males 293, females 12. Total 305. The prison has accommodations for 800, 495 more than are confined therein. In the Ft. Madison institution there were 420 prisoners in confinement, all males. Making a total for the two prisons of 725 persons, only twelve being females. This is one prisoner to each 2,413 of the State's population. We notice that according to census bulletin number ninety-five, the number of prisoners in the county jails were 327, being 171 prisoners in jail for one million of population. Although Iowa was tenth in rank of population, twenty-three of the States of the

Union exceeded Iowa in the number of prisoners in their jails. The ratio of prisoners in jail to population was 171 prisoners to one million population, and forty-three of the States and Territories exceeded this ratio. There is crime in Iowa but there are few States in the Union that have so little crime in proportion to population. We gladly acknowledge valuable assistance from the Iowa Register in the preparation of this chapter.

PAUPERISM.

The great Master, when on earth, said to the murmuring Judas: "The poor ye have always with you." The saying is ever true in earthly conditions. The physically and mentally infirm—the unfortunates are present in all countries. For her poor Iowa makes comfortable provision of shelter, food, clothing and medical attendance. Her alms houses may not be palaces, but they are not prisons nor places of cruelty. There were in 1890, as shown by the national census, in the alms houses of the country 73,045 persons, or 1,166 to each million of population. Iowa had but 848 to the million of her population in her alms houses. The sobriety of her people diminishes extreme poverty. And crime and pauperism alike are reduced to a minimum by the prevalence of sobriety, intelligence and piety, virtues that when observed in practical life alike preclude criminal action and pauperized condition.

THE NEWSPAPER PRESS.

The people of this State are known to be generous patrons of literature. They are liberal supporters of the press. The State, though comparatively young, was settled before the telephone or telegraph was invented. Yet when Iowa was opened for settlement, the newspaper had won recognition as an instrument of power in political and social affairs, and soon after its settlement had its own newspaper establishment. In 1836, but three years after its permanent settlement was commenced, John King started "The Visitor" in Dubuque, issuing the first number on the 11th day of May of that year. The press on which that paper was printed was of the Smith pattern, and was purchased in Cincinnatti. It did worthy pioneer service. After being used some six years in Dubuque it was sold and removed to Lancaster, Wisconsin. After being used there some time it was removed to St. Paul, Minnesota, and in another mutation of its ownership was taken to Sioux Falls, Dakota, where in March, 1862, on the raiding of that place by the Sioux Indians, it was destroyed in the conflagration of the building in which it was located. In its somewhat brief history it served in printing the first newspapers ever issued in Iowa, Western Wisconsin, Minnesota and Dakota. In 1837 James Clark, afterwards Governor of the Iowa territory, established a newspaper at Burlington, naming it "The Gazette." It has survived the mutations of political administrations, commercial struggles and business changes, and is now one of the influential journals of the State, publishing daily and weekly editions.

There are now published in Iowa 951 periodical journals, but four of the forty-four States exceeding us in the number of such publications, namely, New York with 2,131, Illinois 1,560, Pennsylvania 1,478, and Ohio with 1,190.

Newspapers are published in each of our ninety-nine counties, there being but one of the ninety-nine county seats without a newspaper, namely, Concord, the county seat of Hancock county. Two papers are published, however, in the town of Garner but a mile distant from Concord. Newspapers are published in 446 of the cities, towns or villages of the State. Of our "ninety and nine" counties five, in 1892, each had three papers, namely, Adair, Clark, Winnebago, Emmet and Worth. Eleven counties had four papers each, namely, Adams, Audubon, Dickinson, Franklin, Grundy, Hancock, Lucas, Monroe, Palo Alto and Ringgold. Eight other counties each had five journals, while Dubuque had 20, Scott 23, Woodbury 26, Linn 29, and Polk 45.

Of these 951 publications in this State fifty-eight are daily issues, five are tri-weekly, twelve are semi-weekly, 769 weekly, three semi-monthly one bi-monthly, eighty-five are monthly journals and two are published quarterly. One is published in the Bohemian, nine in the German, three in the Hollandist, seven in the Norwegian and Danish, and one in the Swedish languages. Thirteen of the whole number represent collegiate interests, twenty are published in the interests of agriculture and live stock, thirteen in advocacy of the interests of fraternities, seven are educational journals, two medical, two are devoted to the advancement of science, eight specially advocate temperance and prohibition, one is published in the advocacy of Woman's Suffrage, one in the interests of people of color, ten specially represent various industrial and commercial interests, several are published in aid of Sabbath school work, and one is a juvenile journal. There are also a number representing denominational and religious interests, while 568 of the whole number are classed as political journals, 330 advocating the principles of the Republican party, 194 the principles of the Democratic party, thirteen are styled Independent-Republican, twelve are classed as Independent-Democrat, and fourteen are assorted as Greenback, Union Labor, Peoples Party and Anti-Monopoly journals.

The people of Iowa not only liberally patronize the larger city journals but they liberally support their county and village press. All business and moral interests and lines of thought are represented by the press of Iowa. Our newspaper writers have won fame throughout the country, and have borne able part not only in the discussion of matters of national interest but also in the dissemination of intelligence respecting our resources, progress and possibilities and by their work have given valuable aid in promoting the prosperity and happiness of our people, thereby promoting the settlement of our wild lands, and the wonderous development of this fair and noble Iowa. Here the largest possible liberty has ever been allowed the press in the discussion of all public questions. This happy privilege has led to the multiplication of newspapers but it has resulted in energizing thought, quickening activities, inspiring worthy ambitions and noble purposes, and giving to our honored State the world wide fame it enjoys for the superior excellence of its commercial, social and domestic conditions.

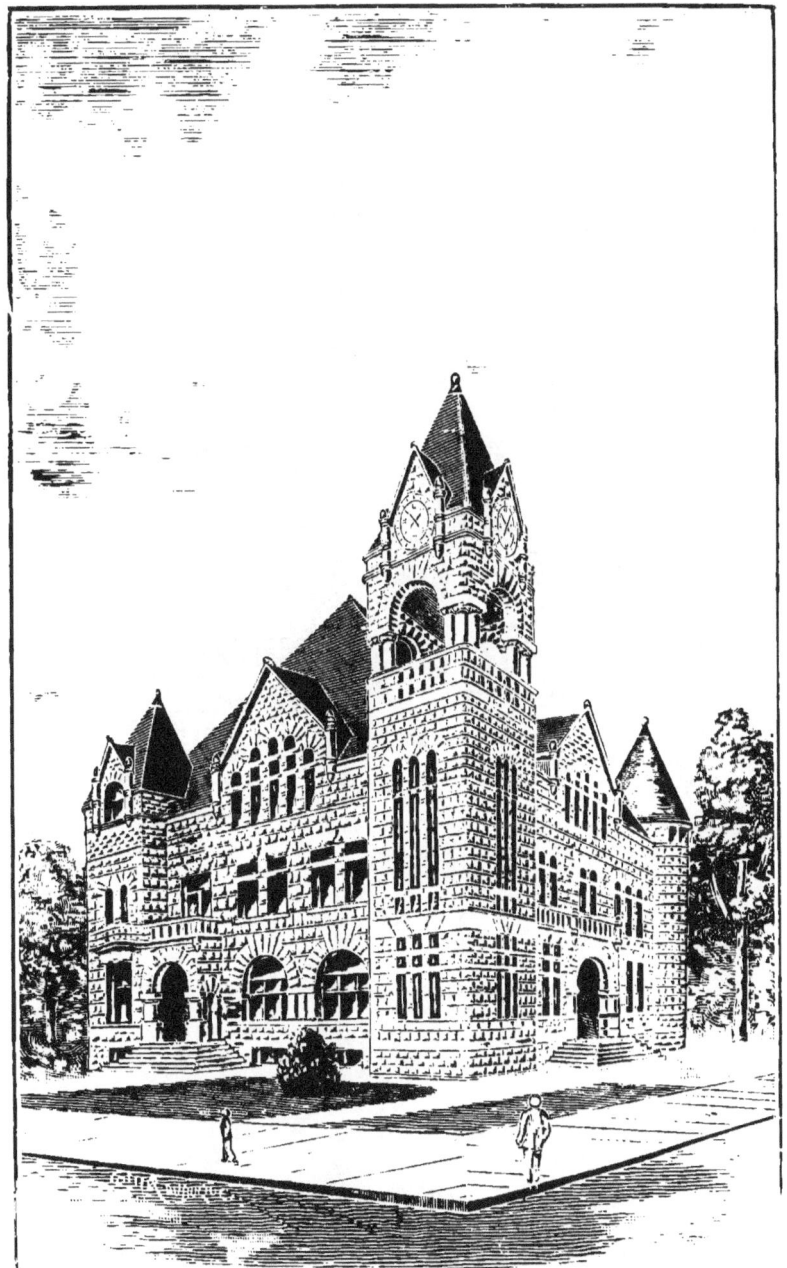

DUBUQUE HIGH SCHOOL BUILDING.

DUBUQUE COUNTY COURT HOUSE.

www.ingramcontent.com/pod-product-compliance
Lightning Source LLC
Chambersburg PA
CBHW031447160426
43195CB00010BB/888